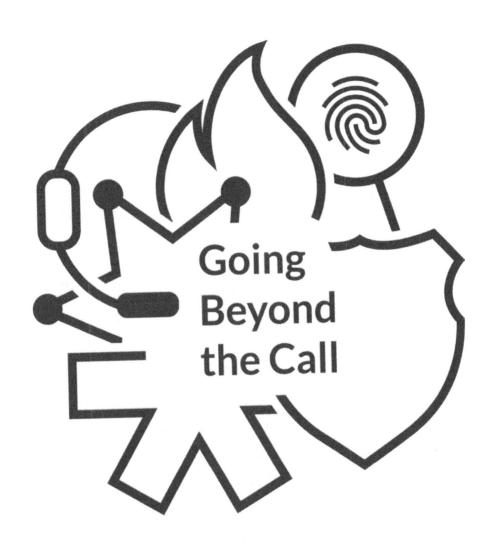

Going Beyond the Call

MENTAL HEALTH FITNESS FOR PUBLIC SAFETY PROFESSIONALS

Authors:

Deirdre von Krauskopf
Sean Wyman

PRAISE FOR GOING BEYOND THE CALL

Going Beyond the Call teaches why the importance of communication and emotional intelligence is critical! It's what we do near 100% of our time, from gathering vital data to de-escalation & dealing with people in crisis. This is how you create positive interactions.

~ Chris Summers, Chief of Investigations, Leon County Sheriff's Office

The reason I believe so strongly in this content is it helps us to realize we are communicating all the time; our thoughts and feelings come through in actions, reactions, and words. Through this program, they are given the tools to communicate effectively, in any situation, helping them enjoy success on the job and in their private lives, which I believe are inseparable.

~ Chief E.E. Eunice, Director, Florida Public Safety Institute

Going Beyond the Call is an outstanding workshop providing good knowledge and interesting content. I learned a lot about stressors, recognizing, and mitigation. The statistics were eye-opening, and the interactive presentation was excellent.

~Jeremy Radney, District Chief, Walton County Fire Rescue

We not only deal with folks coming in with severe mental health issues we have to deal with the ongoing issues, including suicide. This course will not only help me manage the people I deal with, but it will help with my own stressors. It allowed me to learn to manage my own emotions better.

~ Keyera Wilcox, Corrections / Law Enforcement, Leon County Sheriff's Office

Going Beyond the Call was very interesting, great content, and so helpful to work and home success. I gained great insight and information about the development of stress and reactions in mind and body. Recognizing the different levels of stress, burnout, hypervigilance, depression, PTSD, and all the different stress reduction techniques to manage it all.

~Rachel Barker, Paramedic, Walton County Fire Rescue (Mental Health Committee)

I think this information is critical for officers. I've never really gave thought about how stress could impact me over my career. We are told this is a stressful job, you will hate it at times, you'll get divorced, but not taught how to combat those realities until now. The communication tactics are great!

~ Tazaia Weilhammer, Florida State Police Department

I attended a Going Beyond the Call workshop with members from all public safety professions, great dialogue on how trauma affects each area across the board. I really liked learning how to disengage in a heightened stress situation with the calming and redirection of thought tactics. The instructors were so relatable, using personal experiences on the job and from personal life to relay the message. It really impacted how I view my life and reactions, it has lightened my load and given new meaning. So grateful to have taken this class! I definitely want the new hires and others to learn this.

~Brittany Mosley, Communications Training Officer, Walton County

Communications training is as essential as emotional Intelligence training. We often manage social and emotional interactions. Understanding how people react the way they do and how they may trigger us from our own past gives an advantage not often learned without years of experience. This training is essential for success.

~ Mark Saunders, Chief of Police, Toronto Police Service

This learning is groundbreaking on issues we are behind the ball in. We handle others in crisis but not trained in how to help each other, lessen suicide, and depression. This content teaches this and more. The understanding of the brain, body, and relationship impacts is outstanding! This will change your life!

~ Robert Hunter, Florida State University Police Department

Going Beyond the Call delivered outstanding training that is helpful to all areas of life. I enjoyed learning the biological and neuroscience aspects of psychological responsiveness. How stress reactions work and can be managed. It was interesting to learn the legal liabilities related to stress impacts.

~Jeremiah Gile, Detective, Bureau Fire, Arson and Explosives

Going Beyond the Call provides excellent knowledge that is helpful for both personal and work life. Understanding the science behind communications challenges (push-pull) and the emotional intelligence components is very useful. The awareness of mental health stressors, including ACE's was insightful. Deirdre and Sean are well informed and passionate about this topic.

~ Ramona Rumph, Director of Communications, Seminole County Sheriff's Office.

Fascinating information, some things are really hitting home. Understanding ACE's and trauma in a whole new way. That in itself will be so helpful on the job. The emotion wheel, taking how we manage stress to a whole new level and working with citizens in their crisis moments.

~ Will Blanton, Emergency Communications Training. Officer and Recruiter, Consolidated Dispatch Agency

Going Beyond the Call is outstanding! Beneficial information on trauma-informed care, how to develop mental fitness in a high-stress career and understanding, mitigation of burnout before it grows into worse, like PTSD. This was, by far, one of the best workshops, I learned so much. It has helped me realize some of my own signs and how to start working on them before they impact in worse ways.

~Larry Long, Deputy, Liberty County Sheriff's Office and Training Officer, Department of Child and Family Services

I learned so much! I believe this content would be great for everyone, academy, and veteran officers. We need this for the people we interact with, and for ourselves and our wellness as officers. We are here to help others but also have to save ourselves and our peers.

~ Justin Reed, Florida State College Police Department

DIRT ROAD PUBLISHING

A DIVISION OF NORRIS VENTURES, LLC

Going Beyond the Call ~ Mental Health Fitness for Public Safety Professionals

First Published in 2019 by Dirt Road Publishing Dirt Road Publishing
Jamestown, NC
T: 1-336-477-3693

BULK PURCHASE: Please contact the publisher and author at:
info@goingbeyondthecall.com | **1-844-411-GBTC (4282)**

Logo Design: Lynn Wyman, Graphic Designer
Cover Design: Benjamin Peddycord, Visual Designer
Editor: Marlo Francis

ISBN

Softcover: 978-1-988995-17-5
Hardcover: 978-1-988995-14-4
eBook ISBN: 978-1-988995-1

DEDICATION

This book is dedicated to:

Those who, day and night,

bring order to chaos,

extinguish the flames,

breathe life into the lifeless,

remain calm in the storm,

bring civility to hostility

and are all willing to provide light to complete darkness ~

while unknowingly getting captured in their own

~ truly going beyond the call.

The Public Safety Professional

PROLOGUE

NORMAL REACTIONS TO ABNORMAL EVENTS

"You hold in your hands one of the most important books of our time. A hidden impact, a stigmatized secret that overshadows the men and women who sacrifice every day. Going Beyond the Call, is nothing less than an action plan for the magnificent individuals who "go beyond the call" every day - and for our very civilization - to survive and thrive in the midst of death and darkness. We must begin a process, a movement, a revolution in which every public safety professional is equipped with the information in this vital book."

~Lt. Col. Dave Grossman, author of
On Killing, On Combat, and Assassination Generation

Going Beyond the Call is asking you to take a big step in faith, one that has to open up your defenses and acknowledge the muted reality within your professions. To understand the critical information causing a toll on your mind and body that is not yet part of mandatory rookie training, college curriculums, or annual requalification. As much as that is our long-term goal, we know we have a long road to travel, and it begins with you.

Our starting point is to impact a common denominator, your desire and commitment to rescue others. The rates of suicide, mental health concerns, critical illness, and relationship challenges among your professions are unforgivably high. We aim to help you help your peers, those in your charge, and by the end, by learning the logic of the material may be enough for you to look inward and, if needed, rescue yourself.

You see, hear, touch, smell unimaginable, and with your incredible resilience, many make it through a long career unscathed. Some of you will fall back on the industry standards of stoicism, disassociation, depersonalizing, or putting the troubling aspects of your experience in a vault. It is a sound psychological defense strategy, and every defense has a weakness, so we are going to enhance whatever approach you use.

The most important thing for us to remember when it comes to a psychological trauma injury is there are no preset absolutes in the span of trauma experiences. Our childhoods, personality, resilience, ego states, mental health, emotional intelligence, DNA, cumulative trauma events, and more all build a unique perspective and outcome. Wherever you are on your life path when trauma strikes, how you respond is perfectly normal, including no reaction, even when all those around you seem severely impacted. An intense fear response or sense of helplessness or hopelessness can ignite the same internal chemical brain reaction as other forms of trauma. Over time something that would not cause you to blink ten years ago may have an emotional response that catches you completely off guard if not trained to be aware and knowledgeable on what to do about it along the way or when it gets personally intense.

Some may scoff that members in these professions are conditioned to manage the unthinkable, and in truth, the resiliency in these fields is extraordinary. However, consider the international impact on those watching the devastating events of 9-11. There are very few members of the public that were not riveted in horror as that act of terrorism unfolded on television. Members of public safety professions have the training; many have experienced enough events to have watched that same event unfold with a knowing lens that gave a more profound sense of fear, helplessness, and horror. Many of you had a painfully clear picture of what those at the scene were managing. You comprehended the enormity of the rescue efforts before the collapse and cringed at the challenges of fighting/containing fires of that magnitude and locations. Many were initially watching with an innate drive to want to be there and help to know the overwhelming aspects and then to watch; one; then, the other building collapse to feel that impact with all your knowledge. The average person was flooded with incomprehensible helplessness and fear. I do not have to emphasize the heightened emotion felt as it rippled through each and every one of you. We mourn nationally when any member is lost in the line of duty, but this had a truly unimaginable grief and helpless anger impact that still raises intense emotion as we continue to lose brave men and women that worked the event and recovery.

As we work through the impacts of psychological trauma, respect that it is not just the direct or even indirect events that can damage your mind and body; we cover the peripheral elements many tend to dismiss or shove into their vaults without considering. Even the strongest among you have breaking points or cracks that form that impact quality of life. For all that you give, you deserve the very best awareness, prevention, mitigation, and treatment tactics to gain and maintain a healthy mental fitness.

We urge you to send in your comments, share your stories, and help us spread the word that no one among you is alone should darkness creep into your thoughts, or cracks show in your armor. To further support you, our next goal is to bring you an app that provides a source of hope, information, and unity across these professions. It will provide information, self-assessment quizzes, resiliency tactics, updated training, awareness, and help links that can serve you and your peers when needed. We seek members from every area to participate in surveys to build the national and inclusive data required for administrators and government funding bodies to approve training in this area of knowledge. Finally, we need your help to create the necessary momentum so that this topic becomes as critical as the initial and annual training you undertake for your safety, protection, and outstanding service to the public.

Connect with us:

Twitter.com/GBTC911

Facebook.com/gbtc911/

Linkedin.com/company/gbtc

Instagram.com/@gbtc911

GoingBeyongTheCall.com

GBTC911.COM (Non-Profit)

info@goingbeyondthecall.com

1-844-411-GBTC (4292)

Table of Contents

ACKNOWLEDGMENTS

We would like to acknowledge James MacNeil, contributor, for his brilliant communications program; whom Sean is a Licensed Business Partner and I, a Global Business Partner. His work significantly improved the communication savvy in our professional endeavors and more importantly, with those who matter most to us. The aspects of this program we will share here will, in turn, change yours.

Lynn Wyman, a talented graphic artist that embodied all public safety disciplines in the creation of our amazing logo. She also patiently listened and interjected to help collaborate when our sibling-like debates and discourse in the creation of this work was stalling progress.

Lastly, to our experiences and life lessons, however painful; without them, we would not have the drive to serve and help others in the capacity we are able to.

Partial proceeds from the sale of this book support the non-profit GBTC911 (.com) aiding families and retirees impacted by the stressors and trauma of these high-risk professions in partnership with grants, funding and angel investors for online, in-person training and our annual relationship retreats.

FOREWORD

By: Lt. Col. Dave Grossman, author of
On Killing, On Combat, and Assassination Generation

You hold in your hands one of the most important books of our time. A hidden impact, a stigmatized secret that overshadows the men and women who sacrifice every day. We can understand the trauma impact of warfare; but often overlook the trauma that prefaces and impacts the daily interactions with those who cross paths with public safety professionals every day. We do not learn the toll of these interactions, nor understand the underlying cause that impedes an enlightened system of care that can make or break our resident's wellness and contribution to society, or, our public safety professionals psychological, physiological and biological wellness.

Stay with me a moment, while I outline to you:

1. The magnitude of the threat
2. The essential role of our "public safety professionals" as the vital "lubricant" in the friction points for our civilization
3. The critical role of this book in assisting those individuals to rise to the dominant challenge of our age while maintaining internal and interdependent wellness to the direct, indirect, cumulative and vicarious trauma they see, feel and bear over the course of their careers.

The Threat: The Toxic Realm of Human Aggression

We recognize the big threats after they take place. We understand and sympathize with horror when human life is made meaningless in the eyes of domestic and international threats. We "get it" when it hits the news; but rarely consider the daily toll that the readiness, vigilance, investigative and insider knowledge takes on the mental health of those who prepare for that potential threat, every day. Take a moment now and consider:

- The attack on the World Trade Center on September 11, 2001, with 2,996 dead; generally considered the most horrendous terrorist attack in history.
- Over 600 massacred, many of them children, in the Lutheran Church in Liberia, in 1990; possibly the single worst church massacre in modern history.
- 69 murdered and 120 wounded on Utoya, Norway, in 2011; the most horrendous massacre by a single individual using only firearms.

- 59 murdered by a single person, with firearms, in the Las Vegas Mandalay Massacre in 2017; the worst such crime in American history.
- 15 murdered by a 17-year-old student in Winnenden, Germany, 2009; the worst massacre, committed by a juvenile, in human history.
- 17 murdered in Erfurt Germany in 2002, and 17 murdered in Parkland Florida in 2018; both crimes committed by 19-year-old high school dropouts. (That is not an error, an identical crime to Parkland happened in Erfurt, and these crimes by 19-year-old perpetrators do not qualify for our "juvenile hit parade".)
- 26 murdered in Newtown Connecticut, 20 of them 1st grade students with ages ranging from five to six years-old, in 2012.
- 33 murdered in Virginia Tech University, Virginia in 2007, and 20 murdered in Kerch College, Russia in 2018.
- These are not the events of some ancient history in some distant land. This is us. This is now.

In the US, the FBI tells us that the number of mass murders is doubling every decade and the average body count is going up. You do not have to go any further than the front page of your newspaper to find similar examples in your own part of the world.

This all points to a new twist in terrorism: body count. Whether the perpetrators are school killers, workplace killers, or international terrorists, they are not interested in negotiating; their only goal is to kill as many people as humanly possible. This new twist in terrorism creates a call to reconsider the previous psychological effects of terrorism on society - especially the effects on those directly in the pathway of this new violence.

During the deadly 9-11 events in the United States, terrorists murdered over 3,000 citizens; the stock market crashed; the US invaded two nations and our world changed - instantly and dramatically. Interestingly, we find that in that very same year, over 30,000 Americans were killed in traffic accidents - yet life continued on at a seemingly, unchanged pace. The reason behind this stark contrast is the very reason that terrorists have adopted this new twist into their evil plans. Even though the latter number is 10x's greater than the former, the traffic-related deaths were accidents that happened over time, instead of a mass attack that claimed so many at once.

The Diagnostic and Statistical Manual of the American Psychiatric Association (the "Bible" of psychiatry and psychology) tells us that when the cause of a traumatic event is "human, in nature," the degree of psychological trauma is usually more severe with longer-lasting effects.

In our minds, we still recoil from the memories and shock of these events - yet, empathetically, let's take these feelings a little deeper for those that hear and are briefed on these kinds of potential and imminent threats, every shift. Add to that, the additional anxiety of never knowing whether or not a simple violation stop, medical transfer, vehicular accident, suicide call, or domestic intervention will end by taking a bite out of their soul.

These things considered; how you would respond to the following two scenarios:

> A tornado (or earthquake or fire or tsunami) hits your house while you are gone and puts your whole family in the hospital.
>
> What is your initial reaction? Most people would say, "Thank God, they survived!"
>
> A gang hits your house while you are gone and beats your whole family, putting them all in the hospital. How do you feel about that one?

Most people would agree that there is a vast difference between these two scenarios and the emotions they conjure; thus, we have to recognize that this toxic realm of human aggression is what we are asking our public safety professionals to deal with and most often, clean up. If they fail, the very existence of our civilization is at risk. For these public safety professionals, every day deposits more residue into their memories and feelings; impacting the lens through which they view and the manner in which they engage every additional human interaction.

The defining, societal challenge for the future is to protect our way of life from this ever-encroaching violence that threatens our civilization on every front. This is what we ask our public safety professionals to deal with, on a smaller but no-less-toxic scale, every day; this is what we ask them to deal with when the massive, major incidents occur; when gunshots are being fired; when people are dying; when every sane rational creature flees from the danger - we find these magnificent humans going towards the danger. Many would say, "Wait! Fire and EMS responders do not go into the fray while shots are being fired; only law enforcement does that, right?"

Wrong.

Today we are teaching our fire and EMS responders what "going beyond the call" literally means - moving into emergency zones directly behind or even, in some situations, shoulder-to-shoulder with our law enforcement brothers and sisters. These magnificent men and women are dedicated to "going in" as soon as possible, to be there during that precious "window of time" when there is a greater chance of saving lives, especially in situations where horrifically wounded citizens have injuries that won't wait. Our dispatchers talk desperate folks out of pulling triggers while simultaneously hearing those, with whom they serve alongside, enduring those high-risk scenarios in real time. Our forensic technicians count body parts and piece together humanity's diabolical aftermaths. Our corrections officers live in fear and readiness for that one, last, desperate act of a long-lost soul, housing an unquenchable evil that longs to express itself. Every single day, our terror and disaster response teams manage the unimaginable.

Thus, the threat to our civilization is extraordinary; yet, the conundrum is that the more lives our public safety professionals save, the less the "body count" and the less we are aware of the threat. Indeed, there is quite a paradox here, in that, the murder rate is being held down, not by an improvement in societal behavior - but by improvements in medical and other public safety technology!

In 2002, Anthony Harris, along with a team of scholars from the University of Massachusetts and Harvard, published a landmark study in the journal: Homicide Studies. This study concluded that medical technology advances since 1970 have prevented approximately 3-out-of-4 murders. That is, if we had 1970s level medical technology, the murder rate would be three or four times higher than it is today. And that data is almost 20 years old! The leaps-and-bounds of medical technology in the last 20 years is astounding. The situation is much worse than it looks.

The Response: The While Blood Cells of Our Civilization

In the midst of these violent and desperate times, at the critical "friction point" of our civilization, wherever and whenever it is the worst, that is where you will find our public safety professionals: the vital "lubricant", easing the friction points of our society.

We must rise to the challenge. Our public safety professionals are the white blood cells in our civilization, and we must "super-charge" those white blood cells, if we have any hope of survival in these desperate and violent times. We must empower and equip them as never before - both psychologically and physically. And it is within our ability to do so!

Above all else, this book should give us hope that great minds are rising to the occasion and answering the call to rise to new levels of performance. Our public safety professionals are "going beyond the call", every day, to save lives and to preserve our way of life. They must be equipped, trained, empowered and prepared to a higher level of human performance that goes beyond technical skills and must include the psychological and emotional intelligence to manage the stress and horror of daily events. It must rip off the band aid of "awareness" and dive deeply into the mind, body and soul of these professional callings.

That is what this book is all about. That is why you hold in your hands one of the most important and critical works of our time. With this book, Deirdre von Krauskopf and Sean Wyman have given us a "universal survival manual" for all public safety professionals. The array of resources in this book is simply astounding. I cannot begin to encapsulate the information in this book, or to communicate my great respect for the authors. People cannot manage, control and improve what they do not know or understand; therefore, the knowledge gained through this training fortifies the inner strength of these sacrificing professions. Anything less does not honor the impact these careers have on the psyche and wellness of those who serve our daily safety and security.

Going Beyond the Call, is nothing less than an action plan for the magnificent individuals who "go beyond the call" every day - and for our very civilization - to survive and thrive in the midst of death and darkness. We must begin a process, a movement, a revolution in which every public safety professional is equipped with the information in this vital book.

Thus, I welcome you to an amazing book. And I encourage you, I exhort you, to not just read it, but study this book, and apply it to survive and thrive. Because those who go beyond the call; those who bring light to the dark places where others fear to go - they deserve the very best that we have to give them.

Well done, Deirdre and Sean!

INTRODUCTION

This book was developed for public safety organizations, nationwide, knowing they are seeking solutions to halt the growing trends in member suicide, unhealthy behaviors, rising turn over, and mental health wellness.

We hope that this book enables you, your family and friends understand and mitigate the unavoidable impact of these professions, which will reduce self-harming and detrimental behaviors. The trauma you see, hear, experience and manage on a regular basis, negatively impacts your mental health fitness when left unmanaged. Our unique approach identifies issues and solutions from a psychological, physiological and relationship perspective. At the end of this learning you will optimize your health through:

- Trauma informed care
- Mental health fitness
- Body language interpretation
- Human behavior neuroscience
- Advanced communication techniques
- Emotional intelligence
- Resiliency tactics

Let's start with trauma informed care: a trending psychology discipline that enables an in-depth self-awareness on how our internal wellness impacts every interaction. Secondly, you will learn more about the majority of people we interact with, including those with mental health challenges, learning how to approach them with a calm, safe, confident mindset. Understanding the basic neuroscience of human behavior and mental health challenges lessens stress inducing situations and provides members with a powerful pre-escalation approach.

Delving into mental health fitness we share the hard facts of the psychological, physiological and relationship impacts common across these professions. While some embody a strong resilience as their career builds, many do not, as seen in growing suicide and self-harming numbers. Even those who have convinced themselves their emotional vaults are impenetrable, will soon discover their coping mechanisms are unlikely to be the best for long-term health outcomes. In discovering the science behind brain plasticity, you will learn how easy it is to develop resiliency at any stage, rookie through retirement.

It starts with self and controlling the controllable. Through emotional intelligence, personality profiling, and body language techniques you will learn to be the best version of yourself in every situation. These professionals live to serve something bigger than themselves. They seek ways to rescue others during their worst possible moments; yet, it is a challenge to turn that ability inward and rescue themselves - or reach out for a hand for help. It is imperative that we do everything possible to bring light to those living in the shadows of traumatic inputs.

In addition, we will share what you need to watch for within your peer groups and within yourself for stress, health and relationship impacts. Our mission is to reverse the trends and avoid losing one more soul to suicide because of a lack of information or stigmatization.

Lastly, we cover the power of effective communications. When interacting and influencing others the tools and tactics provided will give you a significant advantage in attaining your interactive objective. The questioning techniques are ideal for gaining insight and cooperation with those you serve in the community. However, our vision incorporates how to improve the home life of every public safety professionals we serve with this knowledge. Advancing the member wellness goals of every agency by encouraging the healthiest and the happiest version of oneself when showing up on the job.

This knowledge is imperative to public safety professionals, given a large percentage of interactions do not center on the standard training provided. While critical for member safety and protocol, a large percentage of daily work interactions will center around someone having a bad moment and your presence either triggering an escalated response or keeping them calm and focused. This training will develop healthier reactions to others; enable stronger cooperation from someone in crisis mode; gain faster information to aid your objective; improve your mental fitness and most importantly, enhance conversations with your loved ones.

The need for a comprehensive training program that gets to root-cause answers drove us to develop this work together. The statistics tell us what is available out there is not working; yet, advances in neuroscience, behavioral science, communications strategies, mental health, emotional intelligence and trauma informed care, provide us the knowledge to reverse unacceptable trends. This is how we brought it together:

Co-Author: Deirdre von Krauskopf

Resiliency and an anti-victim mindset have been the cornerstone of my mindset from a young age. Being a tough, focused, strong-willed woman served me well in overcoming the adversity of my trauma-infused childhood and also aided my advancing success in male-dominated positions, both in the military and throughout my career. At 18, it also gave me the grounded foresight to choose a man that was a rock: stable, secure, calm, and strong. I thought that I knew exactly what was needed to create the life I had dreamed of as a child.

Considering the trauma as a teacher in strength-building lessons, I was a master of vaulting emotions; managing the unthinkable and adapting to challenges. My husband moved through the sections and ranks of policing into high-risk positions and I was the perfect partner in managing the stress - even the stress of several attempts on his life and multiple accidents over the years. I felt that this was where I could be the rock for him and ease the burden of the traumatic impacts of his chosen career. He shared more with me than the average "public safety professional couple"; finding strength in that closeness, something we often wished for our friends and colleagues whose marriages we'd watch falling apart. Until that "one thing" happened, we seemed to have it all.

We were unprepared; both individually, and as a couple, when this one, direct trauma changed this rock-of-a-man that I had married - which then, in turn, changed me - then in a very short time, changed us. Watching our near-perfect union dissolving, I grew more desperate to find what might fix the growing disconnect and sense of spiraling loss between us. He, on the other hand, pushed it to the back of his inner-vault - ignoring all the changes and coping in increasingly, unhealthy ways.

Along the way, I read psychology books, learned about trauma and PTSD impacts, and received counselling - all of it offering me great insights and information. None of it, however, taught me the tactics and skills necessary for mitigating the imminent crash. I reverted to an instinctual and foreboding dread that beckoned me to escape. After 26 years, I made the most difficult decision of my life and left - hoping that the rock that I married would resurface and take on the challenges necessary to fix us; but unfortunately, he did not. As soul-crushing as that was, I knew I needed to persevere if I was to understand and find the answers that I needed in order to adapt and overcome my indescribable heartbreak.

In attempting to heal, I jumped into psychology from an "other" perspective - because what had happened to him is what made such a drastic impact on us. Fortunately, we had a good co-parenting relationship - there was no bitterness or hatred - just an overwhelming sadness for the loss that greatly mirrored the grieving process. I convinced myself that he was like a twin of himself; looked familiar to me, but no longer the same man. It allowed me to focus on easing his burden by being the best ex-spouse I could be; not triggering his PTSD by my actions. This masked-effort did not really heal anything thing and it was beginning to show in my health, my inability to authentically connect in another relationships, or to fill the ever-empty feelings inside.

In 2015, friends introduced me to a communications and emotional intelligence course that was mind-blowing. For the first time, I learned how much my actions and reactions fueled the end of my marriage. Immersing into a deeper study of myself and how I contributed to the realities of my past, allowed for true self-healing. For the first time, it wasn't just about my ex, or about the man who tried to kill him - or about the cumulative trauma of "the job" or his unhealthy coping mechanisms. I could not fix or change those things; but, if I knew then what I know now, I would have had the skills to respond differently. I would have communicated differently, and I expect the outcome would have been much different. He would have learned to understand the impacts of his cumulative, direct trauma and perhaps made different decisions about coping and our relationship. Although it was too late for us, I was sparked with the hope that I might be able to save others from the same devastating fate as my own.

Courses and studies built upon this learning presented as an opportunity and I jumped at the chance to buy a license and teach the content. For the first time, career-wise, I wasn't helping corporations make millions - instead, I was changing lives for the better. Testing out the content as a protégé and then later helping the founder spread the licensed program, I soon came to the crossroad of retiring my corporate hat and delivering this content, full-time.

The program founder, James MacNeil, was the son of a law enforcement officer, himself, and lived with the effects of unhealthy coping mechanisms, at the hand of his addicted father. He loved the idea of developing content to meet the unique needs within public safety fields. Soon after, we met Sean Wyman in a training session and connected with a plan to deliver this to law enforcement. James and I co-wrote the first program, Communication Tactics for law enforcement and Public Safety Professional, followed by a retreat for public safety professionals that I authored: Relationship 911. After that, I wrote, Behind the Badge ~ The Home Effect of Serve and Protect, for those attending our programs. Sean, also a licensee, taught the program and tested it on the streets.

Sean and I had many conversations about how much this training helped us reconcile our pasts, greatly improve our inner dialogue and manage communications in a powerful way. Through the business partnership and training he and his awesome wife, Lynn, (another trauma to success story) created a strong bond of friendship that quickly morphed to family.

Buying a global license from James, I could now develop new products. Influenced by his program, I grew my education in the neuroscience of human behavior. Developing and facilitating programs for corporate delivery in employee engagement, wellness and customer service, and published my first book, Mistakenly Underappreciated ~ Re-engaging the Disengaged. Since that time, I have formed partnerships with other licensed business partners to deliver programs, globally; but, my passion for making a difference in public safety professions remained a priority.

The law enforcement program was successful, our testimonials outstanding; but it did not take off - something was missing to bring it all together as a truly transformational program that met agency training priorities. Sean supplied the answer. In his ongoing development, he became certified in Critical Incident Training, exclaiming how critical this mental health training was to an officer's success. He also saw a missing link between mental health knowledge and the social-emotional skills learned in our designed program. He further studied trauma informed care and saw the power in combining these elements with the brain science elements I had developed.

We outlined what that would look like – and this book was born. Through researching and interviewing, we quickly decided to open the scope to the broader public safety family. It was the logical advancement, given the aligned stressors and trauma these professions have in common, the similar stigma that hinders managing that stress and alarming suicide rates across the board.

Through Sean, I learned about the Adverse Childhood Experiences (A.C.E.) survey - and that we each scored a 9. He had gained significant expertise, certified in trauma informed care and had acquired a great understanding of how childhood trauma impacted the interactions and triggers we show in adulthood. After gaining my own certification, I saw the power in teaching this aspect. I will now turn it over to my business partner, Sean to share more.

Co-Author: Sean Wyman

As the author of, The M.O.V.E.M.E.N.T Process, I have dedicated myself to helping the transformational development of those overcoming the impacts of trauma. As a strong, energetic, ambitious, never-say-quit innovator, I will show you the path to a stronger mental mindset. With 20-years' experience in law enforcement and 8-years in the military, I found my time as an Army Ranger and LEO instructor instilled the need for excellent safety and tactical preparedness training. What I now know (through the lessons we will teach you here), is that it's only the tip of the iceberg. Understanding the social, emotional and trauma-infused aspects of human behavior are critical to our success in the field; for our ongoing mental fitness; as well as for fulfillment in our important relationships. There is a lot of valuable information that will provide essential tools for your toolbox that can:

- Help you bridge gaps in your community
- Improve your mental and physical health - both on and off the job

- Reduce agency liability
- SAVE YOUR LIFE

I have experienced the impacts of trauma from both sides. Thriving after surviving an abusive childhood and movement through the foster care and group home system, was not easily achieved. My adverse childhood experiences fueled drug and alcohol addiction by the time I was 13. The next phase of life was no better, as 27 found me carrying a failed marriage and $100,000 in accumulated debt. My military experience came with a near-death experience, followed by a tremendously painful recovery. If there is anything I understand in this world, it is the effects of psychological trauma.

For a long time, I allowed these events and experiences to be anchors. Moving into law enforcement, I was still carrying emotional scars and anger from my childhood and it showed with how I managed interactions with the public. Working in an environment that triggered my early experiences and not understanding that lessened my effectiveness in avoiding escalation.

Recognizing this and wanting to achieve greater success within my second marriage, I took a long look at myself; realizing I needed to revisit and face the brokenness in my past to be able to move forward in my professional and personal life. With that one, watershed, self-development decision, came the blessings to do everything I ever wanted to do within law enforcement. I have been happily married for over 15 years and I am a proud father of three amazing children.

As I continued on this "best version" journey - both for myself and for those I was coaching, I discovered the communications and emotional intelligence course where I met Deirdre and James MacNeil. Throughout their training, I saw the benefit of sharing the content with law enforcement - but not until I tested it, myself. As a Defensive Tactics and Firearms Instructor, I understood the need to test things to make sure they pass the street test. They passed - and for the last several years I have been applying this training on the streets and on a consistent basis and have been amazed with the results.

Through my own self-awareness and growth, I discovered a positive outcome when I began to learn about childhood and psychological trauma and the effects of these experiences over the long term. It was disheartening to watch public safety professionals across the nation falling into depression, burn out and committing suicide. I wanted to know why this was happening and what I could do, on a larger scale, to reverse this increasing trend. As I began to educate myself, I met and learned from people like Dr. Vincent Felitti and Tonier Caine, as well as leading global trauma experts like, Judy Crane. The more I trained and studied, the more I came to scary realizations that only served to fuel my ever-growing desire to help lead in a movement for change.

When I went to the law enforcement academy back in 2000, we learned a lot of amazing things that helped me be a more effective officer - but they missed one critical aspect that is still overlooked today; understanding self and others from a social and emotional perspective. Ensuring that public safety professionals are trauma-informed with mental-health-readiness training is the key to optimizing success from Day 1 on the street - when their boots hit the ground. We added in both communications and emotional-intelligence strategies to further supply the necessary tools for managing the social and emotional issues faced over 90% of the time.

When I got into law enforcement, I knew it was a calling - I truly wanted to help people and serve at a high level. The calling to serve something bigger than oneself is a common thread amongst public safety professionals. Through this training, you will come to the same realization I discovered. The people we want to help are being triggered and often hurt worse from our interactive approach because of the re-traumatization taking place subconsciously. Our hope is that with the knowledge learned here, change will result - and with that change, a huge impact on escalation-avoidance; truly helping people through traumatic experiences.

Further realization of the changes needed within training comes when you understand, not only the impact of direct traumas, but also the cumulative events and vicarious traumas that impacts the mental and physical wellness of public safety professionals. There is a need for focused intervention. Today, I can understand there was a purpose behind all the adversity I faced earlier in my life. This understanding allows me to not only overcome my own past, but also creates an ability to identify a problem that needs a solution. There are many resources available that identify and report the startling statistics of public safety suicides; but, there is no denying this wake-up call when find that the numbers of lives lost on the job does not eclipse the numbers of those who are choosing to end their lives by their own means. This cannot be ignored.

However, it goes deeper than that with statistics showing us there is a direct impact from the daily stress that results in heart disease, increased safety violations, lost time attendance issues, unbecoming conduct and lawsuits. Through my continued studies in psychological trauma impacts, I learned the outcomes they have on a public safety professional in both the short term and the long term. You cannot gain this knowledge and not want to share it far and wide because lives will be changed. Our training, more than anything, is committed to this one thing: saving lives and enhancing the quality of life.

The communication and emotional intelligence skills and tactics will provide fantastic inroads to improving interactions on the job and more importantly, off the job. We will ask you to give yourself some grace throughout this book as there are things we know and things we do not. After reading this work for yourself, you will be very aware and can then make a conscious decision to use these tactics or not.

It is smart to identify where we find ourselves within the learning cycle and open ourselves to new ideas and new ways of looking at things. There is a psychological aspect to learning competence from an original teaching model by Martin Broadwell that helps us understand. This model relates to the psychological states that occurs while learning any new skill bringing us from a state of incompetence to competence.

The Four Stages of Competence

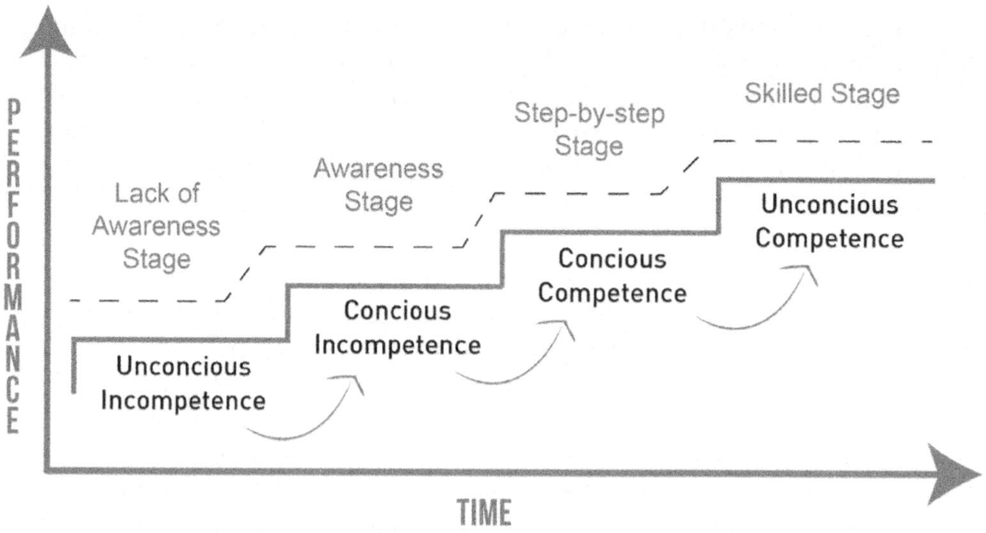

When I partnered with Deirdre to develop this program, we committed to writing direct, honest truth. Truth that goes far beyond awareness and provides tangible knowledge and tactics that can be used immediately to enhance lives. PTSD and suicide are real problems in this industry, but these tragic outcomes often manifest from cumulative inputs that are mismanaged due to lack of knowledge.

This book will improve your understanding of mental fitness from a whole-person perspective. You will discover simple street-proven communications and pre-escalation tactics that will serve you in the field or at home. The emotional intelligence and ego state management will assist your self-development. The awareness, prevention, mitigation and resiliency learned will create improved peer-to-peer support and lead the trend towards building trauma informed public safety organizations. It is time we focus not only on being the first line of defense but also the first line of healing so, #letskeepmovingforward.

CHAPTER 1

IT BEGINS WITH UNDERSTANDING

The disillusion of carrying the weight of the world on your shoulders is you do not have to stare it in the face so it remains hidden.
~Deirdre von Krauskopf

Public safety professionals see the worst in people on a daily basis. You are the guardians, rescuers, life savers and authoritative bodies over the tragedies, traumas and offences against humanity. In the not too distant past, there was more reverence for the work you selflessly did by the general population, now there is a camera catching every wrong while overlooking many saves In this book we will solve three key issues to help reduce the impact caused by the nature of these professions:

1. Bridge the gap between public safety professionals and the communities they serve

2. Create higher quality of life and improved wellness for public safety professionals

3. Reduce the liability, risk and political impacts to organizations

Clearly there is a significant need for understanding and training in both trauma informed care and mental health awareness, prevention, mitigation, self-care tactics and treatment options. Knowledge and tools for resiliency and self-care are as critical as the tactical and safety training every member receives. Too often, the outcome of uninformed trauma build-up is tragically impacting public safety professionals who:

- Take their own lives
- Turn to addictive coping methods
- Chose negative and career impacting behaviors
- End up as unintentional, viral, social media sensations

Mental Health studies on public safety professionals show that depression from direct, indirect and long-term exposure to trauma are key factors that contribute to higher-than-usual suicide rates. Suicide and depression are still a small percentage of a bigger problem. Untreated stress and mental fatigue lead to poor physical health and impaired decision-making skills.

National statistics are challenging to find so numbers are pulled from studies around the globe to show an international concern. PTSD and depression rates among firefighters and law enforcement officers have been found to be as much as 5 times higher than the rates within the civilian population; communications and corrections are disturbingly high with EMS in some areas reporting critical numbers.[i] Imagine, this is only what is reported.

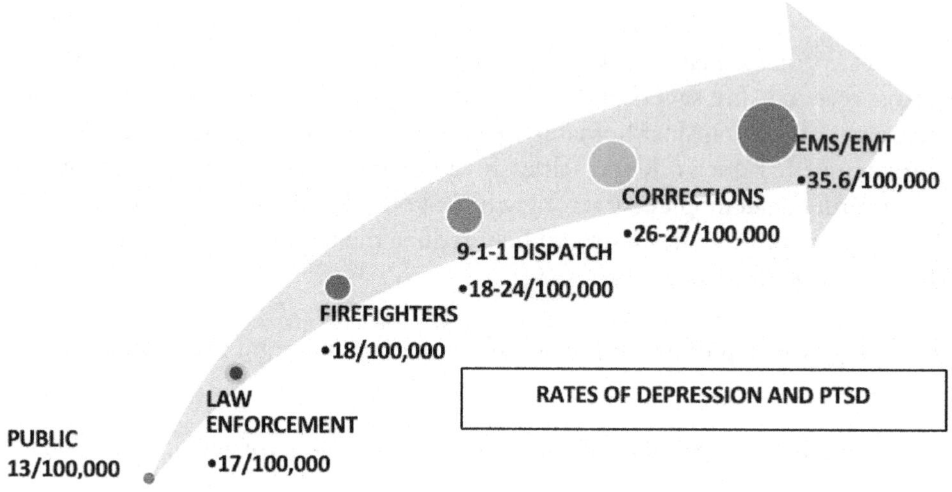

The Ruderman Family Foundation reported … tragically more law enforcement officers and firefighters died in 2017 from suicide than from incidents on the job. "In 2017, there were at least 103 firefighter suicides and 140 law enforcement officer suicides. In contrast, 93 firefighters and 129 law enforcement officers died in the line of duty. Suicide is a result of mental illness, including depression and PTSD, which stems from constant exposure to death and destruction. Even when suicide does not occur, untreated mental illness can lead to poor physical health and impaired decision-making."[ii]

The Firefighter Behavioral Health Alliance (FBHA) further estimates that approximately only 40% of firefighter suicides are reported. If these estimates are accurate, the actual number of 2017 suicides would be approximately equal to 257, which is more than twice the number of firefighters who died in the line of duty.

The Journal of Emergency Medical Services (JEMS)[iii] clearly identified that critical stress has the same devastating effects. This survey result showed that:

- 3,447 (86%) of the 4,022 respondents experienced critical stress

- 1,383 (37%) of the respondents had contemplated suicide
- 225 (6.6%) had actually tried to take their own life

These EMS statistics are roughly 10 times greater than the national average for adults in America, according to a study done by the Centers for Disease Control and Prevention in 2012.[iv]

The Journal of Traumatic Stress summed up the critical need to address dispatchers when developing mental health awareness plans. Listening and responding to traumatic and life-threatening situations can cause fear/anxiety, helplessness and horror, just to name a few - which, if left unaddressed, set the stage for Acute Stress Disorder (ASD) and Post-Traumatic Stress Disorder (PTSD). 3.5% of survey respondents reported symptoms, "... severe enough to qualify for a diagnosis of PTSD." (Pierce. H, Lilly. M, 2012).[v] An interesting finding was that not knowing what happens "after calls" were also significant stressors for dispatchers. An ABC news article stated:

> "The men and women who field 911 emergencies hear some of the most soul-searing sounds imaginable: the anguished wailing of gunshot victims, the final words of someone they can't deter from suicide, or the last thoughts of someone gasping for breath in a fire; however, the stresses of their experiences sometimes haven't been considered traumatic because the dispatchers haven't left their computer consoles."
>
> "I think this is a really important study because dispatchers are the forgotten public safety professionals," said Francine Roberts, a clinical psychologist in Marlton, N.J., who treats public safety professionals with PTSD. "They carry a high level of responsibility for coordinating the response to the incident, but they are very remote from it. High levels of responsibility and low levels of the ability to influence the outcome equate extremely high stress.
>
> Recognizing that times of high stress will cause adrenal and cortisol response, while mindful practices help release the chemicals and ready them for the next call. Fire, law enforcement, forensics and EMS also have extreme stress responses however, Francine Roberts states an opinion that there is, "... some adrenaline release in the physical action and exertion of the event." Lastly, there is also the recommendation to share some formal feedback with communications after stressful calls, so there is some closure to the disturbing thoughts and traumatic inputs."[vi]

Correctional officers are another group (often overlooked) that require trauma-informed care training and practice. A 2012 national study of nearly 4,000 correctional officers and staff conducted by Caterina Spinaris, Ph.D. with Desert

Waters Outreach in Colorado found a 27% PTSD rate among correctional staff and a depression rate of 26%.[vii]

A New York Post article shares the distressing story of a correctional officer who left for work and never made it home, his suicide note citing "The job made me do it." The article shares:

- About 10 percent of correctional officers say they have considered or attempted suicide - a rate nearly 3 times that of the general U.S. population, according to data provided in a survey completed by California's 30,000 correctional and parole officers. It's even higher among retired guards, about 14 %, similar to the suicide risk among military veterans.

- Half of the correctional officers expressed at least one symptom of post-traumatic stress disorder, due to officers' frequent exposure to violence and injury, their perception of constant danger and their reluctance to share traumatic experiences with family members or counsellors.[viii]

Forensic technician suicide statistics tend to fall under the law enforcement umbrella, so statistics are scare. One article in PubMed.gov on Factors Influencing Post Traumatic Stress Disorder in Crime Scene Investigators, shares that the mean score for PTSD in law enforcement crime scene investigators was 13.69%.

> "When Richard Shepherd was diagnosed with post-traumatic stress disorder, the mental health nurse told him he was really worried. 'Most people say they're going to commit suicide,' the nurse said, 'but you actually know what to do.'"
>
> Shepherd's daily life was made up of blood-spattered corpses, anguished relatives and scornful lawyers. But it wasn't a particular incident that left him immobilized by dread, struggling with sleep and plagued by panic attacks; instead, it was the gradual accumulation of stress from 30 years confronting violence and the steady buildup of emotional damage from 23,000 dead bodies.
>
> "You don't notice it," Shepherd says, "because you think you're good enough to do it without giving in; but, actually, it's like little fish – nibble, nibble, nibble – such tiny pieces go that you don't notice the individual bites. And yet, when you look back, you realize it is having an effect."[ix]

It is challenging to pinpoint nation-wide cumulative data when it comes to public safety services in the United States. The Canadian Journal of Psychiatry compiled the first results from a national survey for public safety professions (PSP) regarding operational stress injuries. It included law enforcement, firefighters, paramedics, correctional workers, and dispatchers from a wide variety of municipal, regional, provincial and remote PSP's with widely varying access to services in their communities:

- The current frequency for incidence of mental health concerns among public service professionals (44.5%) is much higher than the frequency of diagnosed mental health concerns in the general population (10.1%) [x]

These studies place the disciplines under the umbrella of public safety professionals which is more encompassing to all members that are impacted directly and vicariously by regular trauma on the job. Resiliency is also high in these professions however, the statistics that are available clearly show more time and investment into effective training and preventative measures is required.

Trauma induced suicide, PTSD and depression indicate the extreme outcome of unmanaged stress impacts. It is important to recognize that there is often preceding stress and trauma exposure that shows up in the higher-than-average divorce rates, addiction and unhealthy behaviors that also plague these professions. Why, then, is there so little focus on it? Why is basic training in these fields missing when psychological injury is pretty much guaranteed to impact member safety and wellness throughout their career? We want to bring this mental fitness and resiliency training to every college and agency worldwide from rookie-to-retirement transition. The time to put a halt to these trends is now.

Surveys and studies show that mental health stigma and shame are still mainstream within public safety professions who prioritize a culture of bravery and toughness. Experts in each of these professions report a dismissal 3-5% of agencies have suicide prevention programs.[xi] There is an even lower percentage when it comes to understanding and developing higher social and emotional intelligence to gain pre-escalation communication and interactive skills along with advanced mental fitness. As you learn and share the information within you will be leading the way to change the cultural gap.

Beyond the cultural stigmas there are common dissociations when public safety professionals interact with people who have significant mental health, emotional/social or substance abuse problems, from an authoritative or caretaker role. When one is charged with rescuing or controlling people in their worst possible moments it is difficult to associate that extreme view of mental health issues to one's own dark thoughts and unhealthy behaviors. Interviews showed a common internal stigma reported as the challenge of looking in the mirror and identifying a similar trauma, within. Not many in these fields can recognize the need to rescue themselves.

As resiliency builds, empathy often lessens over time with repeated exposure to trauma, and a high majority of public safety professionals have an altered threshold that likely extends to themselves. While resiliency is positive and necessary, we must promote the need to understand signs and symptoms to aid your peers and mitigate those larger trauma moments that may catch you off guard or bypass the resilient core you have built.

Slowly, leaders within agencies are recognizing the need for a cultural change on stigma and seeking ways to reverse the trends of suicide, PTSD and trauma stress within their organizations. With this acceptance comes the need for a deeper understanding of human complexity. Trauma-informed public safety professionals will gain that insight and dramatically increase their ability to lead and guide people under duress, as well as those with mental health challenges. You are learning the tools to meet interactive objectives safely, swiftly and without causing undue harm to achieve the best possible outcome in the situation being managed. Trauma-informed skills will greatly enhance community-relation issues even challenges prevalent in many lower socioeconomic neighborhoods.

However, it is not only in those neighborhoods where these skills will be well-utilized. It is safe to say in today's presiding self-focused culture, there has been a shift away from community connectedness. People are more polarized and influenced by organized groups, providing unverified and conflict enticing information. We are in a disoriented world that increasingly thrives on drama and chaos. This is not a new subject. It has been addressed through psychological, philosophical and spiritual studies - the research showing us that the modern world is feeling increasingly unsafe.

One might think that this shift has occurred within our last decade of instant access to information and disinformation; however, the crack in humanity started much earlier. Back in the 1920's, a societal "shift" began - growing from seeds of desperation with compounding effects still affecting our society today. Like a poisonous weed, it has spread itself across the globe. It seems we are devolving from the tribes of community we were meant to be, towards a society of desperate individuals. As a society, we simply haven't been trained very well on how to remain human centered.

The communications-intelligence that was once learned from watching elders interacting around us is now learned over a lifetime of hits and misses as we struggle to understand ourselves and others. Families, neighbors, spiritual leaders, engaged educators and trusted adults once shared local and regional values on how to behave within a civilized society and how to respect authority. Wisdom that was passed from generation-to-generation to maintain and adapt local culture to a changing and evolving world. At times this has been less than positive, as some of those cultural norms created illogical racism and anti-humanity extremist views. Generally, it aided the personal development of each child.

With the growth and necessity of both parents working - and with family units more scattered, many traditions, values, and life-lessons are being highly influenced by drama-infused TV and social media babysitters. Neither a teacher of healthy emotional intelligence, by design, we would be bored of shows that always showed positive, effective communications. We want the drama and excitement - it's what makes it entertaining. Sadly, however, it is a poor substitute for learning how to manage and influence others or managing oneself in trauma, duress, stress, conflict or complex conversations.

What was once understood by early adulthood is now most often delayed; the trials and tribulations of life teaching the individual along the way until, "one day" they "sort of figure it out." Emotional Intelligence is necessary to learn "how to manage me" in society. By the end of this book you will discover, "How to best manage ME in the world where I touch and influence those around me."

> *"Accompanying the dramatic developments in science and technology and modern civilization in modern times, is the aggravation of human spirit with experiences, restlessness, insecurity and loss of direction."*
> *~ Kisshomaru Ueshiba, author of The Spirit of Aikido "*

There does feel like an increase in restlessness, insecurity and loss of direction in the world - and perhaps if we look closely, also within ourselves. This feeling can exaggerate stressors and reactions to psychological trauma. "Going Beyond the Call", means we are dedicated to delving into a deeper understanding of human behavior and brain science. This depth ensures the learning in this book and program is not limited to PTSD, suicide or other more harmful outcomes of the worst-case scenarios we started with at the beginning of this chapter.

While emotional intelligence and mindful wellness are threaded throughout this book, we haven't written a "woo-woo" book on loving all mankind without any context. There are times when clear authority, direction and power are absolutely necessary. What we hope to impart here are tools and knowledge for those higher percentages of times when levels of command and control do not need to be so overt. The powerful mind that accompanies healthy mental fitness provides a beneficial internal edge, as well as direct benefits for those with whom you interact.

CHAPTER 2

STIGMA BUSTING

I conceal what's in here, in my brain, what I live with. You can't see it, feel it, or know it. I do, though. It claws at me. It tears at me. Like it or not, it's a part of me. It squats on my chest when I awake in the night, glaring at me…daring me to remember those things I work to forget. It molds me, holds me, and has changed me forever. I wish you'd known me before; I was different then.
~ Anonymous

What are the issues and challenges a stressful career with traumatic inputs have? Everyone experiences stress, some of which is actually quite healthy. It is the unhealthy stress overwhelming our coping mechanisms that we must understand and mitigate. All trauma, stress, or high excitement moments can trigger our automatic protective response towards fight, flight, or freeze. This response is innate and protective, which is good. It can also become a threat to our overall health if repeatedly activated.

When you are living with unresolved trauma, acute stress, environmental stressors, or hypervigilance, the accumulation intensifies your response reactions which can destabilize and heighten your typical responses to lower levels of stress. It becomes a living cycle of reactivity that negatively impacts interactions and increases maladaptive coping mechanisms. This leads to mental fitness erosion. There is an expanding acceptance of post incident debriefings after the tragic and heart-searing impacts of mass casualty incidents. However, there is much slipping under the radar.

A majority of public safety professionals will have moments of repeated high stress and even overwhelm, so you will relate to some of the symptoms shared in this book. We all feel the impacts of stress. It is recognizing the tipping point or moments when those impacts are having a physiological and psychological effect before damaging our health and relationships.

"People in this profession are resilient - but nobody is totally immune; extreme stress can get to anybody,"
~ Professor Anke Ehlers

Professor Ehlers is a clinical psychologist, leading the study into different predictive factors which might help identify and minimize PTSD.[xii]

In 2017 the University of Phoenix conducted a study on public safety professional's mental health. It included 2000 firefighters, law enforcement, paramedics/EMT and nurses. A high number of which are managing traumatic stress events and also are impacted with mental fitness issues.

"The findings show that while approximately half of public safety professionals have participated in pre-exposure mental health training, the majority report that mental health services are rarely used at their organization. Data shows there are resources available to public safety professionals, but stigmas associated with mental health may be keeping them from getting the help they need."

- 85% experienced symptoms related to mental health issues
- 84% experienced a traumatic event
- 74% are aware of readily available mental health services
- 51% have received pre-exposure training
- 49% received "Psychological First-Aid" after incidents
- 39% have sought out professional help
- 27% have been diagnosed with depression
- 10% have been diagnosed with PTSD

Discouragingly, 39% say there are negative repercussions for seeking mental health help at work. Of the above respondents:

- 55% say supervisors will treat them differently
- 45% say co-workers will perceive them as weak
- 34% say they will be overlooked for promotions[xiii]

Internationally, the results are similar. A Canadian survey researching operational stress injuries among paramedics, law enforcement, firefighters and 911 operators indicate they are considerably more susceptible to mental health issues than the general public. Published in the Canadian Journal of Psychiatry, the survey sought out symptoms that were associated with PTSD, including: depression, social anxiety, panic attacks, and alcohol use. The research shows compared to the general-public percentage of 10%:

- 44.5% screened positive for clinically significant symptom clusters consistent with one or more mental disorders
- Symptoms of operational stress injuries also appear to increase with more years of service and more exposure to traumatic events
- Those who were single were significantly more likely to report symptoms than those with a significant other[xiv]

One of the reasons the stigma must be challenged is the science behind what causes mental health challenges. It is not a problem that can simply be "sucked up and shelved." A medical journal in the Proceedings of the National Academy of Sciences of the United States of America cites:

> "A decade of reports that indicate prolonged, major depression is associated with atrophy within the central nervous system in the region called the hippocampus. This structure plays a critical role in learning, memory and emotions, and the magnitude of hippocampal volume loss; nearly 20% in some reports, (meaning a loss in brain tissue.)...

Ignoring, hiding, or denying this problem leads to physical harm to the brain. Memories and learning impact your decision-making process and how you perceive and interpret emotional stimuli. A collaboration between global research institutes cite:

> The brain magnetic resonance imaging data of 8,927 people, 1,728 of whom had major depression and the rest of whom were healthy. The researchers found that 65% of the depressed study participants had recurrent depression and it was these people who had a smaller hippocampus, which is involved with long-term memory, forming new memories, and connecting emotions to those memories."
>
> So recurrent or persistent depression does more harm to the hippocampus the more you leave it untreated. Co-director, Professor Ian Hickie stated there was good evidence that with treatment, the damage was reversible."[xv]

Dr. Anthony Walker, PhD, a firefighter is additionally linking the role of occupational hazards to PTSD, Acute Stress Disorder (ASD) and Depression. In "Extreme Physiology and Medicine" he writes:

"Elevated rates of depression and PTSD in vulnerable occupational populations, in addition to acute traumatic events, could be linked with exposures in their working environments. Studies show sleep restriction and deprivation (quality/quantity), heat/smoke exposure and physical exertion/overtraining /injury, elicit inflammatory changes that may be priming public safety professionals to react adversely to acute traumatic events increases the risk of PTSD." [xvi]

Science and research studies are teaching us a truth requiring critical attention whose facts are completely logical to the most hardened of men and women. Impacts to mental fitness tend to develop from the deeply disturbing scenes these professions attend, whether that "one" call or a career long accumulation of calls. Swallowing down the feelings or a mentality of "toughing it out or embracing the suck" has aided the continual rise of self-harm behaviors and suicidal tragedies.

Some of you will have a way of sharing your emotional reactions after bad calls with a close friend or loved one. More often either a stoic or protective mindset does not wish to share the burden with those they care for. Also common is a sense of shame from the inability to manage the stress and overwhelm. We will discuss relationship strategies under communication tactics to show you a way to share emotional impacts without sharing harming details. Having a healthy outlet to communicate is very important!

We have also seen an increase in mass shootings and terrorism which impacts us on an even deeper level. I have yet to meet someone that can swallow any one of these scenes without feeling an impact. According to Gun Violence Archive[xvii], mass shootings reached total of 346 in 2017 and 337 in 2018. School shootings in particular are not something anyone can be "prepared for" mentally. There were 24 incidents with injuries and death at schools in 2018 and 17 in 2017 - a statistic that has been growing. Even the most trained, experienced, and elite members have deep reactions to this type of loss.

In the aftermath of the Parkland School shooting where 17 children and staff were murdered, and another 17 Public safety professionals were injured. Firefighter Lt. Rob Ramirez, states:

> *"I know I'm not the same person I was the morning; I went to work as who I am today. This changes you as a person. Public safety professionals were overwhelmed with victims and had what I called 'battlefield" injuries' - all of them with major traumatic injuries. As you can imagine, these small-frame, small-bodied, high school children taking these large caliber weapons — multiple rounds, to the torso, legs, arms and extremities. The men and women that responded to that call are not the same men and women that walked away from it."*[xviii]

Quinn Cunningham, a SWAT team leader and firearms instructor in Denver, Colorado was so impacted by responding to a school shooting; he now trains teachers and administration staff to carry and use concealed weapons in the school. We can easily imagine a teacher would not choose their career with a mindset they may have to take a young life one day to save others. What we don't stop and consider is that a law enforcement officer would be equally impacted. Our humanity does not change to match the profession we choose and violence towards children hits close to home for all of us. Cunningham states:

> *"The thing I remember most is the crime scene and seeing the student's blood and hair on the ground.*
> *I will NEVER … EVER forget that!"*

He also indicates the reality of what public safety professionals train for and expect is often not what they get when they arrive on scene. He recalls:

"As we entered the school it was a very eerie feeling … there was silence and normally when we train, we add in a lot of chaos and destruction - fire alarms going off and kids screaming and running at you; clinging onto you … but instead, silence. Almost deafening silence. When we evacuated the children, there was this haunted look of lost innocence … I never want to see that look again."[xix]

Even if your role or position is one where you see trauma every day, it doesn't mean you ever "get used to it". An article from, Shots – Health News from NPR, recounts the impact from the emergency room perspective during the 2017 Las Vegas shooting where the gunman fired into a gathered crowd of 2,200+ people at a music festival.

"Nursing Supervisor, Antoinette Mullan was focused on one thing: saving lives. She recalls dead bodies on gurneys across the triage floor, a trauma bay full of victims. But, 'in that moment, we're not aware of anything else but taking care of what's in front of us.' She calls that event, 'the most horrific evening of my life.' In a career spanning 30 years, Mullan has experienced plenty of other tragic incidents in which she witnessed suffering and death. She says she has tried to work through these painful memories, mostly on her own. 'I still have emotional breakdowns and I never know when it's going to hit me,' she says."[xx]

A healthy, prepared mindset dismisses stigma by identifying and realizing that you cannot possibly be trained for every scenario. There will always be those that leave a dark stain on your heart and mind. Cunningham's choice to provide options for teachers to help curb the next event gave him a healthy outlet to manage the trauma. Too many suffer internally, quietly, and end up with unhealthy coping choices and relationship impacting maladaptive behaviors. So now when considering the symptoms that can negatively impact mental fitness within you, your peers, those in other responder roles, keep in mind trying to lock it away and forget about it is simply not logical.

Dr. Chuck Russo, program director of Criminal Justice at American Military University, in an article from, In Public Safety, states that his team:

"Helps responders understand that they are having a normal reaction to an abnormal event. Many responders end up playing the, 'what if' game. Some feel guilty about not helping more people or think they could have done more to change the outcome. This adds to the stress; it's important to prepare to experience an array of emotions, including the highs and lows, sleeplessness, changes to eating habits and sexual dysfunction."[xxi]

Without preparing yourself with healthy coping mechanisms, singular or cumulative stress can create a harmful internal challenge. A lonely existence grows where recurring thoughts, nightmares, triggered emotional reactions, and even feelings of hopelessness are trapped. Science proves that humans do not lock away feelings inside the mind and simply dissolve them. The phrase, "It's eating away at my mind" is truer than we realize.

If you are not dealing with your stress or trauma, your brain is physically shrinking, and damage is slowly impacting your cognitive functions. Seeping through in self-defeating and self-harming behaviors or brain health and immunity that impacts later in life with higher risks of diseases like Parkinson's and Alzheimer's. It also lowers emotional intelligence and your ability to manage interactions. Especially the ones that matter most, both professionally and personally.

I interviewed Dr. Jeff Morley, and he had some interesting insights in trauma reactions both personally as a 23-year veteran law enforcement officer; professionally as a psychologist, counselling in Critical Incident Stress Management. He advocates that Acute Stress and PTSD is:

- Not a "Disorder" it's a physiological injury
- Involuntary
- Not a moral failing
- Changes brain, hormones, body physiology
- Changes emotions, beliefs, behaviors, relationships
- Changes worldview, spirituality
- Affects our ability to make meaning

Dr. Morley also addresses the issue of organizational stress as an additional threat to our psychological well-being. This can simmer and become the "last straw" moment where emotional control is lost, or trauma is deepened. He discovered the tipping point often appeared as agitation or frustration with peers, administrators, leadership and the justice system. Whether unfixable social issues, irritating peers, toxic inter-office, inter-agency, or other organizational dysfunctions, this last straw stress can also lead to burn-out.[xxii]
Dr. Morely shared this story:

> *"When treating a public safety professional involved in a horrific shooting many years ago, I presumed that he was ready to talk about that traumatic experience. When I suggested that was what he was there for he said, 'No, actually, that was really difficult, but I kind of made peace with that.' I asked what brought him in then, and he started relaying issues of stress in the workplace - a new boss who was changing all*

the rules. He said, 'He's not communicating with us and there's conflict in the team.' For him, the organizational stress that was the last straw."

The DSM the Diagnostic and Statistical Manual of psychological disorders would say that for an event to be considered traumatic, it needs to involve a serious threat to the physical integrity of oneself or others close by - involving feelings of fear, helplessness, or horror. These feelings are common moments in the world of a public safety professional. This is why it's important to remember that everyone manages traumatic moments differently, even you, from one event to another.

Dr. Morley shared:

"It's interesting what gets considered traumatic and what doesn't. I remember as a young officer my parents had come to visit me. I had just finished a shift where it was my very first high-speed chase, a long chase, that was followed by the car crashing, then followed by a foot chase and that was followed by a fistfight. I remember coming home at the end of the day and telling my parents about the event and as I'm talking, my mom leans over, puts her hand on mine and asked, 'Are you okay?' I remember thinking to myself, 'YEAH! Am I okay??' [scoffs] I was like, this is what I joined for! Personally, I thought it was one of the best days on the job so far. Did it meet the parameters of primary trauma? Yes, it involved a serious threat to my physical integrity. I could have been injured or worse. Yes, it did have an element of fear, but in my opinion the elements of helplessness and horror part were experienced by the bad guy, not me."

Ask any firefighter, paramedic, law enforcement officer, corrections officer, or communications professional about one of their big events and the war stories begin. Often with embellishment, dark humor, and excitement. We can all experience the rush of our chosen careers which is why trauma can be so confusing when it rears its ugly head. So, it becomes a challenge to convince yourself that an internal threat is looming, when it is easier to convince yourself that it's nothing, you've been here before, you'll get over it, or locking accompanying bad feelings in a vault. To wonder why you are experiencing an event differently "this time" can be confusing and it is often easier to try and ignore it, bury it, or as an example, drink it away.

It isn't always the big events that trigger a traumatic moment or the secondary trauma that builds over time; often, it can be the moments that leave you feeling frustrated with a sense of helplessness that is contrary to why you joined your particular profession in the first place. I asked Dr. Morley about it and he shared:

"I remember taking a domestic in progress call and the dispatcher says, 'It's being called in by a 9-year-old boy. Please don't identify who's calling it in.' We arrive, this big guy is fierce looking, and he is an angry, angry man. We did absolutely everything we could to try and arrest him but there was no overt physical evidence and the wife wouldn't say anything, so we're unable to make an arrest. I remember as we were clearing the call, standing in the driveway watching him

clenched up, looking around saying, 'Who called it in then … who called it then?' I said, 'Someone in the neighborhood did, sir … half the neighborhood heard what was going on.' But he zeroed in on his kid. We knew exactly what was going to happen as soon as we left there. So, the sense of fear was for that kid; a sense of helplessness because being able to protect a child was as important as any critical incident. But, were we going to get a stress debriefing over things like that? Not a chance! So, it just accumulates."

The same type of situation is common for fire and paramedics services who see obvious signs of abuse, neglect, and danger in a household but are powerless to do anything about it. Dispatchers experience this when trying to calm someone until help arrives, when they hear the danger in the background, or someone dies while they are on the phone with them. Forensics can process scene after scene and feel that inability to change the outcome, they are always there after the horror has occurred. Corrections see many victims that have been abused and used until they "get caught" and feel that poor person never had a chance given their circumstances.

That helplessness can eat away at you. It is familiar to all because it is so common; it's part of "the job." It is good to recognize it and be mindful that it can take a toll. It is healthy to seek guidance, talk it out, or call attention to it when it hits home. This knowledge makes it easy to remove the stigma that you may have associated with an experience that you or others had.

Another logic factor in erasing the stigma of PTSD is to trace its origins. Historically if we review the evolution of PTSD and stress injury diagnosis, we will see where an understandable and traumatic shock was manipulated and changed to ease the financial burden of the government. That change created the stigma we are now seeking to eliminate as advances in neuroscience and psychology have created better understanding and clarity on the very real impact. An article from, The Conversation[xxiii], shares the history and continuing effort to define and treat PTSD type symptoms. In WWI some soldiers were sent home wounded with variations of amnesia, partial paralysis, inability to communicate, and dissociations that had no apparent physical cause.

Shellshock was the predominant consideration after English physician Charles Myers, wrote the first paper on "shell-shock" in 1915, whose theory was the symptoms stemmed from a physical injury from the repetitive concussive blasting to which soldiers were exposed. He wrote that brain trauma was the cause behind the increasing wave of symptoms being seen in soldiers being sent home.[xxiv]

This theory did not hold up under more thorough examinations, research and testing. There were too many veterans who had not been in an area with the concussive blasts found in trench warfare. They were complaining or showing signs of shell-shock similar to those exposed and plenty of soldiers who were returning without any symptoms of shell-shock who experienced the same concussive blasting."

Shellshock has morphed into current day PTSD and the brain impacts are now clearly identifiable on neuroimaging scans. There isn't a cohesive explanation of trauma that explains how it impacts different people in different ways with a multitude of symptoms yet. Studies from your DNA to childhood experiences are now emerging on top of differing breaking points for every person. Back to history from, The Conversation:

"A rapid decline in available soldiers halfway through the war and far too many coming back with "shell-shock" symptoms a new definition arose. Soldiers were archetypically heroic and strong. When they came home unable to speak, walk or remember, with no physical reason for those shortcomings, the Military and Medical establishment concluded the only possible explanation was a personal weakness. Treatment methods were based on the idea that the soldier who had entered into war as a hero was now behaving as a coward and needed to be snapped out of it. Shellshock went from being considered a legitimate physical injury to be a sign of weakness, of both the battalion and the soldiers within it. The British Medical Journal provided alternate nonphysical explanations for its prevalence. Poor morale and defective training are one of the most important, if not the most important etiological factors: also, that shell-shock was a "catching" complaint as written in the British Medical Journal, 1922"[xxv]

It was estimated around 20% of men developed shellshock, the figures are unclear as doctors were protective of veterans and did not want to label them with a psychological diagnosis that would hurt their disability pension. Speculation that the government could not afford the rising cost of medical pensions so by making shell shock symptoms a psychological failing they saved considerable taxpayer money.

"Commissioned to work to prove that model of character weakness, Dr. Lewis Yealland subjected soldiers who could no longer speak with months upon months of inhumane torture, including severe electric shock until he had one subject shocked so hard the soldier spoke asking for water. This led to a book in 1918 called, The Hysterical Disorders of Warfare,[xxvi] where this clinician stated he proved his theory that, "Shell-shock was a disease of manhood rather than an illness that came from witnessing, being subjected to and partaking in incredible violence."

WWII was no different with soldiers coming home with the same "shell-shock" diagnosis:

"However, enlightenment came from a Veteran's Bureau psychiatric clinic Dr. Abram Karkiner who countered the manhood weakness claim. In his book, The Traumatic Neuroses of War,[xxvii] he proclaimed these symptoms stemmed from psychological injury, rather than a soldier's flawed character. More theories, studies and clinical work began supporting this new concept. Public understanding of war itself had begun to change, too, as the widely televised accounts of the, 'My Lai Massacre' brought the realities of war into the living room for the first time. 'Veterans advocated for their own health and PTSD acceptance working to redefine it … not as a sign of weakness, but rather a rational response to the experience of atrocity."[xxviii]

Veterans returning from WWII and later Vietnam often moved into public safety careers. With them came the muddy belief of what PTSD meant, and the old school belief that PTSD was a weakness, remains an unexplainable stigma given the medical evidence to the contrary. Awareness and advocacy are finally expanding our understanding and recognition; however, we have a long way to go. More North American agencies are being legislated to offer training and provide occupational health benefits for PTSD and organizations are being nudged towards cultural change.

In Canada, 6 Provinces are now covered under their worker's compensation benefits, and about one-third of the United States are adopting legislation like the one advocated for and signed by the state of Florida.[xxix]

"PTSD is a hidden killer. This benefit is needed, so we ensure that our firefighters don't have this as their only option, our public safety professionals don't look to suicide as the outlet to sort through the demons they deal with and these horrific images."
~ State of Florida Fire Marshal Jimmy Patronis[xxx]

Research efforts are focused on increasing psychological resilience and trying to identify the underlying physiological mechanisms that predispose individuals to develop depressive disorders or PTSD. Not all public safety professionals or military personnel experience PTSD after exposure to stressful events. However, exposure to maimed or fatally injured persons is recognized as a substantial contributor to increased prevalence of health care utilization and mental health care access by public safety professionals. Unlike the general population, many public safety professionals will be exposed to traumatic events numerous times during their career.

Building resiliency is essential in preventing and mitigating the stress and trauma impacts of these professions. Peer to peer support options and one on one debriefings after troubling calls also go a long way to helping avoid the toll many pay for a life of service. Becoming a trauma informed organization will reduce stigma and create a new norm that improves mental fitness across the board.

There was a time when peers would meet up for beers after shift and have a chance to decompress and talk it out after a bad day. The modern world of two working parents, kids in multiple activities and frequently more than one job has lessened the stress relieving activity considerably.

Allowing a personal debriefing to talk it out and release a little of the impact it may have had on you or others at the scene can ease the build-up. This can be a quick five-minute check-in conversation. It doesn't have to be a touchy-feely exchange where you are crying on each other's shoulder, although pending the situation, now and then, it may well be.

While evolving your cultural response to trauma debriefing remember to loop in your communication operators, as they may have been impacted by the event as well. Whether they participated for the whole event or just the beginning of it. If any group or peer support referrals are recommended to those attending a traumatic event, then it is likely they would be well served to be part of that or have their own should they not be local to your organization.

"Pain shared is pain divided. The more you share, the less you keep for yourself."
~ Lt. Col Dave Grossman

We need to lessen the stigma of "swallow it all down, no matter how bitter," as this may instigate someone who was genuinely impacted by trauma to believe they are not "supposed to" feel or be impacted by it. We need to make it acceptable and available to reach out and recognize they aren't alone when something hits them hard. When each of you opens the communication option to admit "that one hit home" it becomes a conscious awareness for others to make it understandable norm.

This new norm will also heighten awareness during interactions with the public. Knowing that victims and witnesses are even less prepared to process the trauma impacted by the event they experienced will enable stronger empathy. Being able to add a few sentences to better serve the moment by asking them, "You seem pretty shaken up about all this, how are you doing?" A curious empathy creates an opportunity for you to be part of a recovery-oriented system of care and when appropriate you may even offer a referral.

To be Trauma-Informed means you have the foresight to recognize, be aware of impacts, and mitigate the worsening of the personal implications. Building a culture of understanding that not all rescues are immediate. It means becoming the first line of healing in a moment when you have the most significant advantage to help someone manage the trauma they were exposed to. Both for the public and within your own professional circles.

- What if sharing a resource with a DUI or their passenger stops grievous bodily harm to other people and children the next time that perpetrator ignores their alcoholism and gets behind the wheel?
- What if offering a number to call stops a domestic abuse from turning into a homicide the next month?
- What if sharing a number with a drunk and disorderly interaction with a Veteran and his girlfriend at a bar fight gets him the help, he needs for PTSD reactions?
- What if opening up a scene that was pretty traumatic with a peer on your shift gives them the incentive to reach out to counselling and prevents a suicide?

This is as simple as sharing options like:

Peer to peer counselling	Helplines, local, specialized to career, National	Victim advocate groups, career specific peer and spouse groups
Social Services	National Alliance on Mental Illness (NAMI) or Canadian Mental Health Association (CMHA) in Canada	Psychiatrists and Psychologists that specialize in trauma
Substance Abuse & Mental Illness (SAMI)	Substance Abuse & Mental Health Services Administration (SAMHSA)	Local and National Veterans Affairs and peer groups

*Links to support lines included in Appendix I

You have now initiated a quiet heroic act and you may never know the true impact it had or the life you saved. It is critical that this starts within your home base. The statistics on suicide and depression are enough incentive to understand the impacts of trauma and indirect trauma. Overall improvements to mental fitness and relationships are a welcome bonus. By now we can all agree that lessening the stigma of reaching out to talk or seeking assistance to manage trauma impacts is a worthy cause.

It starts with administrators and leadership. The stigma may be locally accepted to keep problems in-house and promote the protective "family" element common in public safety professions. This creates a high-risk environment for personnel and public safety concerns. While the "ideal" is to keep the problem "in-house" and avoid causing career limiting actions against a member or peer may seem noble, the impact of avoidance can have significant performance management risks including;

- Unhealthy and self-sabotaging behaviors may harm self or others
- Unhealthy personal relationships, affairs, high divorce rates can impact emotional reasoning and attentiveness
- Self-medicating with alcohol and drugs often coincides with short staffed shifts, high absence rates
- Reaction and impulse behaviors that may lead to risky or crossing the line choices that challenge partner safety, or even job security

Agencies need to evaluate these additional risks as they increase litigation potential and impact the budget. Add in the potential media crisis that has its own social, political, financial, and career impacting costs. Stigma related suppression is no longer an acceptable solution for any organization. Psychology Today states:

"Research suggests that for many public safety professionals there is an underlying personal fear of being subjected by ridicule, prejudice, discrimination, and labelling. Sadly, the truth is that these issues are often perpetuated by those who lack a clear understanding of mental health care, or mental fitness, and psychological illness. After all, stigmatization is about placing a barrier between the 'perceived normal' and the 'perceived abnormal' of society… the way of viewing the worst of humanity that public safety professionals see regularly.

The nature of stigmatizing is to separate 'us' from 'them' and is a source of pride for many within these circles. There is not only a sense of pride but a deeply ingrained fear that prevents many from seeking care. For many, the stigmatization has created a deep divide between the need for self-care and the willingness to seek care"[xxxi]

A poem called "It's not normal"[xxxii] published on the website, The Officer Next Door is written for law enforcement officers, but the sentiment holds true for a broader public safety professional-perspective and adds some reality to this chapter because what you do for a living is not normal… the poem is worth linking to this site and sharing on your social media.

CHAPTER 3

TRAUMA AND MENTAL HEALTH AWARENESS IS CRITICAL

Every day, public safety professionals put their own lives on the line to ensure our safety. The least we can do is make sure they have the tools to protect and serve their communities.
~ Joe Lieberman

As public safety professionals, it is fair to extrapolate that people are experiencing some level of trauma during the time you are interacting with them. You don't often show up for the good times in a person's life. The crisis or stress of the moment is also exacerbated by whatever life experiences a person has brought with them into that moment in time. The Substance Abuse and Mental Health Services Administration (SAMHSA)[xxxiii] states that:

"1 in 6 U.S. adults experience mental illness within a given year"

This same reference from SAMHSA shares that correlate lack of access to mental health and addiction services with increased incarceration. Some states show a marked increase in jail time when services are not available. For a public safety professional, that means you will interact with more people having mental health challenges in direct proportion to the available services in your area. In those states with less access to care, you will interact with more people who have made life decisions that were not in their best interest which increases the threat of escalation. Keeping these people calm and responsive becomes even more critical. 6 out of the 10 states with the lowest access to mental health care also have the highest rates of incarceration. The following States top the list:

Florida, Alabama, Arkansas, Mississippi, Texas and Georgia

The unfortunate truth is that you are not dealing with people in a state of optimum wellness - and few are taught to recognize and manage their own psychological trauma. Our approach reduces escalated situations, how to effectively use your presence and communication choices to create calm in a crisis. This happens by developing and practicing a preventative perspective.

This does not preclude the importance of de-escalation training and situational awareness to safety threats. Going Beyond the Call tactics will help a large percentage of your regular calls. For those requiring authority and control to maintain safety and security you are well trained and equipped with other tools and tactics.

Improving mental health awareness is an important step towards improving community relations and reducing incarcerated and recidivism rates. Taking it to the next level and creating a trauma informed workforce goes beyond awareness. When mental fitness is a priority within the organization you are creating a better qualified and able individual to manage public interactions.

It is important to measure these efforts internally and externally. Public safety professional agencies already have mechanisms in place to record and collect numbers for budget, scheduling, and resource allocation purposes - adding the benefits of implementing trauma informed care will go a long way in gaining council approval for the training budget. Most organizations now recognize the cost effectiveness of after-action debriefing, mental health mitigation strategies and providing resources after major incidents. We aim to track and measure a broader scope of calls with an app that is in development. It will provide attendees with life-long updates, resources and the latest information, link to the training videos and surveys will start tracking impacts to regular trauma. This will be helpful to organizations seeking training budget increases.

As a trainer for many years, Sean has experienced how a lack of trauma informed awareness across the professions has hurt member-effectiveness and their health. His presentations to law enforcement reflect this:

> "For years we have been trained on how to shoot, how to drive, how to fight, how to know and impart the laws and affect arrests. We know the probable cause, reasonable suspicion, how and when to admit someone for mental health assessments and we know these aspects really well. However, we are missing one key factor that leads to more problems, more issues and more depression; not just in the communities, but right in our own agencies. I know from my friends and peers in other agencies that they are the same. The focus on safety and process is huge but they are missing the effort towards an internal workplace wellness. Being trauma-informed, understanding mental health wellness and learning advanced communication and psychological skills gives us the tools to avoid escalation, avoid that dark place in our minds, avoiding triggers and re-traumatizing, and avoid undue harm to self and others."

A veil of secrecy can descend for individuals in some organizations where managing the traumatic impacts to personal wellness is not recognized or normalized. Members may feel required to embrace the darkness in silence due to the stigma or closed mindedness among the ranks. This increases unhealthy coping mechanisms and primes them for long term damage to their mental and physical health. We aim to break down any lingering stigma with the brain science and medical outcomes that prove the sooner someone deals with a traumatic event, the better it is for their personal health and the agency's bottom line.

Statistics are screaming at us to make trauma informed care and mental health fitness a core training requirement. Even when suicide is not a tragic outcome, the mental toll of the job can lead to low physical health and impaired decision-making. Knowing this is enough of a safety risk mitigation and financial incentive to create a wave of change. Consider the budget impacts of poor coping choices to the attendance, coverage and disability payouts and the case is made stronger. Those that turn to addictive outlets increase conduct unbecoming charges, heighten the potential of the next agency damaging viral video and create enormous liability and political fall-out to public safety organizations. One typical city lawsuit pays out considerably more than budgeting a couple of mandatory training days.

Overcoming and addressing the stigma and barriers related to trauma and mental health must be a priority for administrations and leadership across the public safety spectrum. Wellness and communication tactics are a great benefit to service outcomes and engagement of members. They also have significant bottom-line impacts! For example:

- decreased days away or lost time
- less leave claims
- fewer suspensions
- decreased disciplinary actions
- less turn-over due to disengagement

When people are not working, their positions need to be backfilled. You can clock in and out of a shift but unfortunately the effects of trauma don't come with a timecard, the work still needs to be done. How confident are you that each member of your team has the self-control, emotional intelligence, and people management capacity to avoid becoming a social media viral sensation or the next lawsuit?

Sean has collected numerous stories of how effective communications and trauma-informed approaches work to avoid escalation and manage interactions. He has been testing this process in highly challenging neighborhoods for the past two years. Sean sees and senses the difference around him, in the types of incidents he responds to and in the reports that he writes. His partners also see the difference in the community, stating people are calmer around him. Citizens in the community see a difference. He has overheard more than one bystander stating, "Relax, it's okay - it's that cop who listens."

He often shares with LEO management:

> "We need to do a better job sharing with communities, the job law enforcement officers (LEO's) do and also recognizing that the communities we are dealing with are traumatized and dealing with major issues of their own. We will better bridge the gaps if we can teach officers to have a better understanding of the types of people they are dealing with and how approaching them with higher self-control can make a huge difference.
>
> When we have increased awareness of different types of problems - both socially and emotionally, we can succeed in effectively engaging with our communities. We can improve relationships and that serves us well when investigating crimes and building sources. We know deep down that it is in relationships that we build good, solid communities. Strengthening and creating resilience to build trust, loyalty, and commitment to solving local issues.
>
> Bridging the gap also means acknowledging that there are two ends or sides to a bridge, and it is the space between the two ends that must be strongly and skillfully crafted. When your approach is one that extends a hand first, you may be surprised to see who reaches back."

Even with understanding the statistics, knowing the size of the problem and hearing about potential training options, there is another bridge that needs to be built. This bridge is the internal one between the political and governmental entities that control budgets and provide oversight, and the organizational management working to do the best they can with the tools they have been provided.

There is not always funding available to dedicate towards promoting awareness of these issues, or to prioritize prevention, mitigation, and treatment options. Even where budget allows, some agencies are challenged by the implementation due to the time it takes to train programs like ours that will bring about real change.

As an example, with the recent implementation of PTSD being allowable as a worker's compensation claim for public safety professionals in Florida, instead of taking the opportunity to make a significant impact on this topic, a few agencies have told us they can only afford to add a basic mental health video to their employee training curriculum. We all know this will not change the cultural and wellness of agencies or address the underlying issues. It also sends a message about the importance of member mental health wellness. We all have to help to change this budget restriction because the cost of not implementing wellness altering training is significantly higher.

To achieve the budget and time for training, we will start tracking statistics with the agencies we train at so there is tangible financial data that provides city councils what they need to approve budget. We also encourage administration and unions work together as we know both value the importance of a healthier workforce and jointly become agents for change. We are also lobbying for state and federal grants to help organizations with small budgets, with a united front we can make a significant difference.

We recognize that this can feel threatening to some in these professions. It can be challenging to begin inner reflection and emotional intelligence work. It may be perceived as a character flaw or identifying and accepting a personal weakness, when in fact it demonstrates a higher level of self-awareness and resilience capacity. There are hundreds of books written within the corporate realm on the power of emotional intelligence and self-development for success. Whether for career progression or relationship improvement the personal benefits, increased knowledge, and practical tactics will provide stronger wellness for self, and rub off on those in your circle of care.

After training with law enforcement, we often hear how much the new communications skills and strategies assisted at home with teenagers or partners, as well as at work. Across the board we hear exclamations of, "I wish I had been told this on day one!" When increased wellness in personal relationships occurs, it is natural that on-duty interactions improve. It is important that members not begin their day with any lingering anger or frustration that may have begun from a difficult morning at home, which could trigger a negative interaction with the public. A great firefighter saying shows the correlation between positive home life and wellness in the workplace.

"Happy Spouse ~ Happy House ~ Happy Firehouse!"

Even during our first few courses a couple of years back, when we had "voluntold" members put into a class, the value of the training quickly became clear. After the initial aversion to attend training, we tracked desire to attend which averaged 2/5 with post training evaluations which averaged 4.5/5. We regardless of interest level walking in attendees across public safety fields are leaning in and engaged by the first break. Not one class has averaged less than 4.5/5 with a large percentage of comments asking for more.

In our follow up, we heard that learning the pre-escalation strategies, increased capacity to recognize emotional triggers and communication styles in themselves, the public, their partners, and their loved ones that give them an advantage in avoiding unnecessary escalation. They learned to take stock of their own presence, body language, word choices, and acquired the knowledge that they have significant power to change outcomes through self-control, and the importance of self-calming techniques. This optimized personal wellness which positively impacted family life, personal life, and mental fitness.

When these foundational areas are stable, a better-quality person shows up as a teammate and in a better position to serve the community well. Management is the starting point for eliminating the stigma, but members need to accept the benefits as well. Based on the following evidence there is still a long way to go.

The United States (US) National Library of Medicine National Institutes of Health reviewed databases nationwide to identify relevant studies. A quality assessment and meta-analysis revealed:

> "Data from all relevant studies measured stigma regarding mental health care and 33.1% of public safety professionals endorsed stigma issues. The systematic review revealed that the most frequently endorsed items were fears regarding confidentiality and negative career impact. Five of the 14 studies measured barriers to mental health care, and 9.3% of public safety professionals endorsed barriers to care items. The most frequently endorsed barriers were scheduling concerns and not knowing where to get help. Indications were found for more stigma and barriers in individuals with mental health problems.
>
> Stigma and barriers to care are experienced by a significant proportion of public safety professionals, which can potentially lead to a delayed presentation in mental health care and therefore increased risk of chronicity of post-trauma psychopathology* for these groups."[xxxiv]
>
> (*Psychopathology is the study of personality factors that are somewhat out of regular conscious awareness and lead to behavior outside the norm in a particular social group).

What you will truly understand by becoming a trauma informed and emotionally intelligent workforce is, much of what creates escalation is based on long simmering emotional triggers. By learning how to approach during your situational assessment and using the pre-escalation techniques we share, including starting with optimized personal mental fitness you will avoid much of the interactive stress you face regularly on your shifts.

There are times when you still need to rely on your traditional training, so use your authority to direct a scenario or lay hands on someone to take control of them. We recognize and teach that talking to with our approach isn't always the answer. This isn't about changing the way you handle every call; it is about the awareness and tactics to use when you can interject safely and make a big difference. Sean will share a couple of examples that show this difference clearly.

SEAN:
"I get a call one day, I'd already been in one physical altercation, in a domestic violence call and I was still pretty amped up. I get this call that a 13yr old child is violent. He's kicking in doors and glass, he is cussing; he is being disrespectful and not following the rules and they need law enforcement now! While we are headed there, I get an update that he's barricaded himself in a bathroom and refusing to come out. To add to this, he is making homicidal statements saying that he doesn't care and will kill everyone. We are updated that he's also got a history of suicidal threats.

So, we get there, and the first thing I do is connect with one of the women I had built a relationship with through the Department of Children and Families, through the Boys Town. She is one of the facilitators that I know and have developed a positive rapport with because she has seen how I work with children that have dealt with thought adverse experiences. From her, I can learn and assess what my parameters are for dealing with this situation. Often times, those few minutes of understanding the person can make all the difference, especially when dealing with a child in anger, stress, or someone with known mental health concerns.

She says, 'This kid is locked up in the bathroom. His Mom died 2 years ago, and his father is nowhere in the picture. He's been staying at Boys Town, breaking the rules, and not wanting to follow the consequences from doing that. He's become very disrespectful and disobedient - not following instructions.'

While I am gathering this intelligence, my partner gets there, and then my Sergeant gets there. My Sargent is a solid 260lbs; a big guy. This is important because this 13yr old is 5'7' and 245lbs; this is a massive kid. I'm a 5'6' 160lbs soaking wet, if I'm lucky. Well, this 'kid' comes out of the bathroom like a bull in a china shop - charging at us. He's coming right down the middle of the hallway and he's like a linebacker that's not going to let anybody gets in his way. We have the history, we see that he doesn't have any weapons, but we still need to stop the scene, and his charging action removes calming conversation from the immediate response.

The first person that steps in his way is my 260lb Sargent who says, 'Hey man, what's going on? We need to talk to you.' The kid looks at him and still coming, states clearly, 'Don't you F&^%ing touch me!' and Sargent, with some amusement, says, 'yeah right,' and goes to put his hands on him to stop his charge as he gets close. The kid quickly rips his hands away and with escalation yelled, 'I SAID, don't you f&%$ing touch ME!'

The kid is jacked up and he isn't about to be reasoned with. The Sargent becomes a little more physical, grabs him and goes to sit him down in the closest chair and the kid looks him dead in the eyes and says, 'You might as well shoot me if you're going to keep on touching me.' We realize we are dealing with a child that is very angry, volatile, and has a lot going on emotionally. This kid is 245lb pounds, amped up, and on the edge. In this scenario we have to take control of him and get him medical attention. He needs help and a psychological evaluation. He's clearly not thinking in the right frame of mind at the time. So, while we don't want to hurt the kid, at the same time, 245lbs is a lot of mass, filled with rage and you're dealing with an adolescent brain. You're not dealing with somebody that has the same mental capacity and thinks of the same methods that you or I would as adults. He is very agitated and not calming down at all. We have to take control of him to move him out of the location keeping both him and us safe.

My Sargent goes to put hands on. My partner is right there ready to put hands on the right side and they decide they are going to stand him up and put the handcuffs on. Well, as soon as they start to stand him up, the fight is on. He is pulling away, trying to fight, and getting into a position where he can control the situation because he doesn't want us to be in control of him. I take over the right side and we quickly take him down to the ground as gently as you can move 245lbs of resistance. When we are in that process, he emotionally loses it and is screaming at the top of his lungs. His glasses are broken, he's been slammed to the ground, and we have negatively traumatized this kid further, but given his responses and inability to self-calm we did not have another option at the time. We couldn't let him go outside uncontrolled to talk more because he was too agitated and unstable and there was no telling what would happen. He could try to run off and get hit by a car, assault someone as soon as he walks out, or he could physically hurt himself. We could not allow that possibility by letting him out of our span of control.

So, this kid is emotionally off the charts at this point. He is yelling, 'I want my Mama! I want my Mama!' just screaming at the top of his lungs as loud as he possibly can. I'm thinking to myself this whole time, 'Was there something better we could have done?' "

The point is, we recognize there will still be times like in this scenario where traditional training takes precedence because the escalation of resistance requires immediate action to maintain control. What we teach in our tactics is it is the *"Powerful Path to Peace; so Long as Peace is an Option."*

Sean states "that the best news is recognizing a trauma impacted individual is still incredibly helpful. Even in that scenario with a very large person charging towards him, Sean says, "I didn't lose control, take it personally, get angry, or triggered that whole time. It was a professional take-down to put that kid in the best place possible to keep him, the staff, other residents, and us safe. All the while our objective stayed clear as we moved him towards getting the help that he clearly needed."

It is essential for us to all to always be thinking that way and not allow our emotions to overrun us in a fight - even when it's a horrible fight and we're fighting for our life. It is imperative to keep our emotions controlled and let our subconscious and well-honed skills take over when personal safety, the safety of your peers and the public, is in peril. In order to utilize your best talents, we have to manage and control the situation starting with self. Your brain and body will take over naturally when safety is at risk. When you are calm and controlled at the onset and are thinking clearly the higher the chances of survival and safety for all involved.

Conversely, the following story is where Sean was able to impact a volatile situation in a positive and life-altering way.

SEAN:
"We got a call about a guy who is volatile and says he wants to kill himself. My partner and I arrive at his apartment to find that he's really amped up and he's screaming. It was one of those situations where my partner has been around me long enough that I have already shared the Trauma-Informed Care tactics with her, and she is trained and prepared to not allow another's emotions to trigger her. We just don't get hyped up when somebody yells, as long as safety isn't a question. We just let them do what they need to do to get through the emotional moment they are having.

He's going on and on, yelling about how he's being screwed over by the VA (Veterans Affairs). So, we find out he's a veteran and we keep asking information-seeking questions to engage his logic brain (you will learn about this in later chapters). Then we find out that he hasn't seen his daughter since she was born and that's stressing him out immensely. He's got a lot of trauma he's dealing with from his past and the things that are currently going on in his life.

He's still standing up, he's amped up, he's yelling, and he's clenching his fists. He's doing all the things we would recognize as aggressive behavior; but the question I asked myself was, 'It's aggressive; BUT, is it aggressive towards ME?' The truth was, it wasn't aggressive towards me or my partner. It was overall frustration he was trying to manage, and he didn't know what to do.

We finally get him to sit down. I can tell he is still upset. This was somebody we had been asked to do a mental evaluation on because of his behavior. So, I got him calmed down and we had a conversation. I said, 'Hey man, what's going on? What happened to you?' He then tells us about what he suffered from, while in the military and that he was in lawsuits over it. He was waiting for insurance money, but it hadn't come in. He had not seen his daughter or been allowed any contact and that was super stressful for him. It was all really overwhelming for him and caused a moment of crisis. He needed somebody to help him get through it. As law enforcement officers, we have to realize that our role doesn't always have to be enforcement-based. We also serve and protect."

In this circumstance we were able to do just that. We had the time, the opportunity, he was becoming calm and then began engaging in a receptive manner. I shared my story with him about all the challenges I faced growing up and agreed; "It's okay to be angry; it's okay to be upset; but what I am really worried about is your intent to want to hurt yourself?" He kind of looked at me and said, "No, no, I don't want to hurt myself - I'm just really upset right now; I'm really angry right now."

I said, "Okay good; I can work with that. It's okay, if you want to be angry, be angry. If you need someone to talk to, we are here to talk to you or to refer you to someone you'd be more comfortable talking with."

Due to some of the issues and struggles he was having, I gave him a copy of my book, The Movement Process, and told him I would check in with him again. He had calmed down enough that we were confident he did not want to kill himself and we could end the call with a clear conscious. To this day, I check in on him every once and awhile and talk to him to see how he's holding up. That's what I feel public safety professionals should do when they can, to impact their communities in a more positive way.

It should be about establishing relationships with the people in our communities, people that we know have emotional and social problems. I may be the only person that he gets to interact with; that he feels he can relate to. At least one human being on this planet allows him to have hope that there's a way for him to get through that situation, not feel suicidal, or feel no one can help him and everything's lost.

It was gratifying to know and serve this guy, in this way, especially being a veteran myself. This was another potential volatile situation that could have been a negative law enforcement interaction. I could have put my hands on him. I could have physically controlled him. I could have taken him and done a Baker Act on him (mental health hold) if I wanted to.

However, the reality was, I was safe, my partner was safe, and he was safe. Even though he was showing aggressive behavior, I was able to recognize that the behavior was not towards my partner or me. It wasn't even towards himself. It was simply the overwhelming feelings of frustration that he was trying to figure out how to deal with. He was doing all kinds of different things with his body to work through and release the immense, overwhelming frustration and deal with his circumstances.

With this training, we were able to help this guy to the point where now he's been able to interact with his daughter again and get his life back on track - and to work his situation out with the VA and move forward with his life in a positive manner. That's what public safety professionals should do more. Every public safety professional has the opportunity to do that at least once in their career and make a positive difference in someone's life. It adds meaning to public service and puts us in a new light within the communities we serve.

CHAPTER 4

UNDERSTANDING TRAUMA INFORMED CARE

Beyond the first line of defense, we can become the first line of healing.
~ Sean Wyman

How did psychological trauma gain recognition as a significant medical concern for the public and for public safety professions? Let us begin with some brain science that will adjust our inner judgements and perceptions from, "What's wrong with you?" when dealing with someone reacting to a traumatic situation to, "What happened to you?"

When, as a public safety professional, you arrive on the scene, you are often faced with the worst possible versions of human beings, in those horrific moments. Whether the perpetrator or the victim, they are in their most vulnerable and traumatic reactive states. People's behaviors, actions, reactions and manners may be aggravated enough for the following phrase to come to mind: "What the heck is wrong with you?!"

Alternately, you may be working alongside someone who seems distant, distracted and increasingly different from their norm. They may be unknowingly putting the scene, the community and your safety at risk. You may see someone showing up for work inebriated or brimming with a barely concealed rage. Perhaps they are making ethical or even dangerous risks that also sway your brain to think that thought: "What the heck is wrong with you?!"

Trauma impacts people in different ways and can be an outcome of one specific event or a cumulation of events. An easy way to consider the differences is with the concept of layering. If you and some others were to build a wall with bricks and mortar, you would all be driven to get the job done. You'd all start out with the right attitude and would have received the same training and instruction; however, when that instruction failed to provide you with the knowledge of how to lay a foundation, build securely and safely or stabilize the walls with necessary supports to weather any storms - things would not continue to go as planned.

Even if you all start out with the same bricks and mortar, some of you may naturally layer in a manner that builds strength and fortifies well as the walls get taller. Psychologically that would come from high emotional intelligence and natural resiliency. Some of you may ask for help and seek the answers you need to maintain your structure as it you notice it get wobbly. Psychologically, that would be an openness to self-development and self-care through seeking assistance. Some of you would quietly watch others and mimic what you see and hear them do even when their walls do not look that secure either. Psychologically that would be what a stigmatized workforce looks like, when you follow a bad example and are afraid to challenge the cultural norms that are clearly unsafe.

Many in these professions profess to be able to manage on their own, tough it out, and then just watch the build-up, knowing it's messy, knowing it's unstable but don't know what to do to fix it. Perhaps using dangerous props or quick fixes to try to keep it all from tumbling down or just ignore the problem. Psychologically that would look like emotional vaulting, ignoring triggers and turning to addictive behaviors to mask the pain.

Finally, someone comes by and starts asking, "Why don't you have a good foundation?" Your walls can't stay straight and solid without a good foundation. Where are your supports as your wall grows, or if the wind picks up and puts more pressure on the sides? Why aren't your walls joined, supporting each other, to build something even more solid and strong?

The foundational ground you all started on was not the same. The person next to you happens to be on a small incline, the person on the other side has ground that is a little muddy under the rubble of their collapsed wall, and the big crash that came from the person several walls down from you was on a visible incline. Others may not be able to layer their bricks as resiliently or securely because they started with a different ground and foundation.

Trauma Informed Care and Mental Health Fitness is foundational training to ensure every public safety professional has the knowledge, tools and tactics to succeed personally, professional and within their communities.

So how do we recognize whether the ground we are standing on is solid and has a good foundation? One method was discovered, by accident, in 1985 by Dr. Vincent Felitti[xxxv], Chief of Kaiser Permanente's Department of Preventive Medicine. A study he was conducting led to the discovery of a significant underlying cause for addictive and self-destructive behaviors, along with proven medical connections to chronic illnesses. He expanded his theory with further testing of thousands of people over 25 years. It confirmed adverse experiences in childhood were pervasive, regardless of societal "class" or background, and that these experiences were linked to every major chronic illness and social problems that burden the United States with a loss of billions of dollars each year.

That foundation starts with our childhood experiences. Dr. Bruce D. Perry, an authority on child trauma, shared the impacts of maltreatment in the developing child by saying we become a reflection of our upbringing.

> "When growing up in a safe, secure, predictable environment Emotional Intelligence, specifically, self-regulating, thoughtful and productivity-based mannerisms will develop. Alternatively, if growing up in a threatening, chaotic, abusive environment, void of nurturing and supportive relationships, a child is much more likely to be impulsive, aggressive, inattentive and have difficulties forming and maintaining relationships. This person is more likely to have maladaptive behaviors, mental health issues and eventually interaction with the criminal justice system."
>
> "Studies have shown the priority of emotional brain processes in three other major areas. First is the historical priority of emotion to language in the evolutionary cognitive development of the species; the second is its critical role in laying down a firm foundation for childhood cognitive development; third is emotion's role in shaping the direction of the young self-system."[xxxvi]

We will delve into Ego State development later in the book to share how personality is developed and adapted with nature and nurture contributors. Our relaxed personality can respond very differently when emotionalized or traumatized. In the article "The Biological Effects of Childhood Trauma we learn:

"When children experience repetitive activation of the stress response systems, their baseline state of arousal is altered. The traumatized child lives in an aroused state, ill-prepared to learn from social, emotional, and other life experiences. Living in the moment and may not fully appreciate the consequences of their actions. Add alcohol to the mix, or other drugs, and the effect is magnified. Childhood responses to repeated safety threats that activate the fight, flight or freeze response permanently change the brain's development"[xxxvii]

Even if your childhood was relatively blissful, you can be majorly impacted by direct, indirect and cumulative trauma as an adult. A study of adult stress on the brain shows physical damage and shrinkage of the brain. The researchers at the University of California Berkeley, explain the science of how chronic stress has an ability to create changes in both the structure and the function of your brain.

Psychologist Daniela Kaufer, the researcher behind these ground-breaking experiments, suggests not all stress impacts the brain and neural networks in the same way. Good stress, the type of stress that helps you perform well in the face of a challenge, helps wire the brain in a positive way, leading to stronger networks and greater resilience. Chronic stress, on the other hand, can lead to an array of problems. "You're creating a brain that's either resilient or very vulnerable to mental disease, based on the patterning of white brain matter you get early in life," explained Kaufer."[xxxviii]

A test was developed to help guide mental health and medical practitioners called the Adverse Childhood Experience (ACE) test. It helps us understand that the impacts of adverse experiences in our childhood can become overt and noticeable or can sit deep inside like an internal sleeper agent. One that responds every so often with behaviors and actions that do not serve our health or happiness as adults. One that also increases the likelihood of major diseases like Cancer, Alzheimer's, Parkinson's disease and pulmonary disorders.

Why should this be important to public safety professionals? Beyond the previously mentioned depression and suicidal rates, public safety professionals have high rates of coronary heart disease and the death statistics while on active duty are startling. Environmental and personal fitness play a part of course but add in childhood trauma and you have increased your risks significantly.

After the initial physical fitness standards to get on the job, most organizations do not require those standards be maintained. Many of you work in areas that are primarily sedentary with bursts of physical exertion under high stress. Without a commitment to fitness, that regime is not healthy, long term. Cancer rates in firefighters may be predominantly equipment and environmentally based; however, this test indicates another element. The fire fighter's internal stress management ability may also impair immunity and susceptibility to significant health issues. Statistics in one study showing the percentage of on-duty deaths related to coronary heart disease deaths were:

- Fire: 45%
- Law Enforcement: 22%
- EMS: 11%

There are many reasons why someone enters a career as a public safety professional. A common motivator is brokenness during the developmental years and wanting to help people after personal experiences motivated them. Many watched helplessly as someone they cared for suffered, or they came from a neighborhood where they watched numerous people suffer. If you score 4+ on the A.C.E. test we will increase your awareness and understanding of how childhood traumatic incidents may increase your risk for significant health problems. This information gives you knowledge and intelligence to mitigate those risks.

This brain science also gives us some understanding of the higher percentages of addictive behaviors (risky, sexual, alcohol etc.) and the personal relationship failures common to these careers. Understanding, from a scientific perspective, lessens stigma and helplessness; you will know it isn't all about discipline and self-control. This may be the necessary, logical incentive for someone to seek the right kind of help that will serve their health best. As noble as it is to rescue others, it is intelligent to rescue yourself, once you have the knowledge and tools to do so.

The ACE study was the beginning of a major medical mind-shift that provided significant understanding about the lives of millions of people who chose biochemical coping methods. This includes alcohol, marijuana, food, sex, tobacco, violence, work, methamphetamines and thrill sports. All of these can be used to escape intense fear, anxiety, depression and anger.

When serving the public, this knowledge is also eye-opening. You interact with an exorbitant amount of social and emotional problems in your daily interactions. Understanding the root cause of their reactivity will increase your ability to be more empathetic to their situation. You will be more equipped to offer solution-based options to guide another through their moment of crisis.

For a long time, public health experts, social service workers, educators, therapists, and policymakers commonly regarded addiction as a self-control problem. Slowly, through Trauma Informed Care they are realizing these coping mechanisms are perfectly reasonable and expected responses and often subconscious coping mechanisms that grew from childhood trauma. Until that underlying situation is recognized and managed, the coping behavior is hard to navigate.

Consider the science behind the study and take a moment to relate it your personal experiences and those of the people you interact with in the line of duty. I discover the "why" behind some of the behavioral issues you see day after day in the neighborhoods you serve. To describe the science, I will share some excerpts from a TEDtalk by Dr. Nadine Burke[xxxix], a pediatrician who is a huge advocate for the science and possibilities the ACE test has in the field of preventative and reactive medicine. She shares;

- "That the repeated stress of abuse, neglect and parents struggling with mental health or substance abuse issues has real, tangible effects on the development of the brain. This unfolds across a lifetime, to the point where those who've experienced high levels of trauma are at triple the risk for heart disease and lung cancer. An exposure that in high enough doses would impair brain development, the immune system, the hormone systems and even the way our DNA is read and transcribed.

- Folks who are exposed in very high doses have triple the lifetime risk of heart disease and lung cancer and a 20-year difference in life expectancy and yet doctors today are not trained in routine screening for ACEs or treatment options outside medication."

As a public safety professional, how many times have you judged a behavior problem through a lens of social/emotional issues that are someone else's problem to deal with? There is an opportunity to become the first line of healing by acknowledging and referring services with a new mindset. Dr. Burke Harris became curious while serving an underprivileged neighborhood. She says;

> *"I started noticing a disturbing trend: many kids were being referred to me for attention deficit hyperactivity disorder (ADHD) but when I actually did a thorough history and a physical what I found was that for most I couldn't make a diagnosis of ADHD. Most of the kids I was seeing had experienced such severe trauma that it felt like something else was going on. Somehow, I was missing something important. In public health, one of the things that they teach you is if you see a hundred kids that all drink from the same well and 98 of them develops diarrhea? Well, you can go ahead and write a prescription for dose after dose after dose of antibiotics, or you can walk over and say, 'What the heck is in this well water?'"*

While researching she came across Dr. Felitti's CDC-Kaiser ACE Study that examined the ACE score of thousands of participants against the statistics of leading health issues and it proved that ACEs are incredibly common;

- 67% of the population had at least one ACE
- 12.6% had scored four or more.

There was a close relationship between ACES and health outcomes; the higher your ace scores the worse your health outcomes. A score of 4+ had the correlated risk of chronic obstructive pulmonary disease was 2.5x that of someone with an ace score of zero. This is a primary health issue and high non-duty killer for first responders and greatly impacts health costs for agencies.

1. Risk of chronic obstructive pulmonary disease 2.5x higher
2. For Hepatitis, it was also 2.5x higher
3. For Depression, it was 4.5x higher
4. For Suicide, it was 12x higher
5. An ACE score of 7+ had triple the lifetime risk of lung cancer, and
6. 3.5x the risk of heart disease.

Dr. Burke Harris continues her talk to say, "some people look at this data, and they say, 'Come on, yeah you had a rough childhood, you're more likely to drink and smoke and do all these things that are going to ruin your health. This isn't science, this is just bad behavior!' Well, as it turns out, this is precisely where the science comes in!"

The medical professions are increasingly aware that early childhood exposure to adversity physically impacts the brain and physical development. Dr. Burke Harris explains the scientific impacts:

- The Nucleus Accumbens or the pleasure and reward center of the brain that is implicated in substance dependence; inhibits the prefrontal cortex which is necessary for impulse control an executive function; a critical area for learning

- MRI scans show a measurable difference in the Amygdala; the brain's fear and high alert response center.

Why is understanding brain scans of trauma response so essential to a public safety professional? Over time the repeated trauma you are exposed to will show an overused amygdala in the brain. Responses based on the excitement, risk, fear, and danger of the job. Even if your childhood was idyllic, the increased health risks of an overstimulated amygdala on health and wellness is vital to understand. The reason the MRI scans show measurable differences in the amygdala has to do with the hypothalamic-pituitary-adrenal axis. The brain and body stress response system that governs our fight-flight-freeze response; but, how does it work? Dr. Burke-Harris says, "Imagine you're walking in the forest and you see a bear. Immediately your hypothalamus sends a signal to your pituitary which sends a signal to your adrenal gland: RELEASE THE STRESS HORMONES!"

- Adrenaline and cortisol make your heart start to pound
- Your pupils dilate
- Your airways open up
- You are ready to either fight that bear or run from the bear or freeze like a deer in headlights

This is wonderful ... if you're in a forest ... and there's a bear.

As public safety professionals, you can likely relate to multiple stress reactions over the course of a month, a year, and perhaps several times in one shift. When that hormonal trigger is released repetitively your internal system morphs from healthy life-saving adaptive stress responsiveness to an unhealthy maladaptive system that harms you. This is damaging to an adult however young children are ultra-sensitive to repeated hormonal stress triggers given they are still in a developing stage for both their brains and their bodies. Dr. Burke-Harris informs that; "High doses of adversity in children not only affects brain structure and function they affect the developing immune system, developing hormonal systems and even the way our DNA is read and transcribed."

Some studies are now stating that some PTSD reactions are from your DNA which correlates to these childhood experiences and changes made in the DNA structure. All this indicates a need for new perspectives in both medical and mental health awareness, prevention, mitigation and treatments. It also leads the way for public safety, justice and social services to rethink how we manage people who are heading towards or already in the system. The science clearly indicates neurological reasons why people who have suffered from significant childhood adversity will be more likely to engage in high risk and poor health behavior.

When dealing with the public you may not be able to save every child in an adverse home situation, but you may be able to encourage some parents to seek services to learn about this test and the major health implications. While you are not a social worker you do interact with social/emotional issues and are the first contact for many. You have the opportunity to enhance your already significant contribution to society by becoming the first line of healing.

One thing to note about the official survey, is that the questions represent the top ten of the surveyed group Dr. Felitti was working with, predominantly white, middle class. There are, additional childhood traumas and Dr Felitti has publicly stated we should look beyond the top ten to ensure a broader perspective, including newer trauma impacts that were not as prevalent during the survey, like terrorism and online bullying. Some you can consider include:

Surviving/recovering from a major accident or incident (i.e. mass shooting)	Surviving/experiencing major weather events impacting your home (hurricane, tornado, flood)	Parent alienation (where the child is denied access to parent out of spite, control, or used as a manipulation tool)
Witnessing a father being abused by a mother or grandparent	Generational or environmental trauma (disadvantaged or unsafe neighborhoods)	Being in the foster care system
Bullying or Cyber-bulling	Watching a sibling being abused	Homelessness
Racism and exclusion	Involvement in the juvenile justice system	Losing a caregiver, i.e. grandparent

We have included the A.C.E. questionnaire for your interest and knowledge.

ACE SURVEY **While you were growing up, during your first 18 years of life:**	**YES = 1pt**
Did a parent or other adult in the household often; swear at you, insult you, put you down or humiliate you? Or; Act in a way that made you afraid that you might be physically hurt?	
Did a parent or other adult in the household often; push, grab, slap, or throw something at you? Or; Ever hit you so hard that you had marks or were injured?	
Did an adult or person at least 5 years older than you ever; Touch or fondle you or have you touch their body in a sexual way? Or; Attempt or actually have oral, anal, or vaginal intercourse with you?	
Did you often or very often feel that … No one in your family loved you or thought you were important or special? Or; Your family didn't look out for each other, feel close to each other, or support each other?	
Did you often feel that; You didn't have enough to eat, had to wear dirty clothes, and had no one to protect you? Or; Your parents were too drunk or high to take care of you when you needed it?	
Were your parents ever separated or divorced?	
Was your mother or stepmother (may also be the male in the family) often or very often pushed, grabbed, slapped, or had something thrown at them? Or; Often kicked, bitten, hit with a fist or hard object? Or; Ever repeatedly hit for a least a few minutes or threatened with a gun or knife?	
Did you ever live with someone who was a problem drinker, or alcoholic, or drug user?	
Did any household member go to prison?	
ADD UP YOUR YES ANSWERS. THIS IS YOUR ACE SCORE:	

The A.C.E. test is something you can consider when dealing with situations where a person is not acting in a manner that is helpful to the situation. While you have a specific duty to attend to there is now an opportunity, when safe and appropriate to do so, of becoming part of the continuum of care that helps people move away from unhealthy and harmful choices though the manner in which you engage them, offer support or service options or simply treat them with an empathy you may not have previously considered.

"Adverse childhood experiences are the single greatest unaddressed public health threat facing our nation today."
~Dr. Robert Bloch, President- American Academy of Pediatrics

From a policing perspective, Sean found the ACE test and underlying research profoundly impactful both personally and professionally. He shares his experience:

SEAN:
"I would have to say the ACE survey was a huge personal benefit to me because it helped me to understand that I'm not the only one. First of all, there are millions upon millions of children that face adverse childhood experiences annually. Not just locally, not just in our state but across the country and around the world.

These children are affected by all forms of abuse, either indirectly or directly, and a vast majority of those never end up dealing with it as they enter adulthood with this baggage and experiences that impact how they interact in the world. Now they are trying to manage their emotions that are profoundly affected subconsciously and consciously when stressors and incidents arise and as adults, they are ill-equipped to govern themselves well.

As a law enforcement Officer, it was a massive benefit to me. I already knew I had faced adverse childhood situations. I had triggers and reactions to certain types of calls. While I had already started to deal with the impacts of my own traumatic experiences, being able to recognize the extent and the scope of the issues in this succinct manner helped me identify different challenges that I could face. It helped me understand that where there was a significant impact on the incremental percentages of unhealthy behaviors and actions directly proportional to an ACE score. There is hope though IF you learn to recognize, address and manage those impacts."

When seeing his score of 9/10, plus some after the top ten he says; "It was an incentive to ensure I was serious about addressing these adverse impacts, to not only be the best law enforcement officer I could be - but also to be the best person I could be, the best husband I could be, and the best father I could be. To do this, I had to be open and willing to address all those impacts from my childhood, openly and honestly. I had to recognize that many times my emotions could be swayed or triggered by my interactions with others. By recognizing and managing my triggers, I was more professional and more cognitive when I felt those feelings bubble up inside. That's how the ACE test personally helped me in my professional and personal life.

As a public safety professional, my knowledge of trauma and the ACE scoring indicators made a big difference. Now I recognize it when I'm talking to people - I can tell when someone is coming from a place where they experienced an adverse childhood experience."

In the right moment, Sean can even address aspects in a conversation by saying, "What has happened to you? What has led you to fall into a situation of domestic violence, where you refuse to leave?" He can share the statistics that show how a large majority of people that end up in these situations, either saw it or were involved in it at an earlier time in their lives. It also helps him check his emotional response and avoid getting triggered given domestic violence subconsciously reminds him of his own childhood and questions on why his own mother didn't leave.

Often just asking the question, is the door opening that was never considered and a chance for them to consciously realize their choices. We will hear, "You know what, I watched my mom get beaten up from the time I was born until I was 18 years old and I just began to believe it was natural, it was normal. I guess I became attracted to men that are like the ones I knew growing up, with my mom." Taking those few short minutes, when you can, opens that door to begin those conversations and lead them to a recovery-oriented system of care that can help them from there.

From a personal introspection, Deirdre shares how discovering the A.C.E. was the final piece of the puzzle that answered why her near 30-year marriage fell apart after they had survived so many traumas along the way, just fine. Like Sean, she scored 9 on the ACE test and with several of the extra (beyond top ten) trauma considerations. When her ex was showing signs of PTSD, it was easy to blame him in the beginning because she didn't think she had changed or had anything to do with the failing situation. Understanding ACE and Ego States (which we will get to soon), allowed her to see how much her reactions and triggers impacted the end of the relationship. How she responded triggered him, which triggered her and slowly the erosion of friendship, trust, security and safety was too much to manage. It was never about how much either loved each other, it was about the communications, interactions and inability to see the person they had committed to was suffering due to their own internal struggles. For her, this knowledge allowed healing and self-development to become a better partner for a future spouse and together they are really present and committed co-parents.

CHAPTER 5

TRAUMA INFORMED CARE OUTCOMES

Traumatized people chronically feel unsafe inside their bodies: The past is alive in the form of gnawing interior discomfort. Their bodies bombarded by visceral warning signs, and, in an attempt to control these processes, they often become expert at ignoring their gut feelings and in numbing awareness of what is played out inside.
They learn to hide from themselves.
— Bessel A. van der Kolk, The Body Keeps Score

Trauma is a global and costly public health problem that impacts a large percentage of the calls you attend. How you respond, your approach, body language, choice of words, and actions could trigger someone based on their previous experiences and escalate a situation quickly. For many members of society, it is related to a history of violence, abuse, neglect, loss, disaster, war, and other emotionally harmful experiences directly and indirectly.

Trauma is blind to age, gender, socioeconomic status, race, ethnicity, geography, or sexual orientation. It is shown to be a part of the history of those suffering social and emotional mental health challenges and substance abuse disorders. Trauma is increasingly recognized as a critical component of informed behavioral health service delivery. Before many people get to that level of help though they tend to have interactions with you, the public safety professionals that are meeting them at a very vulnerable time.

Managing this growing health crisis needs to start at the initial point of contact, whenever feasible. This will create an integrated recovery-oriented system of care with a multi-faceted, multi-agency approach including education for the public. It also helps identify the self-care needs of your brothers and sisters in the inter-connected agencies. Knowing that the accumulation of what you see, hear, touch, and do, on a daily basis has an impact directly or indirectly.

"Individual trauma results from an event, series of events, or set of circumstances that is experienced by an individual as physically or emotionally harmful or life threatening and that has lasting adverse effects on the individual's functioning and mental, physical, social, emotional, or spiritual well-being."
~SAMHSA's Concept of Trauma

Most public safety rookie and annual training emphasizes taking command and control of the scene. It is vital that you have robust situational awareness and response actions to manage whatever may come your way. This requirement can cast a shadow on any alternative communication strategies taught with thoughts of, "I don't have time for that - I'm not a social worker." While that is true, you are not there to solve their emotional trauma, you have potential opportunity to manage and influence the best possible outcome for all involved. Less escalation, paperwork, potential risk for you and better community bridge building as a bonus. They get someone who is there to help them "make an informed decision in their own best interest."

Any public service role is going to have an element of people-management and emotionalized behavior can be aided with a little psychology knowledge. This is not about making you work harder, it is about working smarter and using different strategies while taking command and control of the scene and the people in it that may pose a challenge to your effectiveness.

To have command and control over a situation, you first must have command and control of yourself. Then you are better prepared and able to manage from a pre-escalation mindset and influence people away from self-harming or limiting behavior. Without that, you are not "managing" anything you are just reacting to whatever is thrown your way.

"If the only tool you have is a hammer,
you tend to see every problem as a nail."
~ Abraham Maslow

Start your situational assessment with "Am I safe?" and "am I in control of myself?"

- If you are safe, you ask: "are my peers safe, those on scene and on way?"

- If we are safe and in control of ourselves then we can look at the public member who is showing signs of emotional outburst and ask; "Is that person in control of themselves?" If they are not in full control of themselves then you ask; "Are they safe?"

- If everyone is safe, even though they are acting outside of "calm", then consider a broader situational assessment; "Is there anyone else that could be in danger right now?"

- If all the people involved are all safe; "Is the environment safe?"

If you are satisfied with your situational awareness assessment, then consider that a win, in recognizing that at that moment; "I'm in control and we are all safe." Moreover, they may not be in control, but they are still safe. Maybe they are venting, crying, flailing around, or even a little hysterical but everyone involved, and the environment is still safe. That's a powerful place to be to project a calm, safe, confident demeanor that can manage and influence to avoid further escalation.

This provides an opportunity to consider: "Can I evaluate and assess this situation a little more deeply and see what's going on?" As an example, it allows you to offer an empathetic approach and instead of, "You need to calm down." say, "wow, I can tell you are really upset right now, aren't you?" Often, when we acknowledge someone's pain, their issues, and their concerns, we can sway further emotional escalation right there. You will often get an agreement, "Yeah, I'm upset, because ….!"

Psychologically, you interrupted their emotional overwhelm with acknowledgement. They know they have been heard. Now you can focus on understanding the situation further by asking: "Okay, I would like to help you gain the best possible outcome, in order to do that I need to understand, so tell me what is going on?" and get them to start talking. You have just avoided escalating them further via physical control techniques, harsh instructions, and body language that is threatening or unempathetic. You have come at the situation from a help-based perspective and asked them to assist a good outcome. You are providing them an opportunity to start to take control of themselves by opening-up that steam vent with more focus on the issue you asked to hear about, and less on the emotion and overwhelm of the moment.

From Sean's experience using these communication tactics and from the feedback from all the agency members that have taken the core communications and emotional intelligence training; this works! You may not be a social worker; however, you do have to manage social/emotional issues. Doing so from a pre-escalation mindset can save you from many unnecessary confrontations, undue personal call stress, or even being filmed as the next "YouTube" sensation because your own triggers created a two-way emotionalized situation. These strategies and tactics are very similar to what a hostage negotiator would use to manage their scenes.

Sean shared:
"I can't tell you how many times since I took this training, that I have heard from folks, 'You're not like most law enforcement Officers I have met. Most Cops want to talk over me, they want to yell at me or talk me down, but you seem to go with the flow and let me get it out of my system.'"

Sean's peers started asking about these techniques and if they could be coached on them because they saw the outcomes. They saw a closed and perceived dangerous community of bystanders at scenes, lower their bristle and trust Sean enough to approach him and share information; often hearing something along the lines of, "That's the cop that actually listens!"

Sean states; "Here's the thing - when you are known for being fair and willing to hear them out, they will open up to you more. You're going to solve more crime. You're going to get the insights to understand the criminal elements in your neighborhoods. I'm not suggesting you ever let your guard down. In fact, I would argue that with this training you will be more aware of your surroundings because of your heightened level of self-control. This will improve upon any previous training taken because you are fully engaged while being fully detached.[xl] I'm no different from any other public safety professional; but, with this training, I have experienced different results and I go home with a lot less stress on my shoulders than I used to. I have tested these tactics hundreds of times and I see the impact and difference it makes within my community. I use a pre-escalation approach regularly, and it has definitely been to my advantage to influence others in a way that allows them to feel safe, heard, accepted, respected and understood. When you humanize someone, you will achieve a far better outcome 99.9% of the time. It does not mean I agree with them, and it does not mean I am not arresting them, it does not mean they are not going to get checked into the hospital for a mental assessment. However, it does mean that situations that I saw escalate in the past have lessened dramatically. My partner sees it, my coworkers see it, my shift supervisor sees it, and my wife and kids get to see a better man walking in the door after shifts.

Even from a paperwork perspective, when you can calm someone down and gain their full story; when bystanders co-operate; you save time at the scene and significant paperwork. When you help someone, who is 'jacked-up', emotionally gain control over themselves and calm themselves before you have to take 'hands-on' action, it is an excellent thing. As soon as I have elevated the situation to a physical confrontation and put my hands on them, I must complete a use of force report, I have to initiate an arrest using the proper justification, per my jurisdictional authority. I get such great results with advanced communication technique we are teaching you that I don't put my hands on someone unless I know there's a clear purpose behind it. If I must affect an arrest, it's to protect somebody, protect them from continuing an issue with somebody else, stop a resistance or threat against me or other public safety professionals or inhibit them harming themselves, whatever the case may be.

When I go physical, there's double the paperwork compared to when I use a pre-escalation approach, listen empathetically and utilize these communications techniques. Many times, a conversation with them is where it ends, and I don't even have to write up a report. My computer notes cover it with saying, 'After making contact with this guy, we determined that he was upset. We assessed under the Baker Act*; and determined we did not need to take that route.

Nothing more needs to be documented at this point.'" *(*involuntary 72 hour* hold and *examination in Florida)"*[xli]

Another win is with future interactions within the community. Consider all the bystanders and looky-loos with their cell phones videotaping the situation. You are building trust and respect that you will give people a "fair shake" and hear them out. It's not just law enforcement consider;

- You will be the officer with whom they will share the local criminal activity

- You will be the person at the firehall that people will go to and seek help or share fire hazards that could be the next big fire that hurts you or one of your crew

- You will be the ambulance crew that people are forthcoming and share the correct mix of drugs someone has taken, needles in their pockets, mental health issues, or other medical history needed to save a life or protect you.

- You will be the corrections officer who is informed of upcoming riots or other violent acts that could save their life or yours.

- You will be the dispatcher that stays calm and keeps people calm in order to get the information needs to aid the 911 response team.

There are plenty of you out there that use similar techniques. Advanced communications skills taught in special unit training, from self-development or through organizations that value psychology-based training. However, the average public safety professional is not trained in this yet. The reliance on positional power is still predominantly taught. Yet the interaction environment is changing, everything is filmed and generally people are less inclined to submit to authoritative power without pushing back, even when their own safety is involved. These powerful communication and human behavior techniques will help you do the job better, lessen your risk and threats and improve your service to the communities.

The results on the job quickly become quite apparent and others will show curiosity when you have less stressful calls, more cooperation from people at scenes and attain more information quicker, without the argument. Peers around you becomes aware of the advantages and begin to adopt these practices. When you exhibit calm, safe confidence it gets results for you and also helps all the responders in the situation. Ideally a culture shifts towards a trauma-informed organization that will enable us to rescue our own more effectively.

We recognize that there will always be a competitive and overt rivalry between your services. It is the same between the different military organizations. When healthy, it adds a layer of fun to war stories and interactions. However, brotherhood and sisterhood does not end, pending the uniform you wear. We need to look out for our extended family too. It starts with you. What you give in a moment of tragedy can well serve your own and others mental wellness.

Sean recalls how this cross-agency impact can be impactful. "I was called out to a car crash on a single lane road. The guy flipped his truck and he was pinned underneath this SUV. He had fallen out of the truck, and his legs were pinned or crushed underneath, and there's nothing much I could do for this guy, I couldn't extract him because I'd kill him so other than that I could only talk and comfort him. I had to wait for the fire department to get there.

I held the guy's hand, and I prayed with him. We had a conversation and I continued to talk to him, got his name and reassured him that more help was on the way. I was really trying to keep him as calm as I possibly could. He keeps asking me, 'What do my legs look like … what do my legs look like?' I told him the truth. I said, 'I don't know, I'm going to stay up here with you, keep you as comfortable as possible and make sure you know I'm right here with you. We'll worry about your legs when the fire department gets here and can lift this SUV off you, don't worry about that right now. Focus on talking to me right now.'"

When fire arrived, it was such a relief because I couldn't do anything for this guy on my own aside from talking to him and keep him calm. It was a mess and they had to blow up airbags to lift the SUV and then extract him out. This victim is a walking miracle today. From what he went through, not being able to walk, his legs crushed to full rehabilitation and being able to walk again is just incredible to me.

After EMS took control of the guy, I went back and started talking with the guys from the fire department and having the post-event talk. I shared how much of a relief it was to see them pulling up and how helpless I felt not being able to help the guy. Then they opened up to me, with the stress of getting the truck off him and hoping they were there in time to save his legs and how traumatic it was for them too and how appreciative they were that I kept him so calm. It took nothing to open the door and enhance a typical post-event debriefing with a little humanistic venting of the stress caused by our respective work.

Later, we went together to meet with the guy when he held a big celebration for getting out of his wheelchair for the first time it was as teammates. When he walked and then gave credit to all of us for all we did for him, there was pride and joy for each other. That's what it's about because we all do hellish jobs at times. If you can get all your responders to work together and not let their, "Service Ego" get in the way, we can recognize and support each other and help speed the healing process of indirect and direct trauma.

We all must work together cohesively and in unified partnership. When all the egos are balanced, and we can all appreciate what we can do for each other it makes working together that much better. It makes the reality of trauma across the services easier to recognize, address, mitigate, bust down stigma and manage wellness as a collective family.

"We've all seen the headlines implying that people with PTSD are dangerous. We must not resort to thinking, due to fear, that a person with PTSD equals a ticking time bomb. The stigma surrounding PTSD is so negative. It arouses concerns and provokes whispers and worried glances. People don't understand it at all. They assume I'm a potential powder keg just waiting for a spark to set me off into a rage, and that's just not true, about me or any person with PTSD. I have never physically assaulted anyone out of anger or rage. I'm suffering with it, and people are afraid to ask me about it."
~ James Meuer, DAMAGED: A Public safety professional's Experiences Handling Post-Traumatic Stress Disorder[xlii] □

CHAPTER 6

THE BODY TOLL

Danger lurks behind the scenes, you see, sneakily creeping through your cells, heart and brain.
Battling for your vitality, your long-term health ... and for worthy love.
~ Deirdre von Krauskopf

Admitting that stress and trauma have a significant impact on mental fitness is a touchy subject for many in public safety professions. After reading this, you may choose to remain stoic on the psychological impact; but wait, there's more! There are also physiological and relationship costs to these types of careers. As detailed in a 1991 paper on Stress Management Model Program for Maintaining Firefighter Well-Being prepared by the International Association of Fire Chiefs Foundation; *"Stress is one of the most serious occupational hazards in the fire service, affecting health, job performance, career decision-making, morale, and family life. Emotional problems, as well as problems with alcohol and drugs, are becoming increasingly evident. High rates of attrition, divorce, occupational disease, and injury continue... [and] Maladaptive changes in stress response repertoires exact a price in terms of overall mental stability, anxiety, and interpersonal conflicts, both at home and on the job. They lead to morale problems, decreased productivity, increased accidents, early retirements, high medical costs and chronic absenteeism. ... [and] Poor adaptation may also contribute to alcoholism, depression, and a number of mental health problems in the fire service that undermine judgment and adversely affect performance... [and] suicide is a real and tragic alternative for some."xliii*

In EMS World, the reality of shiftwork on the body is startling and that is before we add in the trauma. According to Lt. Keith Ellis, Tennessee's Washington County-Johnson City *EMS uses both 12- and 24-hour shifts. It's recently begun working some crews on 12-hour shifts due to the danger of employee fatigue. The service's average call volume is 32,000 annually, or 10–20 calls per day per ambulance. Each call can take anywhere from 1–3 hours to clear, depending on its nature. Do this math, and you'll find some crews may not stop during their entire 24-hour shift. Half of EMS personnel sleep only six hours every 24, with more than half reporting poor sleep quality and 70% reporting some problems with sleep.3 Loss of sleep, stressful situations, and not eating on a regular schedule could push an already-stressed employee close to the edge. Insufficient sleep has been linked to cardiovascular disease, obesity, metabolic disorders, gastrointestinal conditions, hunger/ appetite, and changes in emotion.3 Research has found higher levels of negative behavior correlating to sleep deprivation and that a person going without sleep for 24 hours experiences impairment equivalent to a blood alcohol level of 0.10%.2"*[xliv]

In a journal article "Post-Traumatic Stress Disorder and Cardiovascular Disease" author Steven Coughlin drives the point home for all fields "*Therefore, in addition to mental health issues, public safety professionals are at higher risk for chronic health issues like hypertension, cardiac crisis, obesity and diabetes. Persons with PTSD, a common anxiety disorder in both veteran and nonveteran populations, have been reported to have an increased risk of hypertension, hyperlipidemia, obesity, and cardiovascular disease."*[xlv]

The cost of these careers is evident, given the chronic exposure to traumatic events. It is not an ordinary human experience to witness and manage regularly. Dr. Robbie Adler-Tapia, a psychologist who works with those impacted by trauma, attachment and dissociation, writes;

> *"Professional trauma is responding to and witnessing an actual or perceived threat to the safety/integrity of self or others, that may result in intense fear or helplessness in response to an event. For public safety professionals, responding to and witnessing a critical incident or a series of distressing life events over time, can lead to medical and/or physical symptoms and long-term consequences."*
>
> *The perception of an event varies, depending on the individual. Consider that most traumatic incidents are commonly considered to be extremely unusual in the range of ordinary human experiences but are daily occurrences for public safety professionals. Organizations are getting better at critical incident briefings for large scale traumatic calls. It needs to grow and provide resiliency tools for all events.*
>
> *"Such critical incidents may include death in line of duty, the death or serious injury of a child, multiple fatalities, severely injured survivors, attempted or successful suicides, natural disasters, personal mishaps involving death or permanent injury and otherwise high emotional impact, deadly force incidents, grotesque injuries, acts of terrorism, acts of violence resulting in injury or death. Ultimately, professional trauma is anything that negatively impacts the psyche and changes the course of healthy development."*[xlvi]

There are very few men and women in these professions that do NOT relate to repeated critical incidents over the course of their career. Trauma Informed Care provides a higher-level perspective of the process of traumatic inputs on the mind and body. This will develop your perception of self-management, aid managing people at scenes, and to better take care of loved ones who also feel an impact to the critical stress you bring home with you.

TRAUMA INFORMED CARE - The THREE 'E' METHOD

EVENT: The first "E" is the event, itself. The medical journals all agree that trauma is different for everyone - our natural and learned resiliency is varied. From our birth, we all start life with different foundations, so what is considered traumatic to me may not be considered traumatic to you - and your response may be significantly different from the next person.

Public safety professionals are often interacting with someone who is experiencing some level of trauma during the situation at hand. Add in previous trauma that has built up prior to that moment and what one may consider a minor event is the other person's worst possible moment! Often triggered by subconscious inputs, their perception is, indeed, their reality, which may show as an exaggerated emotional response up to a full mental health episode.

> *"Events and circumstances may include the actual or extreme threat of physical or psychological harm or severe, life-threatening neglect for a child that imperils healthy development. These events and circumstances may occur as a single occurrence or repeatedly over time."*
> *~Diagnostic and Statistical Manual of Mental Disorders (DSM-5)*

The first step in becoming trauma-informed is understanding how events impact people differently. There isn't a "right way" to respond to what is emotionally, physically, psychologically, or spiritually damaging to someone. This is also true of a partner or peer showing signs of distress or behavioral choices that indicate a crack in their mental fitness. You are now aware that whether direct, indirect, vicarious or cumulative, a person's critical stress reaction is a very personal reaction to an event.

A pre-escalation response saves you time and stress from having to take de-escalation steps that may lead to life-impacting outcomes. Your approach to the situation (being a calm, safe presence), is as important for yourself, the peers alongside you and the person who is experiencing an event reaction. An article in ScienceDirect informs us that trauma leaves a tangible imprint on the brain during imaging scans. Research also consistently identifies post-traumatic stress disorder (PTSD) linked to higher activity in brain areas that process fear and less activation in parts of the prefrontal cortex. The common signs and symptoms are detailed in the following chart, published by Psychology Today:

Feeling threatened or silenced	Seeing yourself as weak or inadequate	Avoidance or blocking of event memories
Believing the worst in people, and that the world is dangerous	Difficulty with trust on anything outside your control	Difficulty trusting and benefiting from relationships
Inability to cope well with daily life stressors, difficulty sleeping	Challenges with cognitive processes and behavior regulation	Criticizing your reactions, feeling you could have done more

Numbness, avoidance or hypervigilance, feeling on-guard	Loss of interest in intimacy, erectile dysfunction	Nightmares and flashbacks
Heightened emotion: sadness, anger, guilt, fear and anxiety	Fear of reaching out for help	Replaying of the memory, seeing danger everywhere
Abuse, giving or taking	Humiliation, Shame	Betrayal

You likely won't see most of these in a public setting but some will shine through. When you are dealing with the public, they may be irrationally interacting with you due to triggered emotions that have nothing to do with the moment, or with you. Your position of authority is a different impactor though, and may trigger fear, pride, or confusion in the individual due to environmental and societal inputs. Their response could be outside of normal expectancy due to childhood or unresolved trauma. These reactions are subconscious and often unknown or long forgotten. Unresolved trauma commonly shows us as:

Uncontrollable anger; excessive for the situation and often, acting on it.	Suicidal thoughts or actions, self-harm or mutilation activity
Addictive behavior to attempt to numb or escape from overwhelming or negative emotions	Flashbacks, looking as if they see something other than the current situation
Avoidance behaviors, towards people or things that have triggered a known or unknown emotion	Reliving or nightmare quality reactiveness
Can include emotion avoidance, not crying or upset when that would be logical given the circumstances	Signs of detachment or vocalizing a feeling of being dead inside, having no feelings
Isolation indicators show they feel alone in the world or stuck in their own mind	Signs of depression, lackluster, hopelessness
Irrational fear behaviors of people, locations or things	Complaints of excessive exhaustion from lack of sleep
Disconnecting or a disassociation to the event, conversation or loved ones	Challenges going or staying asleep
Hypervigilance or showing signs of being on guard, looking/waiting for something in an agitated or pumped up way	Body language or vocal shame indications they feel worthless, they are a bad person or a lesser human
Impatience, irritation and low tolerance that seems out of the norm	Panic attacks, hysteria or anxiety that seems out of context for the situation at hand

EXPERIENCE: The next "E" of Trauma Informed Care is, Experience. What was the experience for everyone involved: responders, victims, bystanders, perpetrators, dispatchers, and all others who get involved at different stages later on? This perspective takes in the social, emotional and psychological aspects that show in your body's reactions. Both the event and the experience will be different for everybody in how it shows externally and internally; both initially and after the event has passed.

As public safety professionals you have the unique opportunity to ease the experience for each other through a strategic and empathetic approach. Understanding the power in your physical, vocal, and communication choices can lessen traumatic impacts. Trauma is often replayed as a movie, repeating over and over in the mind. What role do you want to take in that scene? Do you want to be that impatient, demanding, brutish, angry-voiced person, or the empathetic voice that still moves the situation along but does not add to the negative experience?

We also need to ensure self-care is taken into consideration. As public safety professionals, you experience considerable trauma and you may "think" you are trained to deal with it - some may even feel they are immune to it; but your brain is not. You may not believe a particular moment is hugely impactful; however, the neuroscience indicates it is growing quietly in our subconscious minds and impacting brain health. No one can anticipate or predict when one more input is substantial enough to collapse your thinly constructed barrier.

"I wish my head could forget what my eyes have seen."
~ Dave Darnell, Detroit PD: Documentary BURN

Self-care means you recognize and take actions to gain foundational knowledge to optimize your mental fitness; developing resilience-strength to manage the moments and long-term effects throughout your career and into post-retirement. Talking about it helps your hippocampus (the memory center in the brain) process the experience and settle it into long-term memory rather than an unprocessed event that continually replays in your mind keeping the trauma alive.

Recognize, as a peer and self-care advocate, that there are times when you all need to regroup, talk with someone, and find healthy ways to manage the impacts of both the direct and indirect trauma. Understand that you need to train for and prepare for that one event or combination of events that may trigger an unhealthy response internally with self-harming behaviors, or through your external actions both at work and in your personal life.

When helping another through an event, you may notice them overly focused on a specific part of a traumatic situation. It can be immediately helpful to expand their vision with questions that shake them out of emotionalized tunnel vision by asking what color the house was, or car, or who was working beside them. Odd and irrelevant questions force the person to move to their cortex (the logic center) to think of the answer and respond, moving them out of them emotionally replaying trauma impact.

Sean speaks of a young rookie who he aided through a traumatizing moment:

SEAN:
"I noticed he was clearly shaken as a baby died in his arms. I walked up to him and asked, 'Are you okay?' He looked at me with a haunted look and said, 'No, but thank you for asking.' I told him it was alright to not feel okay, his was a perfectly normal reaction to a horrible event. I asked him if he wanted to share what happened and he nodded and began to share. As he was talking, I could see him getting tunnel vision, staring down as his arms came up, mimicked cradling of the baby. I touched his arm and asked if it was raining when he came outside. He sort of shook his head and looked at me quizzically for a second and said, 'No.' He looked down again and started to talk and I touched his elbow, again, and asked, 'Did fire or EMS show up on the scene, first?' Again, he paused, dropped his arms and reported on that. He finished the rest of the story with his arms down, looking at me. I had stopped the visual replay and brought him back to a professional perspective. I told him I was there for him any time he wanted to talk, mentioning a great psychologist, should he find it eating away at him in the coming weeks and months. He shook my hand and thanked me saying, 'No one has ever asked me if I was okay at one of these scenes before, so thank you!'"

EFFECTS: The last "E" of Trauma Informed Care is, Effects. By effects, we mean both short-term and long-term. Short-term effects can show up immediately, or within a few hours or moments after it happened. PTSD commonly shows up six months later. For many though, the long-term memory can sit deep inside the human vault until years down the road, either something triggers it, or retirement leaves you with too much free time in your head and traumas resurface. These memories can also be set off by a subconscious trigger at any time; emotional and physiological reactions from preceding moments come flooding back, without you even realizing why.

This is especially notable with public safety professionals. Trauma does not need to be direct or top-of-mind to cause a stress reaction that can have career-limiting or negative relationship outcomes. You have a higher trauma cumulative effect than the average person, so many such vaulted memories can surface at any time. It could be people attacking you while you are trying to do your duty. It may be witnessing grievous bodily harm. Any situation that activates a stress response, the hormone flooding or fight, flight, freeze response.

Sometimes the effects of trauma can lead to addiction issues, whether they be mild or severe. To calm the mind, people often turn to numbing or risky behaviors as coping mechanisms. When that becomes the go-to on a regular basis, addiction is born. A high number of people who choose addictive, coping responses have high childhood ACE's. Whether you are the one struggling with addiction, or it is someone with whom you are interacting, it may be helpful to consider this poignant truth in Judy Crane's book, The Trauma Heart, where she quotes Dr. Gobor Maté, physician and author of, The Realm of Hungry Ghosts:

"If people who become severe addicts, as shown by all the studies were, for the most part, abused as children, then we realize that the war on drugs is actually waged against people that were abused from the moment they were born or from an early age. In other words, we are punishing people for having been abused. That's the first point. The second point is that the research clearly shows that the biggest driver of addictive relapse and addictive behavior is actually stress."[xlvii]

This provides us two considerations, one is that we may want to look at addictive behavior with a more empathetic view; two, if we do not manage our stress well it can lead to life damaging behaviors and addictions of our own - especially if our childhoods were less than ideal. Should that happen, we would want others to treat us with respectful empathy.

"A trauma informed approach is distinct from trauma- specific services or trauma systems. A trauma informed approach is inclusive of trauma-specific interventions, whether assessment, treatment or recovery supports, yet it also incorporates key trauma principles into the organizational culture."[xlviii]
~SAMHSA

Deirdre was conversing with a retired, New York S.W.A.T. team officer as he sought further counsel after seeing our training. He said, "I don't know why it's hitting me now, but I will be sitting at home watching a cop show and something in it triggers me and I start bawling like a baby. It never bothered me while it was happening, why the heck is it haunting me now?" As we talked through the impact of a loss in purpose, power and meaning that many will feel after retiring, his job was his life, it provided his drive and kept him super busy. Then add on his recent separation, missing his kids, relocating after retirement and the loss of his peer and friend circle he began to recognize that he was in a more vulnerable place. His brain was being triggered by a commonality in a TV show to a similar event he experienced, and his life wasn't busy enough for the brain to push it away with practiced resiliency to focus on more expedient issues. He was now processing the traumas he shoved in a vault and ignored at the time. This helped him alter his growing habit of drinking at the local bar every night and get back into his physical fitness routine. He also sought some help to manage the transition and process these life altering events he had experienced.

This is an example of why organization administrations need to take the lead in creating a trauma-informed organization. Your members often have no idea why they are feeling, reacting and emotionally responding to issues they believe are well locked up. The discovery of a problem may not surface until post retirement, a long service deserves the best we can offer for a life of managing the unthinkable events many experience over the course of their career.

THE FOUR "R" approach to Trauma Informed Care: Utilizing SAMHSA's guide we will view trauma from an organization perspective. Adapted from (SAMHSA) Concept of Trauma and Guidance for a Trauma-Informed Approach.[xlix] Which informs us that all people at all levels of the system have a basic realization about trauma and understand how trauma can affect families, groups, organizations, communities, and individuals.

REALIZES	The widespread impact of trauma and has understanding on paths to better management and recovery
RECOGNIZES	Signs and symptoms of trauma. Ensure organizational awareness
RESPONDS	Organizationally by full integration of knowledge into policies, procedures and practices
RESISTS	Actively resists re-traumatization through mindful approaches and management practices during and after traumatic situations
GOING BEYOND THE CALL INCLUDES A 5TH R ©	
RESILENCY	Organizational prioritization of helping teams manage the unimaginable by mitigating the impact of other's trauma and their own through promotion of healthy mental fitness strategies

We now know some people's behavior comes from a different life experience than your own and their reaction may be vastly different to the same stimuli. When people are highly emotionalized, the logic center in their brain is incapacitated. Public safety professionals that realize this when interacting with someone understand their behavior is designed to survive adversity and overwhelming circumstances from past, present, and the perceived future. It could be from direct or indirect trauma whether they are the victim, perpetrator, witness, or have only heard about it through another party.

There is a belief that people are desensitized through the prevalence of violent graphic videos and materials online; however, the greatest danger is with exposure to actual violence in your home or community. What people who have electronic exposure discover is perception is not reality and there is a very real difference when trauma hits live and impacts them or someone they care about. Electronic exposure has a risk though, as it may allow a person to feel more invincible than they really are. A research report from Department of Psychology, University of Miami states:

"Exposure to violence at high levels or across multiple contexts has been linked with emotional desensitization, indicated by low levels of internalizing symptoms; however, the long-term consequences of such desensitization are unknown. Exposure to high levels of violence at age 11 was associated with lower levels of internalizing problems at age 13 - as was exposure to violence across multiple contexts. In turn, fewer internalizing problems and externalizing problems at age 13 predicted more violent behavior at age 18. The results suggest that emotional desensitization to violence in early adolescence contributes to serious violence in late adolescence." [1]

We must remember that the very nature of trauma means a person or persons is dealing with something unnatural that has happened. It is not like you prepare for a traumatic outcome for years and years and are ready to take on the shock, stress and emotional hijacking that accompanies the worst moments in your life. Just because we are trained to see the unimaginable and have dealt with some or many traumatic events, doesn't mean we will react the same at the next one. We don't need an in-depth research study to understand soldiers who are highly trained and prepared, yet still get PTSD. It is no different for public safety professionals due to your professional exposure to trauma. The depression, PTSD and suicide statistics make this very clear. Those with higher resilience can be hit even harder because they don't believe it can happen to them. Being prepared is in your own best interest.

Trauma plays a role in mental health and substance use. It is not as simple as a "lack of control" or self-discipline. Having empathy for those you serve; your peers and you is critical. Empathy is not a weakness and it is often confused with pity, sympathy, or compassion so let's look at the difference between these for clarity:

PITY	SYMPATHY	EMPATHY	COMPASSION
I acknowledge your suffering but don't feel compelled to get involved	I care about your suffering but don't take it on personally	I can put myself into your shoes and feel your suffering without taking it on myself	I want to relieve your suffering and I will take on your pain as if it's my own

Empathy can be further broken down into cognitive-based, as in "perspective-taking", which is being able to put yourself into someone else's place and see their perspective. Essentially, "empathy by thought", rather than through feelings. Emotional based where you get choked up as you can feel the impact of the other person's emotions as if you had "caught" the emotion like a contagion. Finally, compassion-based empathy where you feel another's pain and take actions to help from your concern.

Many public safety professionals believe they have lost their ability to care when they no longer have emotion-based empathy; however, they have usually built up resiliency to the events and experiences of other people's trauma. You still have the choice of cognitive empathy to help guide them through their experience.

Being empathetic while listening to another person and suspending judgement shows in your body language. It allows you to honestly, openly, and respectfully "hear" their perspective. As before, we are not advocating that you have to agree with the other person. We suggest you open yourself to the value of empathetic listening to help you meet your interactive objective. This is useful for any productive listening objective, including on the home front.

Another consideration is the rise in mental, behavior and spectrum disorders that pose a challenge for people inflicted or challenged to interact in a logical and purposeful way. An example would be Autism where a person may be so inwardly tuned, they cannot hear or see you to receive instruction, move out of harm's way, or react rationally. An authoritative approach is not going to work with spectrum disorders or those experiencing a psychosis episode. An empathetic, calm, safe confidence, lower tones and meeting them where they are at will have much better results.

We practice reality-based training scenarios in our workshop on these interactions. We do not list all the mental health disorders in this book as the topic is worthy of a book on its own. The communication tactics we share do prepare you to interact with all but violent offenders and psychotic interactions. These require escalated responses better acquired in other training. As introduced our focus is on the 90% of your calls not the extreme 10%. Sean is a certified critical incident and tactical defense instructor however so if desired, time can be added to our program to include this element.

The recovery-oriented system of care requires a shift in culture that lessens repeat calls and escalated incidents that serve no one. It means that personnel at all levels have to change their language, behaviors, and practices to take trauma experiences and mental health into consideration. A critical and empowering shift when interacting with the public as well as with your partners, peers, and support team.

This provides a greater ability to actually help people, which is one of the largest reasons most public safety professionals got into their career in the first place. Unfortunately, we enter into a situation wanting to help people and we often make situations worse. Leading into the last, R.

Resisting re-traumatization is where you can make a significant difference with the public you serve. At times our approach, communication style, lack of empathy, or trauma informed situational assessment limits a calm interaction. If we trigger someone into a higher emotional trauma reaction it negatively impacts us as well, whether from time, stress impact, potential injury, or a paperwork perspective. A trauma-informed approach intends to resist re-traumatization to avoid triggering past subconscious trauma.

For example, it is common to raise our voice in frustration or authority when someone does not follow instruction. If that recipient was mentally or physically abused, had autism, or were tripping on some drugs we could escalate the situation quickly. If abuse was their trauma, they are triggered to a fight, flight or freeze reaction. If within spectrum disorder, a freeze and withdrawal often happen so you are shut out and no comprehension of what you want will be heard. If inebriated or high, it is more likely fear, pride or confusion is triggered, which raises emotions so high the logic center of the neocortex is shut off.

Your approach, your communication skills, your emotional intelligence, and trauma informed understanding can avoid triggering an emotionalized response that does not meet your objective to maintain order and control of a scene. This will provide you a significant tactical advantage with your objective and avoid escalating the interaction. For public safety professionals, it starts with trust and safety. When you exude calm, safe confidence in your dealings with someone you change the interaction dynamic.

"By learning and applying Trauma Informed Care, we have an ability to turn around trauma infused moments for the better - one call at a time."
~ Sean Wyman, Tallahassee PD

CHAPTER 7

MENTAL FITNESS FOR OUR BRAIN AND BODY

"Neuroscience research shows that the only way we can change the way we feel is by becoming aware of our inner experience and learning to befriend what is going inside ourselves. As long as you keep secrets and suppress information, you are fundamentally at war with yourself... The critical issue is allowing yourself to know what you know. That takes an enormous amount of courage."

~ The Body Keeps the Score: Brain, Mind, and Body in the Healing of Trauma
~ Bessel A. van der Kolk,

According to SAMHSA's 2014 National Survey on Drug Use and Health, an estimated 43.6 million (18.1%) Americans ages 18 and up experienced some form of mental illness. In the past year, 20.2 million adults (8.4%) had a substance use disorder. Of these, 7.9 million people had both a mental disorder and substance use disorder, also known as co-occurring mental and substance use disorders.[li]

During the course of your duties, the likelihood of interacting with someone in a mental health crisis is rather high. The likelihood they have underlying trauma is also quite prevalent. Whether the system they move towards is in health, legal, social services, or a judicial context their journey towards those systems often start with interactions with you. It is only with a trauma informed system of care approach that we will best improve encounters with both victims, offenders, and the general public within an increasingly damaged society.

We will start to explore the intersection of sociology, psychology, neuroscience and human behavior. With a focus on providing an expanded view of the human condition when we interact with those we serve, when we look in the mirror, or when we look at a peer. We are scratching the surface of deep and involved science and human behavior from a layman's perspective to bring you the best possible tactics for your personal and professional success.

Many of you will have some training in de-escalation tactics. This may seem law enforcement focused yet the reality of violence and escalation against all public safety professionals is gaining normality, so these lessons are valuable to all. There are many organizations that teach various methods of defusing potentially violent interactions. We recognize suggesting you remain non-adversarial and calm with some very unreasonable people will seem against the norm and we recognize upfront our approach is not for every situation. We know that a pre-escalation approach works with a majority of calls with seemingly unreasonable people because we are often the ones triggering them with our approach and mannerisms in the first place. Everything we teach will help with a large percentage of your interactions; this training is a powerful path to peace; so long as peace is an option! When peace is not an approach to consider you are already well trained in both de-escalation and physical techniques to manage the task at hand.

"I was trained to fight the war on crime, and we were measured by the number of arrests we made and our speed in answering 911 calls," said Kathleen O'Toole, Seattle law enforcement Chief, "but over time," she continued, "I realized that policing went well beyond that, and we are really making an effort here to engage with people, not just enforce the law."[lii]

We will iterate repeatedly; these are some of the many tools available on your larger tool belt and safety of self and others is paramount. Where we are unique, is teaching the underlying dynamics of human behavior that can be managed upon onset so harsher tactics are not required as often. This enhances your wellness and the wellness of others. This learning will also be very beneficial to improving interpersonal relationships where it matters most … off the job.

WHY IS THE RATE OF MENTAL ILLNESS SO HIGH?

Research would indicate that much of it stems from childhood trauma, life-long acute stress, and direct and indirect traumatic exposure. What is clear to us is that trauma creates a very real physical, physiological, and psychological impact to our wellbeing. No person is immune. Even in these professions where most of you have built up a higher resiliency than the average person; even the toughest of the tough can have a breaking point. Trauma will enter your world on many occasions, you need to be prepared. Avoidance, indifference and inaction to understand and prepare oneself with prevention and mitigation tactics serves no one.

As we now know, psychological trauma injury and stress build-up adds complexity by the approach, responses and actions we take and quite often we create the escalation. You may be inviting and unknowingly instigating emotionalized communications. Once a person is emotionalized, they lose significant access to the logic center in the neocortex.

"Emotional arousal has powerful influences over cognitive processing. Attention, perception, memory, decision-making, and the conscious naturally associated are all swayed in emotional states. The reason for this is simple: emotional arousal organizes and coordinates brain activity."[liii]

The brain is complex, with support cells and neurons called "gray matter," where our reasoning ability, decision-making, and problem-solving capabilities are often hijacked by our mid-brain and emotional center. It also has white brain matter where all the axons are surrounded by myelin that helps speed up the communication throughout the brain. Researchers found that there is an overproduction of myelin in subjects suffering from chronic stress which can lead to lasting changes (read: shrinkage) to the brain's actual structure. It has been heavily researched that people suffering from PTSD have notable imbalances in their white and gray matter.

Everyday stress appeared to have little impact on brain volume on its own, but people are more vulnerable to brain shrinkage when they are faced with intense, traumatic stressors. A Yale University study indicates: *"The accumulation of stressful life events may make it more challenging for these individuals to deal with future stress, particularly if the next demanding event requires effortful control, emotion regulation, or integrated social processing to overcome it," explained the study's lead author, Emily Ansell. Dr. Sinha, Professor of Psychiatry and Neurobiology said that "The study illustrates the need to address causes of stress in life and find ways to deal with the emotional fallout. The brain is dynamic, and plastic and things can improve — but only if stress is dealt with in a healthy manner," Sinha said. "If not, the effects of stress can have a negative impact on both our physical and mental health."*[liv]

This background helps you communicate with those who have mental health challenges or are experiencing a traumatic stressful moment. It also aids in your own self-reflection on the stigmatized belief that you should "suck it up" and move on. The science shows a clear understanding this is a tangible physiological and psychological issue that demands your logical consideration.

From a political and organizational viewpoint this perspective will enable positive understanding of the power of emotional intelligence and communication tactics in managing interactions. The skills you will learn in this book lessen the potential of members becoming negative media sensations or a potential litigation liability for the department. As well as create healthier relationships where it matters most, off the job.

We all experience stress. It is the unhealthy stress that overwhelms our coping mechanisms when responding to real or perceived threats that needs more understanding. All trauma, impactful stress and high-excitement moments can trigger our automatic innate protective response towards fight, flight, or freeze. When you are living with unresolved trauma the accumulation intensifies reactions which can profoundly destabilize the median response to any stress life brings your way. It becomes a living cycle of psychological and physical reactivity. This negatively impacts interactions and relationships while inviting maladaptive coping mechanisms and mental fitness erosion.

An adult who feels they have put any childhood trauma behind them may not understand the subconscious still holds the impacts of those experiences, however stoically managed your "vault" may be. On the surface these adults may appear to have their life in order. The science is clear that major or cumulative stress can trigger during new trauma, show up in unhealthy and addictive behaviors, or escalate development of acute stress or other mental and physical disorders. Or, it may sit simmering and show as disease later in life. Understanding how the brain works is the logical first step in managing mental fitness.

Dr. Perry, the Founder of The Child Trauma Academy[lv], thinks we actually become "dumber" the more upset we get. During a lecture Dr. Perry clarified the impact: *"In a state of calm, we use the higher, more complex parts of our brain to process and act on information. In a state of triggered fight/flight/freeze, we use the lower, more primitive parts of our brain first. As the perceived threat level goes up, often the less thoughtful and more reactive our responses become. Actions in this state may be governed by emotional and reactive thinking styles."*

Neuroscience advances understanding of our complex emotions and behaviors. This gives us incentive to build our self-control over how we react to situations and how we can influence others with our actions, body language, and communication skills. Humans are emotional creatures and these emotions have a large influence on our personality, sense of self, work style. They impact our decisions good, bad, big, or small, but they do not have to OWN us.

Advances in science, showing before and after brain scans with and without self-control training and the results tell us we can change our neurological responses.[lvi][lvii] All of us would like to improve those "knee-jerk" reactions that do not serve us well. Understanding neuroplasticity of the brain means we know we have the ability to change our thinking patterns. Like working out to gain muscle we do the same repetitive conditioning to build our brain behavior and reactionary responses.

When we teach ourselves to think a certain way and challenge perceptions, unconscious and conscious bias, outdated beliefs and self-harming thoughts we gain a healthier, stronger brain fitness. This is the science behind repetitive thoughts and actions becoming automated habits. You are systematically creating new neural pathways in the brain's communication system and it is very powerful. You become what you think and do, which is why negative and self-harming internal dialogue has adverse impacts on your well-being. Most people do not learn this and therefore are not exercising their neural pathways with healthy consistent inputs or working to alter the predominant pathways that no longer serve their best interest.

In the 1960's a neuroscientist, Paul D. MacLean, researched and authored a book, The Triune Brain[lviii], which described three distinct structures that emerged as humans developed to where we are today. This theory is outdated and been updated to prove that the brain is a whole system that is highly interconnected but the simplistic break down allows the layperson to understand where predominant functionality sits without needing a brain science degree.

What seems most straightforward to remember is the brainstem, our primal brain, referred to as the reptilian brain for the instinctive nature of its functions. The midbrain or limbic system referred to as the mammalian brain, where emotions and memories are processed. Finally, the neocortex, at times referred to as the Homosapien brain, where self-awareness, intellectual, and executive functions take place like logic and reasoning. A simple description of a highly complex brain system. Modern brain scan imaging has proven that all three of these 'regions' can be active simultaneously for reactions and reasoning, especially with awareness and training.

The truth remains that a good majority of people get hijacked when strong emotions are aroused due to a lack of practiced mindfulness on controlling emotional or arousal reactions. Most of us do not learn controlled response techniques, aspects of emotional intelligence and self-control. This is a skill takes knowledge, time and training to perfect.
Our brains are fascinating super computers that we are only beginning to truly understand. The following highlights the layman basics of our brain structure when it comes to emotions and cognitive thought.

BRAIN STEM / PRIMAL BRAIN / REPTILIAN BRAIN

The brain stem section keeps us alive, controlling our innate functions like heartbeat, breathing, body temperature and automatic self-preserving behavior patterns that ensure the survival of our species and you. At times referenced to as the controller for the four F's - feeding, fighting, fleeing and fornication, although these functions are also tied into the limbic system. This area is where our basic primal drive for self-preservation begins. Our automatic safety responses come from here, like if you were to jump out of the way of a moving car, or duck from a baseball coming at you before cognitively realizing you even saw it coming.

Beyond internal systems and safety management its major function helps us distinguish between threatening and non-threatening stimuli. It immediately distinguishes anything threatening, new, or unfamiliar from the known which we often have a preset behavior or pattern of managing or the random data that is irrelevant.

How does it do this? Consider how much stimuli we process every second, from sights, sounds, touch, taste, smells. Then we have to assess, process and determine the familiar and unfamiliar parameters from a threating or nonthreatening perspective. On top of all that, we prime this system with cognitive thoughts, experiences and emotions to actively seek and find what is most important to us. To organize the billions of bits of data that are flowing in and actively being sought any given moment in time a bundle of nerves called our Reticular Activating System (RAS) is always on, running in the background to protect and serve us.

Our neocortex brain cannot handle all the inputs the RAS intakes, filters and processes. This section of the brain is faster and more efficiently than any supercomputer. We have no conscious idea of what it is doing at any given time. It interfaces with our memories, experiences, knowledge and cognitive demands to determine and process each bit of data as:

1. A potential threat – next stop the emotional control center
2. Worthy of being passed up to the cognitive processor, through the emotional control center.
3. Stored away in the memory center as non-imperative data, for now.

This is why in the din of a loud event our ears pick up our name being called when we have been tuning out the rest of the noise. Why when we buy a new car (important to us) we start seeing it everywhere. Importantly (base survival instincts aside) if we have not taken the time to change the filter and update the data then our RAS may be processing and scanning with outdated, biased, and emotionally unhelpful inputs. If it is pulling critical assessment information from our crappy childhood, old traumas, outdated culture or biased information this system may be a little gunky and in need of a tune-up. This is why understanding some of the science of the brain will help you build your mental fitness. We need to take more command of our filtering system because what served us at one time in a helpful way, may no longer be the best option to keep our super-computer brains in good running order.

LIMBIC SYSTEM / MAMALIAN BRAIN / MID-BRAIN

The mammalian brain and is where our emotional processing system kicks in. For the purposes of our layman perspective we will highlight the amygdala, the hypothalamus, and the hippocampus. This is where all your emotional responses are processed. Scientists using MRI or fMRI brain scanning will see this area light up when you experience any intense emotion or heightened arousal.

For those wishing to research a little deeper, I will briefly note the BASAL GAGNLIA traditionally aligned to motor skills and diseases such as Parkinson's and Huntington's. Neuroscientists today are learning the neurobiological bases of numerous psychological processes in basal ganglia research, including drug addiction and reward, learning and memory, and psychopathology (maladaptive behaviors) is promising future understanding in how psychological and physiological trauma is showing in our bodies and behaviors.

AMYGDALA / THALAMUS / HYPOTHALAMUS

The amygdala controls our early arousal or alert system and is primarily concerned with safety and emotional processing. Without focused training it does not actively seek input from the logic center of our neocortex before reaction or too often, overreacting with help from our memory center. This is what primes instantaneous reactive emotional decisions. Incoming stimuli from the thalamus (motor and sensory inputs) through the hypothalamus (hormone production, the connector between the endocrine and nervous systems) then instigates the chemical and physical arousal or threat responses.

The amygdala receives the alert signal from the reticular activating system (RAS). The amygdala interprets the images, feeling, and sounds in nanoseconds with instant input from our memories, experiences and when trained, cognitive insight. When the arousal alarm is activated a signal is sent to the hypothalamus. What we initially identify as a potential threat kicks what we identify as the fight, flight or freeze response and some research indicates a fourth fawn state. An interesting perspective is that "freezing is not a passive state but rather a parasympathetic brake on the motor system, relevant to perception and action preparation."[lix] This is an important consideration in understanding how to control our initial arousal responses and not take a label like "freeze" as weakened response. Situational awareness and assessments have a "pause" component and are critical in taking the right reactionary response for the moment.

A series of physical reactions to the arousal alarm is meant to protect us and optimize our systems for the best survival response. The brain sends messages to the autonomic nervous system. The autonomic nervous system has two branches, the sympathetic nervous system (which aids in the control of most of the body's internal organs and helps ramp us up and prepare for arousal response and later, to counter the chemical flooding the parasympathetic nervous system (works to promote maintenance of the body at rest) is tasked with bringing our system back down to normal non-aroused functioning. First, to deal with the arousal, chemical secretion occurs that adapts our physiological capabilities to manage the situation at hand. Brain chemicals dopamine, norepinephrine, acetylcholine, serotonin release along with the hormones from the pituitary gland (controlled by the hypothalamus).

WHAT DOES THIS AROUSAL RESPONSE FEEL LIKE?
The physiology of a fight/flight response is as follows:

- The hypothalamus, through the pituitary gland, stimulates the production of "epinephrine" (known as adrenaline) which shoots through our system and…
- The heart rate jumps (boom-boom-boom-boom).
- Blood pressure goes up, blood rushes to critical muscle mass groups.
- Muscles tense for action and a dilation of blood vessels.
- Spinal reflexes disinhibition with body, or hand tremors to release the pent-up adrenaline (shaking yourself, arms, legs, body can speed up this process after threat has passed)
- Cortisol (known as the stress hormone) releases glucose into blood steam for additional energy and suppresses other unnecessary body functions, like digestion (may throw up … may lose control of bladder/bowels).
- Pupils dilate to receive more light to increase vision.
    - May get tunnel vision or loss of peripheral width though
    - May have eye twitching/excessive blinking
- Blood vessels near the skin contract to reduce dangerous bleeding and clotting ability is increased to manage any wounds.
    - May cause you to turn pale or have cold hands/feet.
    - May get goosebumps
- You begin to sweat to keep you cool as your body temperature rises.
- Breathing becomes rapid and shallow to provide more oxygen, bronchial passages widen.
    - Too fast or too much may cause feelings of chocking, smothering, chest tightness, dizziness, blurred vision, feeling of unreality or confusion, hot flushes.
- Blood is pushed to major muscle groups and away from non-essential functions like digestion to fuel and increase in strength and speed for fight or flight (you may become pale in the face or flushed as a result of blood rushing from head to body).
- Pain tolerance increases, endorphins are flowing, and a person may not immediately realize the extent of any damage to themselves.
- Auditory exclusion may occur with some loss of hearing.
- Dry mouth, dry eyes (glands for tear ducts and salivation inhibited)
- Loss of sexual arousal ability

The physiology of a freeze response is somewhat different, it is an intermediate reaction to threat and may precede a fight response or continue and show as some describe as a fawn response:

- A state of attentive immobility serving to avoid detection by predators and to enhance perception.
- Parasympathetically induced heart rate deceleration.
- Originally referred to as crouching.
- Reduced vocalization
- Disassociation, blocking or numbing
- Analgesic to lessen the pain of injury
- Possible paralyzing

Now we consider all these symptoms as it relates to a threat, but the same systematic responses are responsible for extreme arousal or highly emotional spikes. Some of these symptoms would be felt when facing something unknown or where there 'may' be a threat. Consider sky diving, extreme sports, public speaking, phobias, or even those moments before the roller coaster crests the first big swooping dip. We can choose to convince ourselves with cognitive thought that the activity causes us to feel fear OR excitement even with the same chemical reactions being activated.

We can also train our brain to acknowledge that, with practice, a potential threat activity will become part of our known experiences and either no longer cause a spike in the first place or the response will be more controlled by our trained actions. Now we head back into your zone with running into burning buildings, overcoming the panic that surrounds you when dealing with a patient, going towards the threat or gunshots, not getting caught up in the extreme emotion of another's sympathetic nervous system reaction in person or over the phone.

Due to trauma, high stress, anxiety, and lack of mindfulness training some people have overly active amygdala responses. This higher reaction ignores any input from the neocortex, or rational logic center. Have you ever watched someone lose their mind over what did not seem like a big issue and wonder, "What was THAT all about - what were they thinking?" Well, the fact is they weren't thinking they were feeling. This level of emotional reaction is sometimes referred to as an amygdala hijack.

PTSD CONSIDERATIONS: *The amygdala becomes hypersensitized to threats and danger. The amygdala may even increase in size.*[lx]

HIPPOCAMPUS

The last part of the midbrain we will touch on is the hippocampus which is primarily known as your memory center. It is recording every moment, thought, sensory stimuli you have ever had and logging it in short or long-term memory. It also records your emotional reaction to all those moments which it then feeds back to the brain stem and amygdala as part of their assessment and reaction inputs. The higher the emotional reaction the more heightened that imprint will be in the memory recall. Think of it as your internal hard drive that feeds data without any parameters outside emotion until you begin to enter parameters and train it to only provide the files that necessary for the moment that serve you best in the current situation.

Your behavior is often influenced by encoded emotionalized memories that you have no cognitive recollection of. It does not necessarily deliver the actual memory, but it does share the triggered emotion. If you have ever wondered, "Why did I react that way?" It is a good indication that an unknown or buried emotional trigger was lit up and played a part in your reaction.

PTSD CONSIDERATIONS: *The brain's grey matter is shown to shrink in the Hippocampus with prolonged, untreated trauma or PTSD. This decrease in volume may be associated with the dysfunctional emotional memory processing in PTSD patients that leads to symptoms like hyper-arousal or avoidance.*[lxilxii]

One last note on the brain's circuitry and PTSD is based on studies that theories are developing about genetic disposition someone may have to developing PTSD. Research is not clear as of yet but an interesting area to keep an eye on.[lxiii]

NEOCORTEX – HOMO SAPIEN – EXECUTIVE FUNCTION CENTER

Now we get to the thinking brain, this part makes us uniquely human. Sometimes referred to as the executive brain, where we make our conscious decisions. The neocortex has two large cerebral hemispheres divided into four lobes; frontal, parietal, temporal, and occipital. Each is responsible for processing different sensory information that plays a dominant role in human development.

Responsible for speech, decision-making, logic, values, reasoning, empathy, abstract thought, imagination, creativity, and consciousness-awareness. The neocortex is very flexible and has an almost infinite ability to learn. It is a little slower than the other brain areas to interject into the reactionary process, but not by much and even less of a gap when trained. Generally, this delay explains why highly emotional reactions often fail to have logic and reason attached. You can be highly emotional (limbic system in charge) or highly rational (neocortex in charge). Without training and practiced effort to control nonlife-threatening emotional triggers it is unlikely you will have balanced responses.

PTSD CONSIDERATION: *Prolonged, untreated Trauma, PTSD and the Neocortex show that blood flow to the left side may decrease with less ability for language and memory. Blood flow to the right side may increase causing more sorrow and anger*

From a timing perspective there is a few microseconds head start for our automatic reactive system. However, the various systems do work in tandem with primal, emotional, and rational responses. All creating neural activity that collectively gives us our human experience. Very few of us are trained to critically analyze their responsive norms when emotionalized or stressed and then work to build resilience and control into their reactions, even when triggered. Without emotional intelligence and a basic understanding of brain science many simply feel a feeling and run with it. At times over-dramatizing, overreacting, or getting caught up in the emotion even when such a reaction may not serve our best interests.

An added complexity is that the different inputs do not always agree with each other's assessment and reaction. If there is a disconnect between a neocortex input, assessment, and a subconscious or primal driven emotional trigger, you may find yourself feeling overly anxious or fearful as your responsive emotional brain works to dissuade you from your actions. This is where this number one fear of public speaking comes in, in my opinion. Think of people who limit their experiences in life due to a fear that does not seem logical or reasonable to most. Other people are so emotionally charged that their logic and reasoning center cannot get a word in edgewise to stop an action or outcome that may do harm to self or others. This is where stress reactions get folks in trouble and for those with PTSD science shows us over time a hyper-reactive amygdala and the shrinking grey matter in the hippocampus make the neocortex inputs more challenging.

Our brains work optimally when it can effectively remember information and then build connections when an experience has impact or meaning. Specifically, when it has clear relevance to yourself and your known life experience thus far. Learning will take place by connecting new information to old or by uploading brand new experiences. Think of it as updating and re-setting your baseline of experiences and emotions. Some of you may have learned about implicit and explicit bias in previous training. Your brain is constantly seeking linkages to previous memories and beliefs. This system of interaction can explain the roots of unconscious bias, racism, and the judgement of other cultural standards.

Have you ever had a biased thought creep into your mind during an interaction, then almost immediately wonder where it came from as it counters your conscious thinking? That implicit bias comes from the lingering memories buried and served up from your hippocampus. It is an unconscious bias that remains within you until challenged and rewritten. Knowing it is possible and challenging the validity of these reactions is the first step towards enlightened change.

This is exciting to realize as what we were led to believe is that we have little control over our implicit bias. Science shows otherwise, as the neural networks in our brain can, indeed, be changed. Neuroplasticity allows pathways to get stronger or become weaker depending on how they are used. Those used predominantly and repeatedly become very strong neural superhighways that define our emotional intelligence, ego states, personality, morals, values, and cultural norms. Even those with PTSD have choices of therapy that help rebuild and reset emotional processing and memory recall.

We must train and challenge those existing neural connections. Otherwise we may find logic and reasoning will fail us when our emotions, fed by subconscious input, do not give us the whole picture when sending out reaction responses. Other times, our primal desires overcome reasoning even when we know what we are doing may be to our detriment. Knowledge is the starting point to build new neural pathways and take control and command of your personal vessel, aka your brain.

Professor's Joseph LeDoux and Richard Brown conclude in the latest issue of the journal Proceedings of the National Academy of Sciences.

"Emotions are not innately programmed into our brains, but, in fact, are cognitive states resulting from the gathering of information?"[lxiv]

You now know when there is unresolved trauma the limbic system can malfunction. It gets the cues wrong and your body is thrown into physiological and emotional stress response even when there is no actual danger or threat. Therein lies the weakening of mental fitness and birth of mental health issues. Traumatic stress injury also can show in physiological changes one of the most under-treated associated to a hypervigilant acute stress state is adrenal failure. For those who like to lock all those emotions in the vault and ignore them let's talk a little about how your body can rebel against your stoic stubbornness by impacting your physical wellness.

ADRENAL ORGANS

The limbic system sends out the arousal response alarm and let us head downward to the adrenal glands, as they are part of the stress reaction sequence. When we are in a constant hypervigilant stressed out state, they are working far harder than they ought to be and can cause physical health problems. The chemicals produced by these organs are meant to ebb and flow to protect us. The Sympathetic Nervous System (SNS) ramps us up to react to threats then the Parasympathetic Nervous System (PNS) is tasked with the rest and relax or sometimes called the feed and breed cycle, where our chemicals rebalance. If we do not recognize, manage, and mitigate our stress levels adrenal fatigue may set in.

These two triangular shaped organs on top of each of our kidneys have two parts. An outer part called the cortex and an inner part called the medulla. Each part has a different role in our body overall and they are both prevalent when our arousal response is activated.

The outer adrenal cortex produces cortisol to aid our body response to stress and aldosterone to help control our blood pressure. The inner adrenal medulla creates the adrenaline we need to manage the immediate threat level. Then nor-adrenaline is produced to restore calm after that stress response is over or managed.

There are four stages of adrenal fatigue and this one is important because it impacts your personal relationships in a way we rarely recognize. In the book, The Adrenal Fatigue Solution,[lxv] they share how to manage this:

Stage One: Beginning the "Alarm" phase:

- The imminent threat stressor provides increases strength, arousal, alertness.

- The body makes the significant amounts of needed hormones. Lab tests would show elevated levels of epinephrine (adrenaline), norepinephrine, cortisol, DHEA and insulin.

Stage Two: Continuing the "Alarm" phase:

- If the stress response continues or triggers easily and often your body must continue this rapid hormone deployment.

- While you may produce the hormones that you need, your levels of DHEA and other sex hormones may start to drop because the resources required are being diverted for stress hormone production.

- The overexertion of your adrenals creates a feeling of "wired but tired." Maintaining hyper-alertness when needed then a crashing when you don't. A sign of this is often an overdependence on coffee.

Stage Three: The "Resistance" phase:

- Your endocrine system continues to focus on producing stress hormones at the expense of sex hormones, a substantial drop in those needed hormones DHEA and testosterone to keep up with your cortisol production requirements. The key hormone named pregnenolone, a precursor to both the sex hormones and cortisol. This diversion is named the "pregnenolone steal"

- You are still able to function fairly normally (with coffee); however, your lower levels of many important hormones will lessen your quality of life.

- Typical symptoms might include regular tiredness, a lack of enthusiasm, regular infections, and a lower sex drive. This phase might continue for several months or even years

Stage Four: The "Burnout" phase:

- After some time, the body simply runs out of ways to manufacture stress hormones and cortisol levels finally begin to drop. Now the levels of both the sex hormones and the stress hormones are low. Levels of neurotransmitters are also low, referred to as "burnout" (a term coined by Dr. Fredenberger[lxvi])

- During this final stage of Adrenal Fatigue, you may suffer from extreme:

Tiredness or chronic fatigue	Hair loss	Infertility	Lack of sex drive
Recurrent infections	Chronic inflammation	Weak/brittle nails and hair	Irregular menstrual cycles
Apathy and disinterest in the world	Allergies/asthma flare ups	Hypoglycemia	Headaches
Irritability	Anxiety	Weight loss/gain	Dizziness
Craving salt/sugar	Heart palpitations	Muscle/joint pain	Cold/heat intolerance

- To recover from Stage Four Adrenal Fatigue requires significant time, patience, and often a complete change in lifestyle for diet, self-care, exercise and stress reduction techniques.

WHY DOESN'T EVERYONE LEARN THIS STUFF IN SCHOOL?

We would be much healthier earlier in life if trauma informed care was part of the health class curriculum. We are working with local education experts to build this program and hope one day we build this mind/body awareness into standard knowledge. As public safety professionals, you are now aware that a large percentage of the individuals you are trying to help, give direction to, seek answers from, or approach as a potential suspect do not have the knowledge you have just learned. They do not have education or experience understanding their own emotional intelligence and they are highly influenced by an unknown source of unconscious emotional inputs. Because of this, they do not know how to challenge the validity of the situation in their current scenario.

That does not mean you do not take command and control when required and ensure the safety of self and others. It simply means you have an insight that can allow you to change and adapt your approach to communications using the tactics we are providing throughout this book and with our training program. By doing so you can have a significant advantage in lessening trauma impacts and the reactions that come from it. Your new pre-escalation approach significantly reduces escalation that does not serve the situation well and you become the first line of healing with calm, safe confidence which is in everyone's best interest. If we ask people instead of telling them, and if we give them a reason for why we're doing something, we get much less resistance.

If we just started to treat people with dignity and respect, things would go much better."
~ Gary T. Klugiewicz, ret. Milwaukee County Sheriff's Captain
and De-Escalation trainer

CHAPTER 8

STRESS TO PTSD

"Worry and stress affects the circulation, the heart, the glands, the whole nervous system, and profoundly affect heart action." ~ Charles W. Mayo, M.D.

Human responses to stress and trauma vary widely. Some people develop trauma-related psychological disorders, such as posttraumatic stress disorder (PTSD) and depression. Others develop mild to moderate psychological symptoms that resolve rapidly. Still, others are quite resilient and report no new psychological symptoms in response to traumatic stress. Even with incredibly high resilience to stress responses, individuals can again suffer due to the impact of cumulative stress on the body over the long term.

"Individual variability in how humans respond to stress and trauma depends on numerous genetic, developmental, cognitive, psychological, and neurobiological risk and protective factors."[lxvii]

Inherent within your profession is higher than average stress, trauma, and emotionalized interactions. Regardless of how you react and manage each heart-pumping incident, there are health risks due to prolonged and cumulative exposure to stress and trauma. Often symptoms are observed by partners, team members, significant others, families, and friends before being recognized by the individual. Our responsibility to each other once we learn all this is to be the hand extended before the burden becomes unmanageable, coping mechanisms fail, and in the worst-case scenario, suicide thoughts surface.

When we use the term trauma in this book and program, we are referring to it in terms of the psychological injury to the mind, body, and spirit from what one see, hears, feels, and regularly does in these professions. If we can begin to understand the impact of the immediate to long-term damage from how our brain and body manages these inhumane inputs, we will better comprehend the requirement for healthy mental fitness. We will also better understand why many succumb to unhealthy coping mechanisms. Unhealthy coping and self-management do not always show in the form of an apparent addiction. Some trauma outcomes are much more subtle outwardly yet have the most significant negative impact on relationships and inner peace.

Are you guaranteed to have a negative health outcome from your job? No. However, many more do than do not. Therefore, awareness is essential, both for you and for those you serve alongside. Caustic attitudes or addictive behaviors, which result in damage to wellness and relationships, often become our default.

It is not about self-control as much as it is about identifying and repairing the root cause of the drivers that push us to negative coping responses. Dr. Felitti (author of the A.C.E. study) summed it up in a recent speech we attended in a mind-opening way when he shared, *"What we may perceive to be the problem in the individual, they identify as the solution to ease the pain."*

We all experience stress; in fact, a certain amount is quite healthy from a motivation perspective as it helps push ourselves beyond our comfort zones. There are many theories on the pros and cons of stress; however, a straight-forward descriptor is it drives the process our bodies go through from stimulus to response, from fight or flight to rest and digest. It is designed to be a system of balance, and when trauma and chemical changes in our brain interrupt that natural ebb and flow repeatedly, we have health issues.

Unmanaged, excessive, and repeated stress arousal has a mental health and physical well-being impact over the long term. Physiological implications of excessive stress include:

- Increased risk of stroke, high blood pressure,
- Increase in asthma and ulcers,
- Inflammation is known to contribute to diseases such as diabetes, heart disease, and autoimmune disorders,
- Respiratory system flare-ups with asthma and allergies
- Increased risk of infection, colds, viruses, flu due to the lower immune system
- Sleep disturbances due to excess hormones cortisol, adrenaline, and epinephrine
- Cognitive processing changes as the amygdala (emotional reaction center), is shown to grow while the loss of grey matter in the hippocampus affects memory processing,
- Gut reactions, including increased acid reflux, and flare-ups of irritable bowel syndrome and colitis,
- Increases sensitivity to pain, creates muscle tension, muscle spasms and increases inflammatory based pain,
- Hinders reproductive health, suppresses ability for arousal and orgasm, erectile dysfunction and impotence, irregular menstrual cycles

Understanding the impacts of the excessive stress and traumatic events common to these professions is imperative to building a strong mental fitness and better body functioning. Our nervous system plays an integral part in processing the chemical and hormonal interchange of stress, or trauma arousal response (fight or flight), and the discharge after the threat or emotional intensity have passed. A healthy autonomic nervous system (ANS) manages the ups and downs of stress impacts by engaging the sympathetic nervous system (SNS) when our brain triggers a threat or extreme emotion (fight or flight response). Once the moment has passed, our parasympathetic nervous system (PNS) kicks into play to remove the excess adrenaline and cortisol from our bodies and revert our chemical and hormonal systems to healthy functioning to focus on rest and digest.

Those with mental health illness, including emotional and behavior challenges, depression, anxiety, aggression, and even substance dependency, often show maladaptive cortisol responses. When the ANS system gets overactivated and cannot maintain the necessary activation, then rebalance sequence, one of three things occur that start to impact our health over time.

HYPERAROUSAL – overactivation of the sympathetic nervous system by repeated fight/flight triggers start to show up as:
Anxiety, panic attacks, impulsivity, restlessness, aggressive outbursts, anger/rage, self-harming and addictive behaviors, rigidness and obsessive-compulsive actions, overwhelm, emotional extremes, feeling chaotic, over-eating, defensiveness, racing thoughts, hypervigilance, tension, shaking.

HYPOAROUSAL - under activation of the parasympathetic nervous system by repeated freeze triggers show up as:
Disconnected, dissociation, unavailable/shut down, auto-pilot feeling, depression, low emotive response, memory loss, numbness, spaciness, absence of sensations, hopelessness, lower cognitive processing, difficulty saying no or engaging in any level of conflict, shame, embarrassment

HYPERAROUSAL TO HYPOAROUSAL EXTREMES a chaotic switching between fight and flight responses and extreme need to shut down or risk burnout.

We move between these two systems based on activation and the rebalance process to reset our nervous system as part of the typical human experience. We all experience a flow of highs and lows and spikes of stressors in life. This ideal balance of our autonomic nervous system was coined "The Window of Tolerance" by Dr. Dan Siegel in his book, Mindsight- The New Science of Personal Transformation,[lxviii] which shares the neurobiology of emotional and traumatic processes. Given the increased stress shared across public safety professional careers, we have adapted the visual model to show the increased spikes from stress-inducing calls or events. For enhanced self-management, we have included mitigation and prevention tools throughout this book to build your resiliency, emotional intelligence, relationship, and communication strategies, all of which help with self-regulation. Add in pre-escalation techniques, calming and grounding tactics, and you will be better equipped to manage any dysregulation of the nervous system.

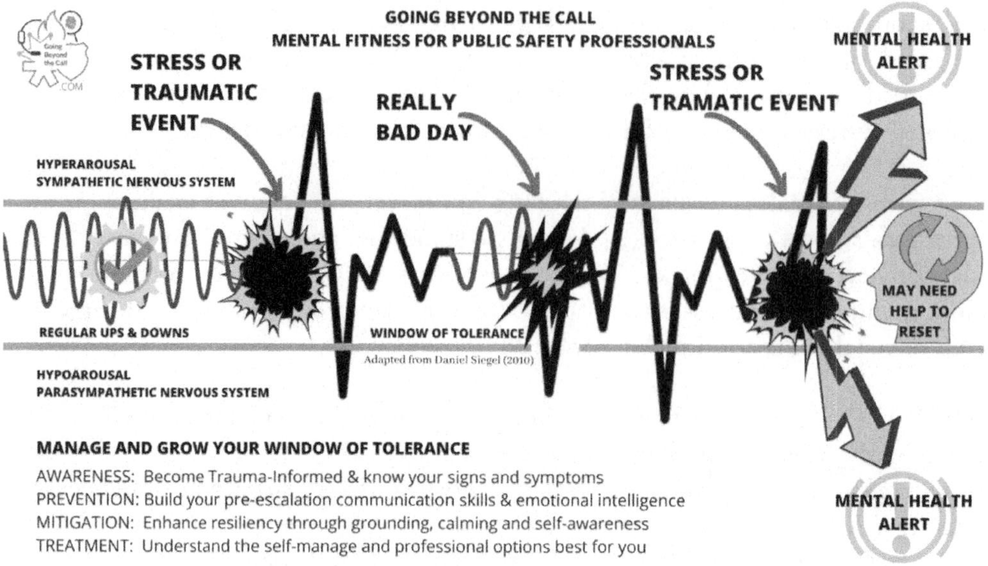

The following trauma and mental health signs and symptoms will seem to co-mingle and overlap in areas. We hear the term burnout and tend to assign it to frontline personnel, yet it is prevalent among all the services and can also co-exist with compassion fatigue. Some references will say that compassion fatigue can be a one-time event or cumulative. Burnout tends to be identified as a cumulative slow build experience. Indirect or secondary trauma is used when you are not personally involved in the trauma but personally impacted. Managing the traumatic scenes and living with the weight of that human suffering falls here and also in compassion fatigue. Hypervigilance cues are seen across many other areas, as it is the nervous system arousal response. Avoid getting too focused on which set of boxes you might best fit in and remember all of them, when ignored, can morph in a cumulative manner to acute stress disorder (ASD) or post-traumatic stress disorder (PTSD) add-in particularly high ACE's from your childhood and you may fit more in complex post-traumatic stress disorder (C-PTSD). All have an impact on the quality of life, so if you see yourself in any area repeatedly or on the higher end of a 1 to 5 scale, take it to the next level and seek some help.

We are going to share links, for self-assessments, support links and helplines in Appendix 1. During our workshops, we do some of these assessments in class and discuss self-treatment, wellness, and therapy options. As we urge when teaching a class, if any score is high, remember two things. One, you will have days, weeks, even months when your stress levels are higher than the norm. It does not mean you have a behavioral health disorder. However, you know yourself, and if any scoring indicates a warning that you need to increase your self-care focus, please listen to that inner voice.

Many therapies like to start with a baseline to assess the overall quality of life. (link in Appendix 1). This baseline is helpful in treatment because you are in your fields for a reason and purpose. One that recognizes that you will be managing the input of human suffering to your psyche but ask if you would change your job and many would adamantly say no. So, balancing the good feelings and accomplishments, you gain with the trauma and stress that comes with it gives you and any counselor a more realistic picture of your mental fitness and can help focus your self-care plan in the specific areas that need the most attention.

"Professional quality of life is the quality one feels in relation to their work. Both the positive and negative aspects of doing your work influence your professional quality of life. People who work helping others may respond to individual, community, national, and even international crises. They may be health care professionals, social service workers, teachers, police officers, firefighters, clergy, disaster responders, and others. Understanding the positive and negative aspects of helping those who experience trauma and suffering can improve your ability to help them and your ability to keep your own balance."[lxix]

We will share the descriptions of burn out and hypervigilance described in Emotional Survival for Law Enforcement, by author Dr. Gilmartin as he does well at aligning these behavioral health concerns to your professions. Dr. Gilmartin explains that "*What begins as healthy survival strategies on the job—distrust, cynicism, and wariness about people who could do others harm—results in chronic mistrust, hardness, and unforgiveness.*"[lxx]

BURNOUT creeps up with the persistent presence of chronic stress, falling outside of the window of tolerance consistently. There are three common indicators to burnout:

- Cynicism. Lessening of compassion and engagement to the people they serve and increasing feelings of anger, blame, or judgment.
- Disengagement. When compassion begins to dissipate, then avoidance of emotional engagement grows, often beyond the public being served. It will start as disengagement, but if left unchecked will often grow into broader avoidance of peers, friends, mentors, and eventually, family members.
- Dissatisfaction with the job or indifference to the work will become more notable and an increase in beating oneself up and expressing thoughts of hopelessness.
- Exhaustion. Burnout goes beyond being tired, it is utter exhaustion but often challenged with insomnia. An increase in stimulant/depressant use, unhealthy food, and other addictive behaviors will become more predominant. Overall it seems like you are not 'all there,' and effectiveness and safety should become a concern for peers and command.

FOR PUBLIC SAFETY PROFESSIONALS "BURN OUT" SHOWS AS:

*Adapted from Dr. Gilmartin's book descriptions

Restricted Social Life: Few if any close friends with whom we can have fun, confide, get recharged.	**Cynicism:** Dark, moody, negative, pessimistic thoughts replace our formerly positive outlook.
Irritation: "I laugh when others share their problems with me. They have no idea WHAT I GO THROUGH!"	**Anger:** Lack of sleep, poor diet, and a sedentary lifestyle leave people in high-stress jobs "on edge" more than usual.
Family Complaints: "Your job gets your best; we get the leftovers." "You're getting grumpier and grumpier these days." "I hardly ever see you smile anymore."	**Job Dissatisfaction:** "I started out loving this job, but now I hate it. I'm counting the days until I can get out of here."
Feeling trapped: "I want to quit/move/retire, but I can't."	**Isolation:** When co-workers, bosses, clients, people, in general, get on our nerves more than usual.
Increased Bias: If we work with incorrigible, unsavory, high-conflict people, we'll be tempted to judge all people as incorrigible and ready to pick a fight—bosses, co-workers, public, politicians, management, neighbors, relatives	**Emotional Instability:** Symptoms include thoughts of, "I hope I don't wake up tomorrow," suicide, depression, debilitating anxiety, and lack of physical energy, chronic negative thinking.

COMPASSION FATIGUE is a term first coined by Dr. Charles Figley, director of the Traumatology Institute at Tulane University.[lxxi] It is defined as: *"an extreme state of tension and preoccupation with the suffering of others to the degree that secondary traumatic stress develops in the individual providing aid."* In the public safety realm, this is often seen as the inability to turn work 'off.' This growing fatigue eventually impairs a person's functionality on and off the job. Commonly, a person loses the ability to meet obligations professionally and personally, and then a decline in self-care begins to show. The spiraling effect creates a disenchantment and belief that what you do no longer matters, or you don't make enough of a difference to care. Compassion fatigue is common to the rescuer position in the drama triangle described in the take the drama out of trauma chapter. In time neglect to personal hygiene, medical care, and wellness are very noticeable.

Public safety professionals have a strong sense of self-sacrifice, but without healthy mental fitness to balance that toll, taking on someone else's worst day over and over will deplete a person's ability to cope. While compassion fatigue can be a singular incident, it is more often a slow-burning decline of mental stamina to receive other's suffering. Training in understanding the difference between empathy, putting oneself in another's shoes while remaining detached, and compassion, taking ON another's suffering, is vital. Barriers and shields go up to try and defend against the substantial cost of caring so profoundly, but in time those walls can lead to defensiveness and bitterness.

COMPASSION FATIGUE SHOWS AS:

Physical signs like a racing heart, shortness of breath, and increased tension headaches	Feeling you are not doing your job well enough, a reduced sense of meaning	Turning to numbing or mind-altering substances (alcohol or drugs) to cope
Anger, Embitterment, Cynicism,	Frustration with self, others, organization	Feeling like a failure, despair
Shattered Assumptions (no good in people/world)	Tired—even exhausted—and overwhelmed	Disconnected from others, lacking feelings, indifferent
Sadness/depression	Helplessness / Hopeless	Apathy, Mistrust
Interpersonal problems and conflict	Worry about the future	Loss of meaning
Spiritual/Relational challenges	Decreased self-esteem	Difficulty making decisions
Confusion/memory problems	Emotional numbness	Irritable/ hypersensitivity
GI tract problems	Neck/backaches	Anxiety
Sleep problems	Withdrawal, disconnection	Feeling powerless

These professionals have also found that their empathy and ability to connect with their loved ones and friends is impacted by compassion fatigue. In turn, this can lead to increased rates of stress in the household, divorce, and social isolation. The most insidious aspect of compassion fatigue is that it attacks the very core of what brings helpers into this work: their empathy and compassion for others.

~ Charles Figley

SECONDARY TRAUMATIC STRESS is associated with all your fields, every bad call, grieving human, hopeless moment, scary incident builds up cumulatively. It also comes home with you, even when you try to hide it. So, this category is also where some family members may sit when they worry or stress about your safety and how your job impacts or changes you. Getting them involved by sharing this work will enhance their mental fitness and will help build connections and understanding of the stress you bring home from your shifts. In later chapters, we will circle back to communication strategies to help share your world, ask for needed self-care time, and communicate emotional impact without sharing the details of what you experience.

SECONDARY TRAUMATIC STRESS SHOWS AS:

Fear in situations that others would not think were frightening	Excessive worry that something terrible will happen to you, your loved ones, or colleagues	Easily startled, feeling "jumpy" or "on guard" all of the time
Wary of every situation, expecting a traumatic outcome	Sense of being haunted by the troubles you see and hear from others	A feeling of responsibility or a strong belief that others' trauma is yours

HYPERVIGILANCE allows you to be instantly ready should someone intend harm to a person or property. Even if your role is not in law enforcement, it is common to see a wary eye scanning people in public places from any public safety professional. You know too much about the ugliness of the world to be oblivious. While a feeling that you must be "on" at all times makes sense for safety, we also must learn to develop and allow our subconscious people reader to work for us and take some of the cognitive burdens off your shoulders when situational assessments provide the clarity to do so. When we consciously ramp ourselves up over extended periods, it becomes harder to shut it off when it comes time for a home focus or self-care. Learning to shift that high alert energy into a relaxed mind or a healing calm that will save the slow slide to the detached, isolated, and apathetic decline often seen with hypervigilance. Regular practice of breathing and grounding exercises throughout your shift will help your body get rid of built-up stress chemicals.

HYPERVIGILANCE SHOWS AS:

Increased vegging out or checking out	Ignoring phone calls	Using the day off to catch up on work-related tasks
Unwillingness to engage in conversations or activities not related to work	Basing one's identity, worth, and significance on the job	Always wary of others even those previously trusted
Tunnel vision on TV, videos, games, phone, internet	Trouble responding to regular conversations at home	Little or no time invested in hobbies that used to give joy

Numbing with alcohol, drugs, affairs, buying stuff	Disengagement from your children/partner	Procrastination for must-do chores
Anger	Isolation from friends	Exhaustion

Next, we consider the increasingly severe health repercussions that can happen, especially without prevention and mitigation tactics: Acute Stress Disorder, Post Traumatic Stress Disorder (PTSD), and Complex PTSD (C-PTSD). There is some research coming forward about using the term Post Traumatic Stress Injury to describe the time of the event to the 3-6 months it takes to receive a diagnosis of PTSD. It may be challenging for you to consider labeling your emerging feelings as a 'disorder' so soon after an incident that may be contributing to many ignoring the internal warnings signs and are not taking adequate self-care measures. Identifying the initial traumatic event as a psychological injury is a more logical first step. As research is published on this, we will update our language and descriptors in our training classes. While we all may have times of excessive stress, the time to recognize and take action is when it becomes a continuous and persistent presence that impacts your quality of life.

ACUTE STRESS DISORDER (ASD) is usually notable within a month of a severe stressor that often involves a feeling of intense fear, hopelessness, or helplessness. Sufferers are likely to have a hard time recalling specific details of the traumatic event that initiated this spike in the hypo-arousal state. Acute stress disorder is characterized by a clear and repeated avoidance of any stimuli that stimulate memories of the trauma. Significant symptoms of anxiety or increased arousal are also present. Also, a diagnosis must include one symptom from each of the three PTSD categories; re-experiencing, avoidance, and hyperarousal in response to triggered stimuli regarding the trauma event. If left untreated, this typically evolves into PTSD.

ACUTE STRESS DISORDER (ASD) SHOWS AS:

A marked decrease in emotional connectivity and responsiveness	Unable to find joy or pleasure in activities, even those previously pursued with vigor	Frequent feelings of guilt even with mundane things
Difficulty concentrating	Numb feeling	World as unreal or dreamlike
Dissociative amnesia	Brain fog/feeling dazed	Depersonalization
Feeling of detachment from their body	Exaggerated startle response	Difficulty sleeping
Jittery / Fearful	Avoidance of people, places, conversations	Irritability
Avoiding trauma-related thoughts, emotions	Hypervigilance	Helplessness / Hopelessness

POST TRAUMATIC STRESS DISORDER (PTSD) can be an immediate response to a life-threatening event or a build-up of cumulative events that are triggered by a specific event. In interviewing people for this book, I noted there is also a commonality among many retirees who are recognizing the onset of PTSD now that their brains are quiet enough to deal with the enormity of their accumulated trauma.

PTSD drastically and negatively disrupts quality of life. What is imperative to understand is that very little success has been found in self-treatment options and evidence indicates when not treated, it usually doesn't get better. In fact, it typically worsens. All the while it is impacting families, quality of service, safety on the job, and one's sense of peace. Unhealthy coping mechanisms may also develop or grow, including high-risk behavior, abusing drugs or alcohol, and impulsive behaviors. We like the identifier PTSI as it is something that makes sense; it is an injury to the senses, and the brain. The frequent feedback during interviews for this book was either a hesitation to identify as having PTSD because it's considered the extreme or a misguided hope that it will just go away with time. The sooner you help your brain process overwhelmingly traumatic experiences, the faster you get your life back to some semblance of normal. In the meantime, Acute Stress Disorder (ASD) is the predicator usually diagnosed before PTSD.

PTSD SHOWS IN A MIX FROM THREE CATEGORIES:

RE-EXPERIENCING	AVOIDANCE	HYPER/HYPO AROUSAL
Unwelcome memories	Emotional numbing	Agitated over small things
Triggers from any reminders	Reduced awareness of one's surroundings	Always on edge
Nightmares	Depersonalization	Jittery/ Easily startled
Spontaneous memories	Sense of suffering	Increased wariness/distrust
Flashbacks	Overwhelming guilt or shame	On-alert for danger
Replaying and beating up self over choices, decisions	Disconnected or detached	Hyperactivity
What-if scenarios	Amnesia / loss of memory	Trouble getting or staying asleep
Blaming	Avoid people that give you any association to the event	Extreme sensitivity to light and sounds

Self or others due to a distorted sense of reality	Burying distressing thoughts	Moodiness or mood swings
Anger towards peers / or others involved	Burying feelings	Recklessness, or
Spiritual anger	I'm OK response, when you're not	Self-destructive behavior
Anger towards the organization, establishment, system etc.	Avoiding external reminders of the event	Increased sexual energy
Negative thoughts about yourself, other people or the world	Feeling isolated & alone	May strive to be super busy to avoid thinking
Event takes predominance in mind over relationships	Disconnection from others including family and trusted friends	Anxiety/Panic/Phobias
Difficulty maintaining close relationships	Uninterested in usual hobbies	Depression
Difficulty experiencing positive emotions	Sexual disinterest / Erectile issues	Depressive episodes
	Trouble concentrating	Fears & helplessness

To have peace does not mean to be in a place where there is no noise, trouble, or hard work. It means to be in the midst of those things and still be calm in your heart.
~ unknown

COMPLEX PTSD (C-PTSD) is diagnosed with people who have been repeatedly traumatized, especially during childhood. If you scored high on your ACE score and *then* have additional cumulative trauma, this is where you may find yourself. Also, typical if you have been a victim of childhood sexual abuse. Generally, C-PTSD is only diagnosed after treatment has started, and specific behavioral indices are noted. It shows most often with a borderline or antisocial personality disorder or dissociative disorders.

C-PTSD diagnosis commonly shows a severe negative self-image and an inability to affect regulation (unable to cope with extreme emotions like anger or sadness). Should you partner with someone with C-PTSD, their emotions can be unpredictable and extreme and flare up without reason. It will likely be followed with an intense need to self-medicate with the self-harming option they use. Additionally, this disorder would show difficulties in forming and maintaining healthy relationships. Sexual abuse shows in risky and self-destructing behaviors and often eating disorders, which are also common to rape victims. Consider the obsessive commitment to starve oneself or purge food for the sake of body image. It is not as much about shape or weight as it is an emotional need to reassert control over one's body. This extreme action creates a sense of relief from mental anguish, similar to those whose addictions are drugs or alcohol. C-PTSD may show as a series of self-harming behaviors or a lifestyle of risky choices that act as self-medication like sexual addiction, gambling, self-harm, cutting, and various substance abuse.

The difference often highlighted between PTSD and C-PTSD is those with PTSD will be very aware of the event that triggered the beginning or worsening of their behavioral health condition with vivid recall. Those suffering from C-PTSD often have little to no recall of the event. It is the brain's way to protect oneself from unbearable memories. With extreme childhood trauma, entire blocks of time may be missing from memory. You may find an adult thinking that nothing in their childhood is related to a current trauma reaction because they have blocked any of that horror from their mind. This missing piece makes therapy more of a challenge as the absence of memory delays diagnosis and proper treatment. Therapy takes much longer and requires an appropriate team of trauma specialists to achieve success.

COMPLEX PTSD SHOWS AS:

Alcohol or drug abuse	Impulsivity	Aggression
Sexual acting out	Eating Disorders	Fragmented thinking
Self-destructive actions	exaggerated emotional difficulties (panic, rage, or depression	Dissociation and amnesia

DEPRESSION

We will look at basic layman science for depression as it will speak to your logic center. Whether that helps you take action if you see yourself in these descriptions or be a better peer with higher empathy should it show in others. We learned that traumatic stress has a specific effect on our nervous system responsiveness that leads to health problems. Depression has a similar startling impact on brain health. Not only from a psychological perspective but the ability to affect physical structures in the brain from inflammation and oxygen restriction to actual shrinking. The longer it is left untreated, the more the negative impact with research showing specific brain regions decreasing in a depressed brain.

The increase of brain scanning has given new insight on what goes on inside our head, and there is lots of competing research working to define more, but the take-away for now is it is real; it is chemical, and it needs help to solve. Including the self-treatment tactic of deep breathing to ensure our brain gets the oxygen it needs. When depressed, we tend to curl into ourselves, restrict our breathing and impair the cellular function necessary by lessening oxygen to the brain (hypoxia), and this can lead to cell injury or cell death.

Researchers have proven that the amygdala, thalamus, hippocampus, frontal, and the prefrontal cortex can be affected. The amount of damage is linked to how long the depression has set in and the severity of it, with notable differences showing around 8-12 months. When these areas of our brain shrink, then the optimized functioning also dissipates. Depression changes a person's emotional responses, their ability to recognize social and emotional cues in other people and reduces empathy or other focus. Damage to the hippocampus reduces the functionality of memory processing, which could lead to PTSD with repeated triggers or traumatic incidents. Cognitively, if our executive functions are impaired, we will have challenges getting things done and maintaining attention.

There are questions in the science community about whether inflammation can cause depression or if it is the other way around, but either way, those with over ten years of depression show 30% more inflammation than persons without depression. Inflammation is not healthy in any part of our body, but in the brain, it can lead to cell death, decreased neurotransmitter functionality, and inhibits the neuroplasticity as we age. Other physical changes include; changes to mood, memory, and ability to learn. Neuroplasticity, as you will read in this book, is what allows us to mend our mental fitness with self-driven tactics.

When you are suffering from depression, all this may be hard to self-evaluate, it tends to sneak in with lowering serotonin chemicals. People go from feeling crappy to feeling like a failure, or hopelessness which can spiral down to suicidal tendencies. Chronic depression can make one feel like a burden to those who care about them and believe they no longer have value to offer. Chemical imbalances and decreased functionality in our brains need to be better understood. I have heard people say that those who commit suicide are selfish and not considering those around them, but they are thinking of others, they are just doing so from the darkest place in their soul when they convince themselves that everyone would be better off without them. So, knowing you may not be able to see this one clearly, trust when those close to you suggest you may be depressed and consider medication in conjunction with self-managed cognitive behavior therapy, so you avoid permanent and damaging impacts to your brain health. Depression is not a sign of weakness or shame; it is as simple as the need for other health-improving medications needed for a short or potentially longer time until lifestyle changes fix the underlying issue. It starts with getting your chemicals checked with your physician; you cannot fix the engine until you open up the hood.

DEPRESSION SHOWS IN FOUR CATEGORIES:

PHYSICAL	EMOTIONS	BEHAVIOR	THOUGHTS
Unexplained aches and pains, frequent headaches	Irritability	Withdrawal from others	Frequent self-criticism
Loss of motivation	Guilt	Slower actions and movements	Confusion
Substance abuse	Anger	Negative changes in personal appearance	Indecisiveness
Lack of energy	Anxiety	Crying	Impaired memory
Too much or too little sleep	Sadness	Neglecting responsibilities	Trouble concentrating
Extreme fatigue	Mood swings	Agitation or inability to settle	Suicidal thoughts
Weight gain or loss	Hopeless or Helpless feeling	Loss of enthusiasm, interest in hobbies	Worthlessness, no good for anyone

SUICIDE PREVENTION

Both suicide and attempted suicides are serious public health challenges, and a devastating way to learn someone was in crisis after the fact. The following points are adapted from The World Health Organization (WHO), which estimates approximately one million people commit suicide every year. This means one death every minute, almost 3,000 deaths every day, and one suicide attempt every three seconds. Astonishingly, people die from suicide more often than from armed conflict and, in many places, from traffic accidents. In many countries, suicide is one of the top three causes of death among adolescents and young adults between the ages of 15 and 24 years, and one of the top ten causes of death overall. Worldwide, suicide rates have increased by 60% over the last half-century. For every suicide that occurs, there are 10 to 20 or more suicide attempts. Knowledge about the extent of this public health crisis is vital for public safety professionals responding to calls and for the mission of peer safety and suicide prevention support. We know most of our services are reporting an increase in suicides among their ranks, this is not a small, isolated issue for a few members, and we believe at Going Beyond the Call, with awareness, prevention, mitigation and treatment tactics we can reverse the trends with your help.

People who feel suicidal tend to share feelings of hopelessness and depression. They see suicide as a way out of solving their mental anguish, removing the burden of whom they feel they have become, and to eliminate their overwhelming suffering and often speak to those feelings in some manner. Although suicide ideation is not always easy to notice, many verbalize warnings or show signs in the time leading up to their death. Sadly, many of us don't know how to recognize those signs or fail to take them seriously, thinking someone is just blowing off steam.

Suicidal ideation and warnings of helplessness, hopelessness, or worthlessness are not harmless bids for attention; they are important cries for help that should be taken seriously. These signs may come with a traumatic incident or a trigger or change in life events like a separation, divorce, parent alienation issues, loss of an anticipated promotion, retirement, or career move that is not welcome. These signals may arise after a significant health warning or problem, a growing depression, or trauma-induced stress triggers. Often common after a recent loss of a loved one or upon an anniversary of that loss. A queue may be hearing about repeated sleep disturbances. There should always be a heightened concern if there is a family history of suicide. Lastly, a notable increase in risky behavior, drinking, or prescription or non-prescription drug use. Some warning signs are similar to those found above in stress and trauma-induced signs and symptoms. Remember, you are not there to act as the therapist, only to be the one who observes and takes action when someone's health is in jeopardy. Observe both behavioral and verbal clues:

- Verbalizing in conversation or perceived jokes and quips that they feel isolated and lonely;
- Post-retirement chat may talk about, loss of status or importance, having no reason, no purpose or a sense of loss;
- Beating themselves up as a failure, generalized expressions of hopelessness, uselessness, notable self-esteem issues Expressing feelings of failure, lack of hope, or loss of self-esteem;
- Talking about a lack of, or loss of, faith or belief system, like, "things just aren't the same" or "I don't fit in anymore." (could be Brotherhood or Sisterhood of uniformed service, changes in command, loss of peers, career changes);
- Depressive comments about a lack of supportive people in one's life, rumination and negative spinning on problems without solutions.
- Whether with a tone of humor or not, discussing a suicide plan, questioning, "how would you do it?"
- Mentioning a need to or starting to clean up one's affairs, get things in order, giving away valuable or prized possessions, unusual talk around

financial, administrative, wills, burial plots to make it easier for those left behind (again with other signs of depression or traumatic stress);

- A growing removal from social systems, no longer wanting to be around or feeling able to relate to friends, family, peers. Noticeable withdrawal from once enjoyed activities and gatherings.

One of the considerations to take into account is whether someone despondent may have firearms at home. Sixty percent of firearm deaths in the US are from suicides. Globally, firearms are one of the most common suicide methods, responsible for approximately 8% of global suicide deaths. In the USA, that ratio is over six deaths per 100,000, more than ten times greater than many countries across Europe. The Center for Disease Control and Prevention (CDC) provides similar estimates: 23,854 deaths in 2017. The number of homicides by firearm in the same year was 14,452. Surprisingly, the number of suicide deaths by firearm greatly outnumber those from homicide. Should a peer or someone you care about say they should just "eat their gun," take them very seriously.
If someone has opened the communication door directly or indirectly on the issue of suicide, the Columbia Suicide Severity Rating Scale (C-SSRS) has a few short questions you can ask. This tool helps assess someone and can help you confirm that action is needed to help the person. It has been showing great results with students as well as the military. "After putting the C-SSRS in everybody's hands, the U.S. Marine Corps reduced the number of service member suicides by 22%.

Columbia Suicide Severity Rating Scale (C-SSRS)

1. Have you wished you were dead or wished you could go to sleep and not wake up?
2. Have you actually had any thoughts about killing yourself? If no, go to #6
3. Have you thought about how you might do this?
4. Have you had any intention of acting on these thoughts of killing yourself, as opposed to you have the thoughts, but you definitely would not act on them? (HIGH RISK)
5. Have you started to work out or worked out the details of how to kill yourself? Do you intend to carry out this plan? (HIGH RISK)
6. Have you done anything, started to do anything, or prepared to do anything to end your life? (E.g. collected pills, obtained a gun, gave away valuables, wrote a will or suicide note, held a gun but changed your mind, cut yourself, tried to hang yourself, etc.? (HIGH RISK if in last 3 months, medium risk otherwise)

Yes, to any high-risk question indicates the need for further care. Please do not leave the person alone, stay with them, get family, a counselor, or a close friend on the scene to manage the next steps, or escort them to professional help. Do not believe them if they say they will seek help on their own. Call the national suicide prevention lifeline for options of care 1-800-273-8255 (TALK) or check the list of some other support options at the end of the chapter. Suicide may be averted with the right care and treatment."

AN INTROSPECTIVE ON ADDICTION - THE NOVELTY GENE

There are many books and online links that help with specific addictions. We will not delve into them all here. What we do want to highlight is how we think about addiction. Perhaps an addiction starts as a novelty or a different way to "cope" with the stress in your life. Alcohol, gambling, drugs, sex, and risky pursuits do not begin with the desire or expectation that that "release" turning into an addiction. There is a higher than average prominence of public safety professionals who struggle with trying to manage a vice that has grown out of control. We want to complete this chapter with some intelligence on the origins and power of addictive behavior.

Researchers state that initially, novelty ignites brain systems to become activated with a chemical release, with dopamine being dominant. The chemical release in the brain from "addictive" behaviors and substances is far greater than you would gain from the "natural high," obtained from accomplishment or love. Dopamine is called our "feel-good" neurotransmitter. As research continues, a newer theory is being tested, which indicates that dopamine may provide more of a "get me more" response rather than a feel-good response and that the "get me more" response is the "addictive" button which is ignited rather than the feel-good outcome. That makes sense when there are so many things that cause addictions. Nearly every drug a person may abuse affects the dopamine system, as does gambling, sex, thrill-seeking, power, chocolate, shopping, money, and more. It is essential to understand that there is a chemical instigator; it's not just about willpower. That instigator is driving the craving that will keep you coming back for more - even when your most cognitive self knows the danger, and the activity has lost its novelty and pleasure.

"Dopamine ... it's often touted as a "reward chemical" or part of the brain's "reward center," but more recent research has shown that "like the midbrain novelty center (substantia Nigra/Ventral), it's actually more closely related to our motivation to seek rewards, rather than being a reward itself."[lxxii]

Armed with this knowledge, we can overcome those habits that lead to addictions by understanding how much dopamine is involved in learning and memory. Learning and memory happen with the way neurons connect. Earlier, we talked about neuroplasticity and the ability to dramatically change those neural networks. For this change to happen, however, there still needs to be a control system. Dopamine is one of the neurotransmitters that help control this as it is released; it signals it is time to start learning something.

We can tap into the novelty center known as "Substantia Nigra/Ventral." Marketing and advertisers have used this for years to gain our attention. Our brain loves new stuff, so when we introduce new concepts, activities, and actions, it engages that rewiring process. This newness is why the 12-step program, counseling options, exercise, new environments, and other "new" activities can be so helpful to combat addictive behaviors. New activities are developed into habits that give us pleasure because we are achieving something important to us.

TRAUMA FOCUSED THERAPY

Trauma-focused therapies are proving the best results in research globally. Ideally, choose a counseling option with experience working with public safety professionals or veterans. Trauma-focused options focus on the memory of the trauma and the meaning attached. Treatment usually lasts in the three to four-month mark, pending how long and whether a resolution is required for multiple traumatic events. Military research lists CBT and EDMR as highly effective for PTSD with Cognitive Processing Therapy (CPT) and prolonged exposure (PE) receiving high accolades. We are all different, so research the options and choose something that clicks with you.

Cognitive Behavior Therapy (CBT) is a psychotherapy acclaimed in over 2,000 research studies mixed with new and effective treatments that target the specific aspects of PTSD. CBT has a structured and present-oriented self-work design that helps identify the goals that are most important to you, then adapt and overcome roadblocks through guided and self-work. CBT engages our cognitive processing, how we perceive a situation or trauma, and how our nervous and emotional systems can react outside of rational consideration and balanced processing. It helps build one's ability to adapt and change thinking behaviors and improve mental processing and decision making. CBT integrates several cognitive and behavioral techniques to suit each person. Therapy may include mindfulness, solution-focused therapy, motivational interviewing, positive psychology, dialectical behavior therapy, commitment therapy, Gestalt therapy, interpersonal psychotherapy, compassion-focused therapy, and even psychodynamic psychotherapy to aid personality disorders.

- *To help jump-start a CBT program, you may wish to consider Cognitive Hypnotherapy. The American Journal of Clinical Hypnosis states; it "can be used in conjunction with evidence-based practices for the treatment of post-traumatic stress disorder (PTSD). We review cognitive-behavioral interventions for PTSD, including mindfulness and acceptance-based approaches, and contend that*

> *(a) empirical support for the use of hypnosis in treating a variety of conditions is considerable; (b) hypnosis is fundamentally a cognitive-behavioral intervention; (c) psychological interventions with a firm footing in cognitive-behavioral therapy (CBT) are well-suited to treat the symptoms of PTSD; and (d) hypnosis can be a useful adjunct to evidence-based cognitive-behavioral approaches, including mindfulness and acceptance-based interventions, for treating PTSD.".*"[lxxiii]

Cognitive Processing Therapy (CPT) helps you learn to identify and change the negative thoughts that spiral after a traumatic event. When our arousal systems are stuck thinking something was "your fault," "you should have done such and such," or the "world and all the people in it are dangerous," we can get caught up in reoccurring obsessive thinking. Learning to change how you think about the trauma can help improve how you feel about it. Through discussions with a therapist and structured work, you will break down the negative thoughts and beliefs that are spinning in your head. Your therapist will then work with you to challenge those thoughts and think about your trauma in a way that has less of a grip on your overall thinking and move towards better coping mechanisms for handling stress-inducing feelings.

Eye Movement Desensitization and Reprocessing (EMDR) is rapidly gaining top choice for people living with PTSD. Reviews and results are showing amazing results with this therapy, especially with veterans who are more closely aligned in their trauma experiences than people from non-paramilitary backgrounds. EMDR helps process the memories and feelings in a new way of assisting the brain in getting past the broken record looping and settling the event in your long-term memory. With time it allows you to change how you react to the trauma triggers. Therapy will choose a specific memory and identify the emotions, adverse body reactions, and areas you over-focus on while your brain is paying attention to other sensory inputs like sounds or movement. As the memory loses its power, you will work to add in positive thoughts and associations.

Prolonged Exposure Therapy (PE) works to face the reality of your trauma. People with PTSD often try to avoid things that remind them of the trauma. Disassociation and avoidance may help you feel better in the moment, but in the long term, it can keep you from recovering from PTSD. In PE, you expose yourself to the thoughts, feelings, and situations that you've been avoiding. It sounds scary but facing things you're afraid of in a safe way can help you learn that you don't need to avoid reminders of the trauma. Your therapist will ask you to talk about your trauma -injury over and over. Repeated and guided retelling will help you get more control of your thoughts and feelings about the trauma and lessen the impact of it on your emotions. It can help remove fears that cause you to avoid thinking about or being hostage to a traumatic event.

Mindfulness-Based Cognitive Therapy (MBCT) is a form of cognitive behavior therapy that incorporates mindfulness practices such as breathing work and meditation to distance and detach negative thinking patterns. The ability to halt the spiral of negative feelings that lead to a depressive state before it takes hold of oneself. This therapy is often practiced in conjunction with options for addictions and anxiety.

Medication is something that may be suggested, along with any of these other treatment options. PTSD or the depression aspect of it may reduce the chemical balance in your brain that helps you manage stress. SSRIs (selective serotonin reuptake inhibitors) and SNRIs (selective norepinephrine reuptake inhibitors) are medications that raise the level of these chemicals to help you cope while other treatment aids your healing. Different drugs react differently with each of us, so be patient with your doctor as there will be frequent check-ins and potentially a need to try different medications before settling on one that works well for you. Medications are helpful to manage chemical imbalance, but they will not heal PTSD, the only therapy that deals with the root cause of your brain's processing and emotional reactions will do that.

WHAT CAN I DO BEFORE COUNSELING?

TALK it out as soon as you realize your reactions are out of normal parameters, the best action is to reach out to someone you trust and talk it out. It could be a family member, friend, through your peer-to-peer program or faith-based counsel. You may wish to ask a supervisor for an after-action debriefing if the event impacted more than you in a heightened manner, your peers will be thankful. Many of you have an employee assistance program where you can find anonymous counsel. Please make use of your benefits and find a local EMDR specialist, trauma trained hypnotherapist, or one of the other therapy options and make a choice to get ahead of it.

> **PEER TIP**: As a peer wanting to help another by listening actively and when you can inject a question, ask for expansion details that go beyond the emotional center of the trauma. By asking for further information outside the emotionally centered feelings, you help them engage their cognitive center and pull them however briefly out of the emotional pull of the moment. If they balk at you for asking odd questions, remind them that by engaging their cognitive brain in the retelling, you are helping them process the disturbing scene.

BODY works. As soon as you can after the event starts shaking or swinging your arms helps your body physically release the cortisol and adrenaline. Relaxation through individual muscle tension and release can work if you are still at work, again with focused, mindful attention on each muscle movement. A more advanced approach would be Autogenic Progressive Muscle Relaxation (PMR), where sequencing and commands that add warmth and heaviness provides a deeper state of relaxation and mental peace. Videos and audio sessions can also be found online.

AVOID obsessively replaying the event in your head. Catch yourself using the STOP, DROP, and ROLL technique we share in a few chapters. Repetitive mulling overwhelms your nervous system, delays the parasympathetic system from resetting your chemical balance, and keeps you in an emotional spin versus a cognitive and rational mindset.

HALT the negative, our brains soak up what you feed it. Adding additional trauma, drama, or horror, and even negative emotionalized news is like pouring lemon juice on an open wound. Give your brain a break, fill it with positive, funny, enlightening to establish some balance to the trauma you are working through and processing. Especially critical 1-2 hours before you go to sleep, don't feed the nightmare machine!

GROUNDING your body and senses. When our brain is experiencing dissociative symptoms, we have lost touch with connectivity, to self and others. Grounding with mindful attention reorients our bodies to tangible reality, create a sense of safety, and engage our cognitive functions over our emotional ones. I have listed three below but take the time to research grounding techniques and pick two or three that resonate with you and practice them any time you want to calm a stress response.

FOCUS - 5-4-3-2-1 Method by working backward from 5, use each of your senses to explicitly detail what each of your senses is experiencing when you mindfully consider it. Order the senses in whatever way works best for what is around you.

- 5 things you hear,
- 4 things you see,
- 3 things you can physically touch and describe
- 2 things you can smell, and
- 1 thing you can taste.

Make an effort to notice the smallest details, describe as if you are sharing the experience with someone who has never experienced it, make them see, hear, touch, smell and taste what you do.

LIST it out by making lists or categories which must use your neocortex and move away from the emotional limbic center control. Get ridiculous with the topics if you want to add in a little humor.

- Choose one or two broad categories, such as "baseball teams," "types of fish," "items found in the dairy section," "worst movies in history," "ice cream flavors," "animals found in a zoo." Mentally list as many things from each category as you can while physically tapping out the numbers with your fingers or toes.

DESCRIBE nearby visuals in exacting detail. Pick any one thing within your visual range and describe it in detail, use all your senses if you can. Choose the next thing, and the next until you feel your body calm.

MOVE and get physical. Your emotional arousal system is heightened and using physical methods to sooth and put a focus on body sensation over emotionally draining ones can be helpful. Popular choices include exercise, either calming or energizing, pending your preference. Exercising will help burn off that pent up adrenaline and release feel-good endorphins to comfort your brain. Options can be hard-hitting like boxing, martial arts, a gym work-out or more relaxed like Yoga Tai-chi, or dance with mindfulness to the movements.

JOURNALING. Trauma can be debilitating to the senses, and perhaps the overwhelm is too much for you to share within the first day or so. Journaling helps define a narrative structure that requires your rational, cognitive brain to get down on paper or computer screen. That process of engaging the non-emotional part of your brain helps it process and settle the memories into long term memory.

PRAY/MEDITATE with a grateful focus. The idea is to move into a semi-trance state to aid the body in recalibrating your chemical and hormonal balance. If you are unsure how to learn meditation skills then look on YouTube, there are many guided meditations choices or also consider self-hypnosis tracks for sleeping and relaxation. Following a guided program can help if you are having some difficulty settling your mind. If you are not faith-based and meditation sound too whoo-whoo for you, I challenge you to download F*ck That: An Honest Meditation. It walks you through the same mindful breathing but adds in colorful language along the way for unexpected laughs. ***warning, if you are easily language offended, the swearing is advanced!

GO PLAY! Whatever sport or activity makes you happy, cook, play with your kids or significant other, try something novel or new.

ROUTINE, routine, routine … even if off work, commit to a routine, and make daily goals. Even if it seems silly, set alarms to eat, do chores, exercise breaks, focused time with family. Having something to focus on and giving your brain established parameters will lessen feelings of hopelessness and fogged thinking.

INVESTIGATE FEELINGS. Become a detective and use the emotion wheel in this book to identify specific feelings. When we can drill down exactly how we feel, it helps our brain to process the jumble of emotions swirling around inside, especially if we are not traditionally a touchy-feely type. Identify, mark, track without judgment, but as an investigator. As you work through what those feelings mean, question how they are associated with our past experiences and our childhood experiences.

SLEEP well using any of the above techniques to create calm before you sleep. If you are on night or extended shifts, then create and maintain a routine to your sleep patterns, ideally go to bed as quickly as possible after your shift. Wear sunglasses on your way home, even when cloudy to start to dim the light getting into your eyes. Soundwave machines or apps may help as may self-hypnotic programs. Avoid caffeine and sugar 4 hours prior to your planned sleep time. If you are restless, then use non-stimulating distractions like reading, journaling, calming exercise, yoga, or stretching over any electronic device as these wake your brain up. Darken the room as completely as possible with blackout curtains, blocking clocks and other light elements. There are scents associated with calming the mind like lavender, vanilla, valerian, rose and jasmine. Use the Do Not Disturb function on your electronic device to avoid unnecessary sleep interruption (you can program favorites to ring through or if someone calls repeatedly it will ring through) when necessary for emergency contact.

SENSUAL BODY MAPPING. If you have a willing partner to do some self-care work with, explain that you need to take a complete sensory picture of their body using as many as your senses as possible. Both of you need to agree that sexual release is not the goal, so no expectation of that outcome is there. With slow and precise detail from the tip of the toes to top of the head, inch by inch touch, smell, look at, taste, and hear the reactions. Sensual mapping is not about achieving a specific result as much as it is about the process of using all your senses and cognitive processing to balance the emotional overload. *If sexual arousal does not happen due to the traumatic stress that's okay, it wasn't the purpose of the connection. If you are concerned about the performance factor, then take the intimate parts of the body off the exploration map or leave them until last in case you want to go in that direction. Removing this pressure helps relax the mind.

We hope this overview of signs and symptoms helps from a peer perspective and dealing with the public. When managing the reaction of others, our approach, body language, and words have more power than we tend to consider. If the event could be traumatic to someone and you take immediate action to mitigate the impact, there can be a lessening of the emotional toll on the individual, including how a peer is handling a disturbing scene. At the onset, your ability to project calm, safe, confidence creates physical safety for all involved. "Immediate action is important in lessening the effects of traumatic stress," says Valley Trauma Center Executive Director, Patti Dengler. *"Most people who are exposed to a traumatic, stressful event experience some of the symptoms of in the days and weeks following exposure. These symptoms generally decrease over time and eventually disappear. However, about 8% of men and 20% of women go on to develop post-traumatic stress disorder, and roughly 30% of these individuals develop a chronic form that persists throughout their lifetimes."*

Because a healthy home significantly aids a healthy mindset in the workplace, we have included chapters to grow your communication skills and emotional intelligence to help your most important relationships off the job. If this area is particularly problematic, we also offer a workshop called "The 911 Relationship Retreat." At our retreats, individuals from the public safety sector, including the military, gather for an intensive educational retreat to repair, enhance, and strengthen the bond with their significant other. We delve further into the impacts "the job," cumulative stress, and PTSD can have on relationships, as well as the actions that can promote healing when trauma hits home.

PTSD has harmed many families. *"We see higher rates of divorce, family strain, and social isolation*, reports Dr. Ash Bender, medical director of the psychological trauma program. *You lose your ability to feel pleasure and love. Since many individuals do not know the symptoms of PTSD, the spouses and partners of many first responders only observe the relationship as failing. Or they note that their significant other has changed and has become more angry, distant, and combative. Sometimes the actions may include extreme alcoholism and physical abuse, characteristics that were never present in the relationship prior. In frustration and hurt, the spouse often looks for a way out."*

PTSD can create problems in relationships including, trust, intimacy, communication, decision-making, and problem-solving, often growing a divide that eventually destroys the relationship. Add in the loss of interest in social activities, family connections, hobbies, or even sex can lead to one's partner feeling unwanted, confused, and being pushed away. A PTSD spouse can feel very alone, isolated, alienated, and frustrated from the inability to communicate with and work through the problems and help his or her partner. Partners will begin to feel hurt or helpless because their spouse has not been able to get over the trauma, and they do not have the knowledge or skills to help the one they love. Let's move forward informed with this foundational knowledge, eager to embrace new insights that will create a better future within our daily interactions, whether professional or personal.

CHAPTER 9

CAN WE DO SOMETHING ABOUT THE PEOPLE?

Two things are infinite: the universe and human stupidity:
and I'm not sure about the universe.
~ Albert Einstein

Trauma informed care shifts the construct of our questions, meaning, "What's wrong with you?" will soon transform into, "What happened to you?" This subtle shift in mindset allows us to ponder the direct and indirect trauma that influences a person, while also changing our approach, producing better results. We are going to touch on some broader societal shifts that have impacted humanity on a larger scale.

Have you ever wondered why loyalty to one job, one career is a thing of the past? Organized shifts in people-management led to a ripple effect that requires course corrections. Without giving significant attention to culture, wellness and leadership-strategies, employee turn-over will continue to increase and impact budgets.

A significant shift in organizational management occurred a few decades ago, (it isn't all about social media and millennials!) In the 1920's the astounding growth of the Industrial Revolution took hold. Experts on "efficiency" were teaching businesses how to improve return on investment and be more process efficient. The efficiency experts were asked the inevitable question to the industry leaders who were enjoying the bursting growth to their wealth and power: "Can you do anything about the humans?" We got the efficient assembly lines, mechanisms and processes. With all the growth, however, the numbers showed that the biggest expense, the greatest variable, and the secret to success or failure was the humans. How could they become more productive?

It was from this question that the dehumanizing idea of using efficiency models on humans, was born. Instead of being valued as an overall effective contributor, it began to change to how efficient can people be. This dangerous shift in society meant humans would now be judged on efficiency-versus-effectiveness. Efficiency did increase speeding up production which positively impacted profits. It also created a very narrow-minded idea of human value and diminished creativity and inventiveness within individuals.

With the inclusion of the Japanese systems of manufacturing, they learned that they needed to add a quality control loop along the assembly lines. This greatly increased the numbers even more, while decreasing errors, leading to a refined process-based system of manufacturing exclaimed as, "The Great Industrial Revolution." Our educational systems altered from an agricultural-based preparedness, to one of making really good, quiet, efficient worker bees - and hasn't evolved much since. Our educational system does not value and enhance the multiple intelligences and learning styles humans have which put limits on individual development and emotional intelligence.

Psychologically, it was destined to create a disconnect that has rooted and grown ever since. When people are treated as "things", the efficiency model breaks down. People must feel appreciated, have a genuine connection and be made to feel secure or a humanistic violation steps in. People start losing hope or start lashing out to rebuild the feelings of value they have as an individual. The sad truth is, we are still seeing the outcome of this cultural shift today with a growth of individual, not community mindset and small, angry movements that cry, "It's us against them!" A lost trust in government, education and authority will likely continue to deteriorate the value of tribe mentality where the good of self, oversteps the good of all.

This dangerous shift in society was first mentioned by philosopher, Martin Buber[lxxiv], who saw the changes happening. Buber stated that we are going from being transformational to being transactional. He called it moving from an "I-Thou" to an "I-IT" culture where people are becoming objects. This, instead of having the traditional and normal human interactions which feed our transformative mammalian nature. In reality, neuroimaging shows when two people meet and connect, they are no longer have the exact same brains. Our brains are always altering and creating new connections.

Scans have proven that the sensory input which makes brain function light up greatest, is the presence of another human. Every interaction leaves an imprint and we are changed from the experience; however, as we move away from transformational to transactional, the opposite is happening. Many of us are overwhelmed by too much "peopling" and work to tune out or shift away from meaningful interactions.

So, what is a good example of a transactional relationship? Consider the last time you picked up morning coffee at your favorite shop - the interaction of, "I've got the cash and you've got the caffeine," and it is nothing deeper than that. For public safety professionals, the transactional relationships they encounter would include all of those routine calls that require an exchange of information or documentation, but not requiring much probing or follow up. Where it has become problematic is when this robotic transaction mindset overrides a desire for relationship building - missing the opportunities that could better serve our professional and personal lives.

The transactional mindset has permeated into places it does not belong - places where we need transformation interactions. For example - at the dinner table, instead of engaging in conversation with the family, everyone has their cell phones out; more intent on reading their screens, than on investing in their meaningful relationships.

A professional example for public safety professionals would be the complacency and desire to, "just get the call over with." You find yourself going through the motions, where you could have an opportunity to make a meaningful difference in another's life, if you would take that opportunity. Perhaps saving a life, a future escalated return, building a connection that could aid your future calls, or giving just enough care to help someone change a direction in their life to a better outcome. It could be dealing with a homeless person or someone suffering from mental health, abuse or addiction issues. Many of these calls would offer a chance to make a difference which serves your soul as well as theirs. It may be easier to tune-out and turn people off, but it isn't necessarily a healthier option.
Deirdre shares in her book, Unquiet Warrior, that during a childhood of abuse, neglect, homelessness and trauma there were 5 adults: 2 known and 3 strangers. These individuals took time to intervene, look her in the eyes and provide wisdom that profoundly changed her perspective. A few sentences spoken with care and good intentions, in a world of adults that had written her off as defiant and troublesome, directed life decisions that likely saved her from a life of delinquent and criminal outcomes. It only takes a few words to make a difference, when said at the right time for them to receive it, knowing not everyone is ready to hear you. Even one life saved or improved by words, makes for a pretty good day; as rescues are not always physical or immediately realized.

Alternately, there is a potential risk if transactional complacency causes you to miss psychological and physiological signs that could endanger you, your partners, or the community. Additionally, while you are humanizing the situation, you may establish some trust with those watching from the sidelines. By witnessing your empathetic and transformational communication tactics, when safe and appropriate to do so, you may motivate someone you least expect to step up with helpful information or have your back in future situations when you need it the most.

We are not promoting a requirement to have long, drawn out conversations with every person you interact with; however, as a public safety professional, you often require a real connection fast to better achieve your objectives and that comes from transformational interactions, not dehumanizing transactions. By the time you finish this book you will know how to create transformational moments with simple communication tactics, instant rapport strategies, quick body language assessment strategies, and easy psychological questioning techniques.

Through situational awareness, you are reading every scene you go into and every person with whom you interact. The unacknowledged truth is they are reading you, too. Transformational interactions also lessen triggered escalation and group volatility, creating a safer environment for you and the people around you. Trauma, social/emotional and environmental impacts contribute to a lot of people being "triggered" by your approach, words and actions. Add in your own trauma and triggers and then escalation happens far more often than needs be. Our society, as a whole, seems to thrive on adversity and challenges and while we may not be able to change other people, we have considerable power when we learn how to better control ourselves with a pre-escalation mindset.

Increasingly, we live in a world where the expectation of politeness lessens understanding and the openness that is necessary to learn about each other. Because we do not want to come across as offensive, we stop talking about religion and politics or anything that might cause some offense. Show a political stance today and you are unfriended by friends, family and "acquaintances" on social media; getting into a heated exchange over what was once a simple matter of opinion. Perhaps it is a good feeling when you talk to people who always agree with you, but are they, really? Too often speaking our minds can lead people to a point where they would rather just agree, ignore, or hold their truth to themselves rather than engage with you.

We have become politically plasticized. Rarely do folks have tough conversations where two or more sides can be shared without emotionalized outcomes. We lost the muscles of shooting straight and hearing someone out without a need to be right by any means necessary. People see the world differently and that is a good thing, like process efficiency humans weren't designed to be robotic clones of each other. We are unique by design and influenced by different cultural insights and life experiences.

If you are spiritual in any way, the best way to understand this is to acknowledge it is not your duty to judge; there is someone that has that role, already. If you are not, then recognize we are all uniquely imperfect because you will never forcibly change another to truly move towards your way of thinking from a judgement perspective. You may influence, leading by example, offering knowledge, and alternatives but people change when they want to, not because you think you are the only one who is right.

We all know people who have opposing political views and are rigidly set in their ways. Most moderate political opinions are open to reasonable discourse about opponents' views; however, when one side or the other moves towards an extreme view, it becomes a will to win not an interest to inform, educate, and sway opinion. That is a fight and you will evoke a fight back. We have learned this forum as "debating" where the goal is not to understand, the goal is to win. What would happen if people with different opinions truly listened to each other with a mindset of understanding the root of the opposing position? Likely, less emotionalized outcomes would result.

What would happen if opposing sides were working together to create new win-win possibilities instead of a narrow-minded goal of tearing each other apart? This common mindset of debate and argue to win instead of negotiating and compromise creates unnecessary problems and emotionalized escalation. We have been psychologically primed by the powerful teacher within scripted TV, media and movies to create drama and few have figured out that we have been manipulated to believe this is normal.

There is a pattern followed in scripts to entertain through dramatic scene-development and storytelling. This is not meant for our daily interactions; however, we are no longer learning conversational etiquette from watching the adults around us work their way through the good and bad, the highs and lows of life. We are learning from media sources that are developed to create divide and emotionalized reactions.

Powerful communication happens when we understand this and learn to listen to each other with aim to work through the variations of thought and perhaps get to something better than either side would have come up with on their own. That is called "synergy" and it's the goal of good communication.

Good communication skills are also missing from our academic learning, so without self-development it can be challenging to grow our ability. We advanced from the grunts of the paleolithic period; however, with the growth of humanity, the fight for power and control created more manipulative communications strategies being taught than relationship building ones. There is a common mindset in current times that you are either powerful or you are weak - you are a winner or a loser. Your positional power is your pathway to authority, perceived prestige and relationship success; so, you try to dominate. However, there is a difference between those who dominate and those who influence.

"The primary purpose of power is creation and compassion,
not control and consumption."
~ James MacNeil, Author, Public Speaker

When power is properly executed, it grows like a muscle. Examples of power coming from creation and compassion would be primarily taught through spiritual teachings, family units and organizations where one learns to serve a purpose bigger than themselves. The reality is, with broken, busy and spread out family units and lessening of organized connectivity in schools and communities our youth are not learning to think beyond themselves. The opportunity to gain this insight may come with service in paramilitary, health and public service roles, but it is still largely absent within the masses.

It is natural to crave power and positioning somewhere in our life. When it is lacking, people may fall into a victim mindset. Most often a victim mindset is created due to a loss of hope, feeling of disadvantage, or fear of power due to how its abuse has negatively impacted one's life. Society seems to push us to decide at a rather young age whether we will take the side of power and control over others or taking a back seat to those who do. Ideally, we should be taught in our youth to be assertive and influential, not take a position of winner or loser or be rewarded for just showing up. A lack of competitive spirit can create a lack of motivation that hurts people as they take more ownership of their own lives as adults.

For some, this desire for control and power may grow into a split personality. An example would be the typical bully. Someone who is in a position of weakness or victimhood in one area of their life and chooses to abuse whatever power they can gain, in another. The school bully who abuses others on the school grounds is most often beaten at home. The perceived loser in a workplace who goes home and abuses their loved ones, is an extreme example for adults. Others may feel they are in a loser position and drown out the feeling of despair in alcohol or drugs in an attempt to tune it all out and make it easier to accept a place in life they never wanted to be. Some may suffer from depression and unhappiness because they perceive they cannot control their life. Far too many seem to shut down due to overload and are incapable of coping well.

We do an Ego State Analysis in our workshops and training where we share how our logical and emotional states are managed and triggered. One of these states is a called an, Adaptive Child State, where there is a need to withdraw. This is when we have to shut down, recoup, heal, and each of us has different amounts of time required for this regeneration activity. It has become harder and harder to find this time. We are inundated in a way that is causing stimulation and information overload.

"Stimulation overload" was coined when behavioral scientists started experiments in human behavior as we became more urban-centered. In the 40's and 50's, more and more people moved to big cities. There, social science testing identified that their senses got so overwhelmed, they entered a so-called "urban trance." It can still be observed today when you see people walking on the sidewalks like zombies, their faces buried in a screen. A Canadian Psychologist, Eric Berne, whose work we will delve into more in future chapters, emphasized the word "interaction." According to brain wave activity, every time we look at each other, or acknowledge each other, it is called a "stroke." Strokes provide a chemical release.

A "stroked person" is catching or receiving attention from the interaction. We "need" strokes so strongly that we will accept negative strokes when no positive ones are available. That's why kids will push us to pay attention whether it is a good attention or not. Either way, they are getting that much-needed stroke. Berne stated that the ultimate negative interaction is not an insult, angry words or even being hit … it is actually the absence of stroke. The most insulting, damaging, hurtful psychological thing you can do to anyone is ignore them and give them zero strokes. It is why solitary confinement is so devastating to the psyche and such a good behavior deterrent in correctional facilitates; also, why time-outs away from all people or electronic stimulation works well with kids. No one likes to feel isolated from others or void of strokes because humans were not designed to function as solitary entities.

It is fascinating, therefore, to see the rise in interactional avoidance. We would rather text than talk and stare at a screen, than converse. The rise of constant information and connectivity is causing a shift that does not make psychological sense. If our brains are most activated with another human's presence and we chose to ignore them, it tells us we are failing to give ourselves the mindful calm our brains need to connect in healthy ways.

Stimulation overload is increasingly impacting our overall wellness when we are grateful that someone is not giving us a stroke, when we avoid face to face interaction. We especially avoid difficult conversations or those we perceive may drain us. The constant barrage of electronic communications drains our connective energy to give and receive strokes and instead the chemical kick we get from we kick addictive based electronic stimulation drains our mental energy. We do not fully understand the level of negative consequence to our brain over the long term, yet. Your brain will seek the pleasure release endorphins by other means if you do not take care of yourself and manage healthy strokes. Unfortunately, this muting is done with alcohol or drugs in order to shut out the overwhelm.

Information Overload is another major factor to this "shut down" desire. Whether paper, newsfeed or non-stop CNN, how many of you read/watch the news each day? Consider, the contents of a single edition of a major city newspaper today contains more information than the average person living in the 1700's would have been exposed to in the course of their entire lifetime.

Now pile on social media, emails, dating/social and activity apps. How many emails do we receive in a day? How overwhelmed and overloaded are we? How overloaded are the people you interact with on the job? Those whose overloaded day just got worse due to injury, traumatic experience, devastating loss, or simply being pulled over may have reached their limit already. The emotionalized and unwise actions start to make a little more sense when we understand all this.

Even without preexisting trauma impact, many are choosing addictive behaviors to combat their overwhelm. Others are powder kegs of suppressed emotion waiting for that one trigger that will blow up a powder keg of build-up. Are you the potential trigger? Absolutely!

In public safety professions, you directly impact the overwhelm that may be simmering beneath the surface of everyone you interact with. Add this to your own potential overwhelm and one wrong word or show of body language at the wrong time can escalate a situation in a second. Understanding human behavior and being trauma informed with the communications tactics we are sharing will make a significant difference with getting you home at shift's end safe and without adding undue stress to your own personal wellness.

CHAPTER 10

COMMUNICATIONS GONE WILD

We have two ears and one mouth
so that we can listen twice as much as we speak.
~Epictetus

When we understand the purpose of communication and what makes us effective or not, it helps build our comprehension for the more advanced tactics we will share. Much of this will seem like common sense as you read it. Having heard about it doesn't mean that we know it though, as it is not taught in schools or intentionally practiced. Even if you are reading and feel that you already know this, it will be a refresher as we all tend to forget the influencers to great communication. Often when we do remember, it is after we are replaying a conversation that did not go well for us in our head. We think things like, "I should have said this … or why didn't I put it that way?"

This chapter will explore tactics on how we can improve our relationships. Communication effectiveness will certainly help our workplace interactions and with those we serve. The cornerstone of being an effective communicator is to project a calm, safe, confident presence in order to achieve the best interactive objective. People are attracted to and comforted by a calm demeanor; more so when the situation is influenced by an emotionalized or traumatic moment. This cornerstone is equally important professionally and with our most valued personal relationships.

Further strength comes from projecting a safe confidence, but not an egocentric confidence -an important difference. A powerful presence rarely brags; however, you instinctively know they are heroic. When they walk into the room, everyone notices, and they will often be described as a person with humility. It has been said that humility is not thinking less of myself it is merely thinking about myself, less. That is the vision we wish to share for having calm, safe confidence.

That does not mean denying yourself moments of war storytelling or sharing a heroic act. Not only does it help your brain deliver those memories to a safe long-term memory center but also, the world needs to hear about those accomplishments, too, and we all need a healthy amount of attention. Understanding our needs when it comes to how we feel valued, can significantly improve all our important relationships.

We recommend reading, The 5 Love Languages, by Dr. Gary Chapman[lxxv]. Understanding these simple truths in how we give and receive value in love after the "rose-colored-glasses stage" where we typically do it all can provide great insights into family and friend relationships. The best take-away is learning to teach people how you need to be treated and creating better balance in the give-and-take of relationships. When we have the insight to know what we need and how to ask for it, your personal interactions are significantly improved. Most often we find ourselves giving the other person what 'we' want and desire which may not be their 'love language' and vice versa, they are showing their affection from their own preferred receiving method. This can create a significant disconnect on what showing love means to each person.

Another benefit to advancing your communication skills and emotional intelligence is about intentionality. We always have an objective to our communications although it isn't always conscious. Our brains are complex organs that are heavily influenced by every experience we have accumulated, thus far. Learning a mindful focus on the best intention for the moment serves all sides and helps maintain that calm, safe, confident presence.

Very few of us stop to consider the intent and objective of our communication on the receiver. This is critical when you are at the scene and you need to gain the cooperation and attention of others. It is important when you are interacting with peers and associates and it is essential when communicating with family, friends and most importantly your loved one.

When you are communicating with the people who matter most in your life, we would like you to consider psychological gold summarized in the following excerpt from the book, Messages – The Communication Skills Book, by Matthew McKay, Ph.D., Martha Davis, Ph.D., and Patrick Fanning[lxxvi] they discuss the practice of relying whole messages to enhance intimate and close relationships.

Expressing your Observations *What your senses tell you*	**Expressing your Thoughts** *Conclusions, inferences drawn from what you have seen, heard, read and observed*
• Fact over speculation • Tangible observations seen, heard, read or experienced	• Interpret to create understanding • Your values, bias, opinions beliefs and theories

Expressing you Feelings *The most challenging aspect as we do not have a great comprehension of or ability to describe our feelings*	**Expressing your Needs/Wants** *No one knows what you need or want besides you*
• Your feelings are uniquely designed to you and your experiences. • Sharing your feelings and who you are builds intimacy. • Sharing feelings builds empathy and understanding and allows the insight needed to adapt behavior that will enhance the relationship (without changing who they are). • Sharing your true self is the pathway to relationship longevity.	• Without providing a roadmap to how you would like to be treated, acknowledged and loved, your significant other is navigating blind and hoping they get it right. • Intimacy builds when both can articulate and express needs and wants • The only one hurt by holding back your needs and wants is you. When left unsaid it can lead to frustration and anger.

Learning to communicate honestly, openly, respectfully and directly when it comes to teaching those that are closest to us, as well as how we interpret the messages, they are sending us, is an instant relationship booster.

Learning to think about our objective allows us to pause and consider whether there is a subconscious input that no longer serves us well. Whether that is an old bias, emotional experience, memory or perception that hinders the objective we have decided we want. When the conversation is important or emotionalized, communicating partially or holding back can lack authenticity. Your partner will sense context is missing and you lose trust and resonance which builds the strong rapport desired in intimate and close relationships. Consider a time when you were in an important conversation with someone and something felt "off" in what they were saying. You may not have been able to pinpoint exactly what didn't feel true, but you get that gut feeling that something is not quite right.

Ideally, every communication interaction you have with another person involves your intellect, social acuity, and your emotions. Your intellect composes the message, your emotions provide animation and depth of meaning, your social savvy ensures you choose the right time, place and presentation. The closer the relationship the more this trifecta communication approach enhances your conversations.

Social and emotional skills can have an impact on your organization effectiveness as much as your personal success. I use this model when consulting with organizations for hiring, leadership and succession planning; however, it is equally powerful in self-development. It interweaves emotional and social competencies. It helps us determine how effectively a person understands and expresses themselves. It also focuses on interactive skills, stress-coping skills, and adaptability to competing demands.

Intrapersonal	Self-Regard, Emotional Self-Awareness Assertiveness, Independence, Self-Actualization
Interpersonal	Empathy, Social Responsibility, Interpersonal, Relationship
Stress Management	Stress Tolerance, Impulse Control
Adaptability	Reality-Testing, Flexibility, Problem-solving
General Mood	Optimism, Happiness

It has to start interpersonal success and how we perceive ourselves and others in the world. It is our emotional intelligence that influences our behaviors, helps us navigate social interactions and informs our decision-making processes. It affects our enjoyment of life and can impact mental health fitness. We all have emotions however few people can accurately identify what they are feeling and how to express it well internally and to others.

Various studies show less than 50% of people can do this. This weakness may be a severe challenge to successful relationships as unidentified emotions can lead to misunderstanding, irrational actions, and counterproductive decisions.

People that work to develop higher emotional intelligence have a higher capacity to control their emotional reactivity, manage and influence others. They also have a more extensive vocabulary of emotions to define meaning and purpose in conversations. Studies show convicts score very low in emotional intelligence and scope of vocabulary.[lxxvii] Conversely, studies of strong emotional intelligence show up in the top 90% of performers.[lxxviii] This correlation of the upper and lower end spectrum clearly show emotional intelligence and emotional vocabulary impairs decision making that can have life impacting outcomes.

Being able to differentiate between feeling "bad" does not have the same clarity as identifying that you are either "frustrated," "provoked," "irritable," or "anxious." The more specific your word choice, the better insight you have into exactly how you are feeling, what caused it, and what you should do about it. This develops emotional maturity and also, emotional wellness. Ideally, we want to be able to identify and communicate both intensity and depth and manage those feelings with greater understanding and situational wisdom.

How do we grow our emotional vocabulary? Robert Plutchik, a leading authority created the original "Emotion Wheel"[lxxix] to help people understand and expand their self-awareness and communication capacity. He was a psychologist and professor who authored numerous books primarily on his research into emotions, suicides, violence and the psychotherapy process. Variations of the wheel have grown since. Use it to develop awareness and articulation which aids internal self-management and our external communications.

This has been expanded upon by many researchers - one group published research on the correlation of emotional maturity and other aspects of mental wellbeing, stress, self-confidence, and self-esteem. Their findings show when the emotional maturity increases with better identification and self-analysis then stress can be minimized. This ties into our concerns with a public safety professionals self-management acuity and overall wellness. In a research paper, A Descriptive Study on Emotional Maturity, led by Dr. S. John Mano Raj, he shares some interesting research that align to wellness:

- The emotional maturity of an individual can be measured through the way an individual "bears the tension". Therefore, emotional maturity is directly related to the self-controlling power of an individual. (Cole,1954)

- An emotionally mature person is a person with balanced personality, who knows how to manage the disturbing emotions, shows calmness and strength under stress." (Dosanjh, 1956)[lxxx]

A challenge for many, is articulating what they are feeling. The following wheel has been adapted from the original work to show a more expansive view of how we can describe what's happening inside, to both ourselves and others. Clarity in understanding is helpful in addressing how you choose to manage those feelings.

When we connect these communication and emotional maturity concepts, it is easier to see that when everything is fine few of us have communication issues. A majority of our daily interactions have no looming, emotional triggers and we manage ourselves well. We can easily project a self-concept of calm, safe, confidence when emotions are not hindering our messages. It is when emotions muddy the water that you will rely more on the skills within this book as your objective with have higher importance to you.

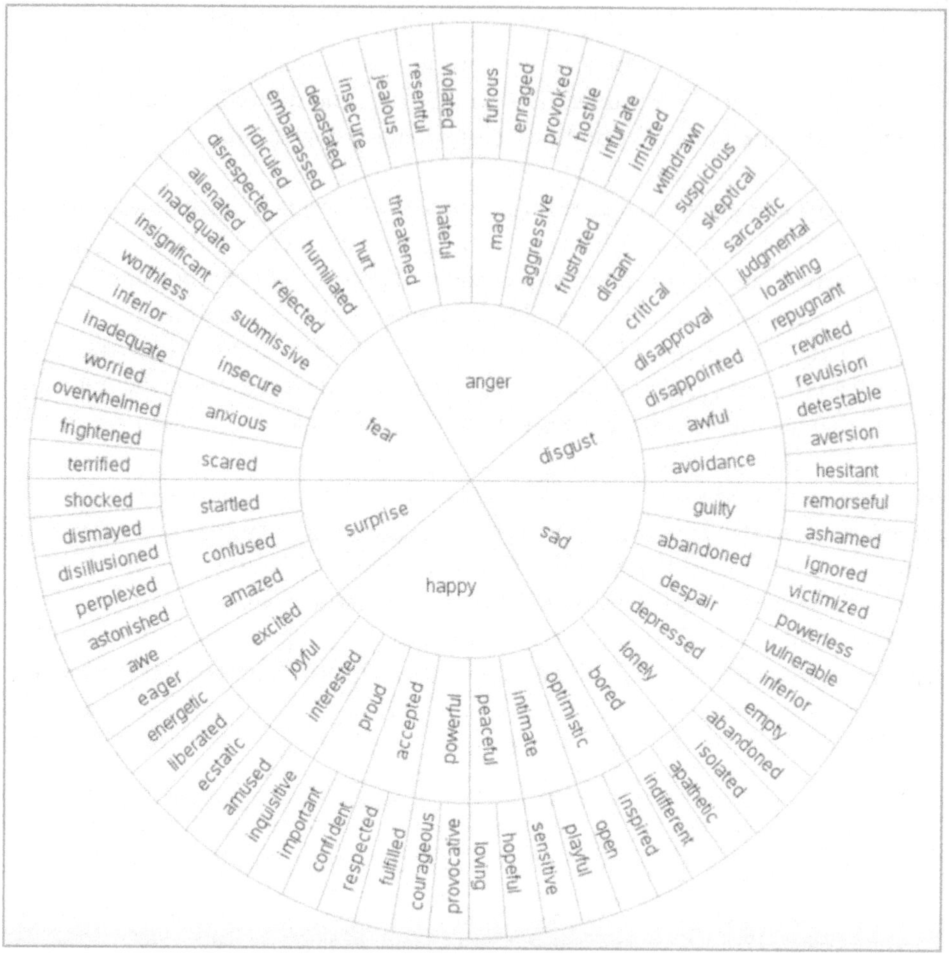

When conflict happens, many of us have never considered the psychological and physiological impacts to the interaction and what it takes to mitigate them. We simply react and if extreme or triggered we enter a fight, flight or freeze response. We share this science in the coming chapters.

When emotions are engaged, your practiced control and communication savvy will have the greatest impact. In these moments, what you believe, what you think and how you approach the interaction is critical. With better control over your behavior, you lessen the possibility of triggering another with your communication choices and body language. This allows you to manage the interaction and influence the other person towards the best possible outcome for the moment. Influencing does not mean controlling, dominating or bullying others into submission.

If you gain understanding and give understanding, then you have succeeded in communicating effectively. At times it may seem onerous to create understanding, especially if you are a result driven and have a tendency to avoid emotional introspection. However, if your objective is to raise a person's understanding of the facts, feelings, intensity, and information important to you so that they can make good decisions, then it is a worthwhile endeavor. Trying to skip over understanding is to your detriment, especially if any amount of meaning or emotion is involved by any party involved.

As public safety professionals, you want people to be able to make their own decisions based on a clear set of information, logic, as well as appropriate emotional intensity. You want that to occur quickly and in the best and safest interest of all involved. Developing understanding therefore is your fastest path to success. There are three distinct ways this understanding is to occur:

1. There is the giving of understanding,
2. There is the gaining of understanding
3. There is coming to a mutual understanding

The other aspect of good communication is building our listening skills. We often believe we are much better listeners than we truly are. How often have you been following someone talking while your brain flips through your possible response before, they have finished speaking? We tend to listen with our next point in mind and that is not effective listening.

There is contrary relationship between confidence and competence when it comes to listening. The fact is in today's world of overwhelm and overload distracted listening is more the norm. How often do you see couples and groups in a restaurant or bar (or at your own dinner table) looking at a TV or device while someone is speaking? We would encourage you to have some humility as it comes to listening skills and admit you, like most of us, could probably listen better.

Part of the disconnect is with those of us who have perfected the art of mimicking active listening cues: direct eye contact, affirming grunts, open body language in what is actually, pretend listening. It could be you started out listening intently and then catch yourself drifting off or having opinions or retorts forming in your mind. When the conversation is emotionalized or important to the relationship, we strongly encourage you to STOP and refocus on understanding the complete message coming at you. If with someone close to you it can be an honest approach to simply state, "I'm having trouble listening right now," perhaps state why, and work on removing distractions or even ask for the conversation to be deferred to a better time.

A listening self-test could be rehashing an important conversation with someone you care for:

- Did you paraphrase what they said to you for understanding?
- Did you take any action on the information received?
- Did you share back in a whole message format so mutual understanding took place?

Those who acknowledge their listening isn't great, often fare better in relationships. They know they have to work at listening when it is really important, so they try harder to pay attention, interact to ensure they got it and address the concerns or information received. It is their humility that makes them more effective listeners.

Mutual understanding is harder when we have to work through a gap in positional power to accomplish an objective. When we are gaining and giving information it is often done without intensified focus on the receiver, we tend to remain settled in what we want to gain. The challenge arises when there is combating interest or differing perspectives. Now you are starting with a problem, emotion or perspective causing one or more of the biggest threats of good communication:

- confusion
- pride
- ego

When you start from a place of opposition and conflict, there is the potential to be quickly triggered into an emotionalized response or worse - an emotional hijack instigates a fight, flight or freeze reaction in one or more of the parties.

With 5 years of feedback from our training courses, we have confirmed people have grown less comfortable with conflict and certainly avoidant of difficult conversations when it comes to those close to them. This fear is triggered because many have lost the capacity to be rationally present. Without emotional intelligence or better understanding that our physiological responses can be controlled, to some extent, it is natural to want to avoid things that flare our emotions. It is unreasonable to think we are always going to get along with everybody or agree on every issue; so, some conflict is inevitable. It is vitally important to develop our capacity to have difficult conversations, to work through issues and come out the other side with mutual understanding.

We want to encourage you to see the positive that comes from these difficult conversations. Relationships cannot grow in silence and inhibition of needs and desires. Embracing tensions and working through them is where breakthroughs emerge, intimacy grows, and synergy occurs. The best negotiators and researchers have the capacity to seek, understand and argue both sides of a problem; giving attention to each segment for well-rounded intelligence. Mutual understanding is easier to obtain when we embrace new inputs, ideas from a variety of people, cultures, and experiences. Accept new information as enriching our perspectives without any commitment to change our minds or values.

Attention on expanding your emotional maturity and communication capacity, along with the trauma informed care insights, will greatly improve your public interactions. More importantly, they will enhance your relationships where it matters most.

CHAPTER 11

EMOTIONAL CONTROL AND CONTAGION

Emotion goes inside-out. Emotional contagion, though, suggests that the opposite is also true. If I can make you smile, I can make you happy. If I can make you frown, I can make you sad. Emotion, in this sense, goes outside-in.
~ Malcolm Gladwell

WHAT ABOUT THOSE CROWDS?

Maladaptive limbic systems impact people individually. However, it is worth noting there is also a theory called social contagion that influences a group think mindset. Whether in social circles, public events, online, within families, or even overarching as a group or organizational "culture", this may be an instigator. This can include:

- Unconscious or conscious bias
- Prejudice, unlawful actions
- Rioting, mobs
- Swarming
- People standing by and filming vs helping during a fight
- Lack of decency behavior where people amass

The Oxford Dictionary of Psychology describes Emotional Contagion as; "The spread of ideas, attitudes, or behavior patterns in a group through imitation and conformity, also known as behavioral contagion."[lxxxi] *It is not a new theory and has troubling associations:*

"Two centuries ago, a wave of suicides swept across Europe as if the very act of suicide was somehow infectious. Shortly before their untimely deaths, many of the suicide victims had come into contact with Johann von Goethe's tragic tale, The Sorrows of Young Werther, in which the hero, Werther, himself commits suicide. In an attempt to stem what was seen as a rising tide of imitative suicides, anxious authorities banned the book in several regions in Europe. During the 200 years since, social scientific research has largely confirmed the thesis that affect, attitudes, beliefs and behavior can indeed spread through populations as if they were somehow infectious. Simple exposure sometimes appears to be a sufficient condition for social transmission to occur."[lxxxii]

A research paper investigating tactical approaches to crowd control conducted a review of five years of media reports on gatecrashing that highlighted: *"Law enforcement intervention could, on occasion, be a source of amplification of excitement for some people: they relished the thought of being chased through the suburbs by the local law enforcement. In other instances, the confrontational style of law enforcement - especially if they showed up in numbers, and in riot gear - was seen to be a precipitating cause of the subsequent crowd violence. In other words, understanding of group behavior and crowd dynamics is also about understanding how the escalation of violence is sometimes linked to the type and intensity of law enforcement intervention itself."*[lxxxiii]

The dynamics of group violence is a more specific learning aimed at law enforcement and can be customized for your workshops. Where we want to make an impact is the understanding that it does not have to be on a large group scale, consider your workplace, or even some family events. Have you ever felt the mood in a room grow instantly happier when a negative influencer leaves the room? Or felt the vibe in the room get quiet and somber when a certain individual enters? This is a less dramatic example of the impact of social contagion.

As public safety professionals, this lesser context is an important concept culturally, as this manner of social contagion can be the underlying reason for stigma, bias, unfair practices, and inappropriate conduct left unchecked. You deserve a fair and impartial culture to work in, as a negative one can have an impact on your health. If you are experiencing symptoms of trauma, depression, or stress this environment may heighten emotionally charged stressors. You owe it to yourself and your peers to speak up and challenge norms that harm a healthy workplace.

From an outward facing perspective this concept is an awareness and cautionary insight when dealing with unsettled emotionally charged groups. It only takes a short while for a group dynamic to create an unsafe environment. You, your partner, crew, or team, and most individuals will have no conscious thought about how they got pulled into their negatively reactive and aggressive state.

NURTURING BIAS

How does our cognitive and neurological processes help and hinder us? In a paper titled, Social Perception: Understanding Other People's Intentions and Emotions through their Actions, authors Julie Grèzes and Beatrice de Gelder reviewed theories of emotional experience to find they are a result of emotional processes:

> *"Emotionally our brain will seek and attach meaning and response to new stimuli based on significant events in our past. Cognitively, our brain has evaluated and determined the content of the experience combining the reactive emotional response with memory infused activation."*[lxxxiv]

Consider this, a law enforcement officer with no previous negative associations to dogs and at a call a large dog lunges with clear intention to attack. The emotional response will be, "A threat is coming!" and a fight-flight-freeze reaction is triggered. A gun is drawn but before the dog gets too close the owner calls it off and the moment is over. As sensory clarity is regained a rising chant is heard from the owner and then the forming crowd yelling, "Don't shoot the dog!" Rather than empathize with the close call of dog attack, the group quickly gravitated to the owner's fear. They were not under attack so did not experience the same emotional response, they may know and love the dog, they saw the dog called off and without the fear response would have a stronger belief it's all good now. However, that could be interpreted as a negative emotional imprint for the law enforcement officer. A belief that no one "in this area" has their back, which may be true or not be true. Because it became a nonevent, there is no factual outcome to support either version.

The threat imprint subconsciously takes in every person, sound, sight, vibe of the moment, and in that is storing a bigger picture than, "Holy crap, that dog almost attacked me!" Without consciously talking it through, internally or with someone to attach some logic and reason to the situation, you may find your emotional memory has attached an additional perceived threat from the group. With that same emotional reaction of the real threat from the dog, your hippocampus may have further imprinted an attachment to include:

- Neighborhood
- Cultural background
- Socioeconomic class of the area
- Heightened threat from that area

Logically, the situation should create an awareness about unleashed large dogs and allow you to mitigate and prepare you for the next encounter. Perhaps it may even create a fear response to large dogs. However, if left unchecked, you may also attach a bias to a group of people who were reacting in a manner aligned to social contagion of, *"Oh my, don't shoot the dog!"* but you interpreted it as, *"they wanted me hurt and they don't have my back."* Then your future encounters with similar people, places, and events could be consciously and unconsciously biased.

Now consider this group reaction was not rooted in a cognitive desire to see harm done to you. More likely, it is an instinctive emotional reaction of empathy that naturally aligned to a known member of their community. Perhaps a fear their children would see something horrible, or their own fearful aversion to seeing a dog they know put down. There is no evidence that they would not rush to your aid if the dog reached you causing a new reactionary process, "harm to human".

An emotionally triggered reaction to the potential trauma created subconscious memories or perceived threats and elevated stress hormones. The people involved had a group-think reaction that imprinted their beliefs and bias based on the response they saw. This will leave them with a specific memory that is layered with past associations that may have an effect on interactions with law enforcement in the future. We cannot control another person's associations, but we can control our reaction and interaction choices from that point on. Choosing to say, "Wow, that group-think reared its ugly head fast!" is less stress causing than, "man, they are out to get me."

> *"Studies of the neural basis of emotion and emotional learning have focused on how the brain detects and evaluates emotional stimuli and how, on the basis of such evaluations, emotional responses are produced. The amygdala was found to play a major role in the evaluation process. It is likely that the processing that underlies the expression of emotional responses also underlies emotional experiences, and that progress can be made by treating emotion as a function that allows the person to respond in an adaptive manner to challenges in the environment rather than a subjective state."*[lxxxv]

> *"Action observation can produce a strong emotional response, and can potentially induce or modify an observer's behavior, particularly when the content of the perceived action is directed at the observer. The amygdala is said to play a key role in fast and automatic evaluation of the social significance of an event – for example, when the event constitutes a potential threat."*[lxxxvi]

EMOTIONAL CONTROL

We now understand the limbic system is primarily responsible for emotions and formation of emotional memory. The hippocampus provides every associated memory into the play and the neocortex is primarily our analytical logical decision-making input. With mindfulness and cognitive effort, you can now develop more effective bridging.

We don't recommend trying to stay too cortex-controlled either … yes, this is for your stoic types. If you have too much analytics in your thinking process you might find yourself in analysis paralysis at times because some emotions are required for effective decision making are impacted. Now let's consider acute stress, hypervigilance, high anxiety, or PTSD continually triggering a person's limbic system. Even if it isn't extreme, there will likely be an inhibiting impact on the neocortex's ability to provide logic, empathy, and good decision-making skills to the situation.

If our tolerance is stressed when it comes to managing emotional or tense interactions, or if we are trying to manage an unhealthy relationship with food, sex, alcohol, or drugs - the neocortex's ability to add a touch of inhibition or reason is challenged. If your stress levels rise, it gets harder and harder to make the best choices or have sound rational thought capacity. We may become so robotic and stoic that social awareness, empathy, and interpersonal connection is negatively impacted.

Now let us add in the extreme stress and challenges that come with all public safety professional careers when you need that emotional and cognitive ability to be at its sharpest. Should something extremely stressful or traumatic happen on shift, that limbic system may flare up and take over which could be a safety risk to yourself or others. It could lead to an unnecessary escalation that leads to career limiting actions.

By approaching someone with forceful, threatening, or aggressive command communication, you can completely disable a person's ability to think straight, be reasonable, and stay in a de-escalated state. When you unnecessarily invoke fear, pride, or confusion in another, you are almost guaranteed to be moving into escalation strategies which adds to your stress burden. There may be times when that level of command and control aggression is required but that should be based on the actions of the person you are dealing with and not your lack of self-control. You will save yourself a lot of grief, stress, and health burden by being cognitive of your approach.

Stress has a memory impact that influences future reactions. The more emotional, the more often stress is triggered, and the stronger the memories. The way you handle your stress today will matter in the future. This is why learning to manage your cumulative stress is important. Managing your approach to communications and interactions now will pay off through a longer-term commitment to healthy community relations in the future.

If you wish to gain more helpful, cooperative, and improved public perceptions, then lead from the front. Do unto others as you would have them do unto you, also known as the Golden Rule. A close version of this rule is upheld in every religion and spiritual philosophy for a reason. When we communicate verbally, visually, and physically with a decent amount of acceptance and respect, we are more likely to get the same behavior in return.

When dealing with addictions or signs of mental health agitation, your initial approach is no different. You want to limit the limbic reaction as much as possible. Even when youth showing higher than normal agitation may seem suspicious to you, they may be acting that way because they are suffering from anxiety from a past adverse childhood experience, or they could have watched hours of YouTube, showing negative interactions with public safety officials, read all the comments from angry group think inciters and be seeing you as a threat to their life. From a mental health perspective, people with high anxiety are prone to exaggerated limbic responses. "A study with college students who scored in the upper 15th percentile for trait anxiety, as in those suffering from social anxiety disorder, showed heightened amygdala responses to both social and non-social highly emotive stimuli as compared to healthy control groups, … like social anxiety disorder. This finding was replicated in various PTSD populations with hyperactivity of the amygdala. Concluding that the amygdala is reactive to fearful stimuli and anxiogenic (control over anxiety, aggression, and depression) situations, and exhibits hyper-function to emotive stimuli, anxiogenic situations and/or symptom provocation in anxiety disorders."[lxxxvii]

WHY DID THEY DO THAT?

Neurobiology helps us understand the decision-making process of risk and reward. Much of what people think is controllable choice or behavior has a deeper rooted and scientific logic. You have likely been at a scene where someone has chosen an action or made a decision that was seriously detrimental to themselves and has left you wondering, "What on earth would compel you to make that decision?" Or it may be closer to home and you are dumbfounded by a partner or peer's decision to do something career damaging or career ending. Research is finding a correlation between addictions, physical trauma, and damage to the brain.

"Emotional trauma is linked to addiction in adulthood. While a number of studies attribute the relationship between childhood trauma and addiction to disruptions in the brain structure caused by the stress of trauma, there have also been a number of other, simpler explanations proposed. In the Adverse Childhood Experiences study conducted with 17,000 Kaiser Permanente patients, many different stress-inducing experiences during childhood have been linked to various forms of substance abuse and impulse control disorders."[lxxxviii]

WOULDN'T THE WORLD BE BETTER IF WE WERE ALL LOGICAL?

"The heart has reasons that reason knows nothing about."
~ Pascal

This might be surprising for the stoic types and Spock fans, as the answer is, no. *You can't be rational when you are too emotional; also, you can't be rational when you are not emotional.*

Neuroscientist Antonio Damasio studied people with damage to the part of the brain where emotions are generated and while they seemed otherwise cognitive and fully functioning, they were not able to feel emotions. They also had an unusual commonality; they could not make decisions. They could be logical and descriptive but when it came to simple decisions, they were unable to do so. This study and others have shown that emotions are a key element in our decision-making process.[lxxxix]

Conversely, overly emotionalized situations don't fare any better and in a legal setting there is precedent about inflaming emotional reactions, too high in Federal Court. Number 403 of the Federal Rules of Evidence,[xc] which says; "*That evidence may be excluded if it is unfairly prejudicial. Unfair prejudice, the rule states, means, an undue tendency to suggest decision on an improper basis, commonly, though not necessarily, an emotional one.*"

In other words, evidence is not supposed to overly engage the jury's limbic system, clearly indicating acknowledgment that emotions interfere with rational decision-making. Scholars Susan Bandes and Jessica Salerno acknowledge; "*That certain emotions, such as anger, can lead to prejudiced decisions and a feeling of certainty about them.*"[xci]

When you are too emotional, you may have a tendency to ignore what you know is best for you. Succumbing to that temptation you know darn well is not in your best interest for whatever reason your logical reasoning has clearly informed you. The best intentions in the world can be tossed aside when we fail to exercise our neural pathways for improved cognitive and emotional responses. When our emotions are in control good people do bad or unhealthy things, smart people act stupid, and many of us question why we did something the next moment our cognitive strength kicks in and says, *"What the heck was that all about?"*

You may be inclined to believe that repression is much easier to control than exercising improved emotional-rational integration. It is important to remember, there is no rationality without emotional input. From the Handbook of the Sociology of Emotions[xcii] we learn:

- The emotional unconscious is most important as the neuronal channels going up from the emotional centers of the brain to the more cognitive centers are denser and more robust than the cognitive centers going down to inhibit and control the emotional structures. Self-conscious efforts to avoid prejudice, fear, hatred, and depression are often rendered unsuccessful by this imbalance.

- Second is the consistent finding that unconscious preferences and emotional leanings exert significantly more influence over our thoughts and behaviors than do conscious preferences. We cannot exert conscious controls over "things we know not of." For example, "mere exposure effect." Unbeknown to us, we tend to respond favorably to objects and statements simply because they are familiar to us.

"It is generally the case that unconscious emotional thoughts will precede and strongly influence our rational decisions. Thus, our much-valued rationality is really more tenuous than we humans would like to believe, and it probably plays a smaller role in human affairs than prevailing theories of rational choice would have it."
~ Walter E. Massey

Another reason is presented by sociologists Wentworth who described:

- It is emotion that puts the compelling imperative into social duties, the thought into morality, the feeling into respect, and the sting into conscience. This observation is why Socrates argued to the effect that thought alone moves nothing.

- Serial killers have readily reported that they knew what they were doing was wrong, but they did not feel this wrong "enough" to have it inhibit their actions. Without appreciating the compelling nature of the embodied "role-taking emotions" of guilt, shame, and embarrassment, we lack a full theory that fuses self-control and social control of behavior in one process.

By definition, then, an exercise in logical reasoning would include a requirement to understand people's emotional states rather than something to dismiss as illogical. The inability to explain a rational process behind emotions does not mean that rational process doesn't exist. Antonio R. Damasio details this as the "somatic (as in body) marker hypothesis." Essentially, he reasons; "*When you're thinking about a course of action, you imagine your body to be in the potential situation, a 'good' or 'bad' feeling about it. It's not that right decisions come from that sort of feeling alone, but, those 'somatic markers' filter away lots of alternatives, as they're a shortcut to decision-making. If you've been through a lot, then you know how you would feel in a wide variety of situations, allowing you to make better decisions (and give, as one does, better advice). Therein lies the problem of the high-reason view without the filtering provided by emotions and their somatic markers, the data sets for any given decision — whether it's what to get for lunch or whom to marry — would be overwhelming. The working memory can only juggle so many objects at once. To make the right call, you need to feel your way — or at least part of your way — there.*"[xciii]

CHAPTER 12

COMMUNICATING WITH HUMANS - THE STRUGGLE IS REAL!

Chapter influenced by James MacNeil's licensed communication program©

The thing that I learned as a diplomat is that human relations ultimately make a huge difference. No matter what message you are about to deliver somewhere, whether it is holding out a hand of friendship, or making clear that you disapprove of something, is the fact that the person sitting across the table is a human being, so the goal is always to establish common ground.
~ Madeleine Albright U.S. Secretary of State, 1997-2001

Knowledge, science, and insights are at our fingertips, but are we advancing towards increased connectivity as humans? Sadly, rather than building stronger ties, we seem to be desperately seeking ways to separate and individualize ourselves. Humans connect most naturally through finding common ground, which provides the foundation of relationship. In a society intent on increasing and expanding the way we label ourselves, finding common ground is a challenge. It is no surprise that we are surrounded by an "us-vs-them" philosophy at every turn.

As public safety professionals, you have the added challenge of connecting with people during times of trauma and crisis, and often where safety is a factor. To avoid escalation, to prevent further safety concerns and to successfully complete your mission, what you communicate with members of the public and members of your team is vitally important. Approaching someone with the intent to build rapport as a path to calmly and reasonably meeting the objective is a great way to avoid escalation.

There are two aspects to rapport: trust and resonance. Ideally, we have both for ultimate rapport, the place where great relationships thrive. Of course, not all interactions are meant to build into relationships. In the book The Speed of Trust: The One Thing that Changes Everything, author Stephen M.R. Covey[xciv] explains there are some people we like, but we don't trust. There are some people we trust, but we don't like. The two are not necessarily connected. When working to build an interactive rapport with someone, trust is a good place to start when in a tense environment. Covey states; "*There is one thing that is common to every individual, relationship, team, family, organization, nation, economy, and civilization throughout the world—one thing which, if removed, will destroy the most powerful government, the most successful business, the most thriving economy, the most influential leadership, the greatest friendship, the strongest character, the deepest love. On the other hand, if developed and leveraged, that one thing has the potential to create unparalleled success and prosperity in every dimension of life. Yet, it is the least understood, most neglected, and most underestimated possibility of our time. That one thing is trust."*

That puts the onus on you, the authority figure, to take command and control without presenting so much authority that you prevent a bond of trust to be established. Pre-escalation is the ability to find common ground, build rapport and ensure the best possible outcome given the circumstances being managed. By understanding some of the psychological and human behavior factors that lead to challenging interactions, you have more resources to find a starting point you can both agree upon. You also have a better chance at building fast rapport to move the moment from an "us-versus-them" situation to an "us." managing a situation together towards the best possible outcome.

In our society as a whole, political, economic, societal, legal, technological, and environmental inputs exist that impact our ability to build relationships, communicate well, and create successful interactions. If we can understand some of the issues that create dysfunction in our society, we can open our perceptions to new ways of managing and correcting where we have control to do so.

Consider how trauma and stress can affect your communication with others, as well as their communication with you. This is a starting point, providing revealing why some of those conversations do not end well. In our workshops we often hear troubling stories about a growing lack of humanity among the public we serve. This may include bystanders choosing not offer assistance, standing by to film the emergency, or not following directions given to safely manage a scene. It comes as no surprise that overload is part of the dehumanization equation. Most of us have felt overwhelmed or overloaded at some point. The pressure slowly builds, and the evidence begins seeping out and manifests itself in our behavior, especially in our responses in emergency or crowd situations.

Building rapport through common ground and trust becomes an important skill to successfully maintain peaceful encounters. This is best accomplished when common ground is desired on both sides and with purposeful focus on a common objective. This is not an easily achieved. Most of the people you interact with will likely be in crisis, and the responsibility to create space for a respectful approach and engagement falls on your shoulders. Demonstrating respect regardless of differences is an area where safety professionals should have an advantage. As a paramilitary organizational structure, you are more aware of respect and acquiescence when it comes to hierarchy, even when you disagree with an order. You understand the concept of respecting others without agreement. The idea of respecting others whose behavior or actions fall outside of your preference is certainly more challenging; however, since the underlying goal is to avoid escalation this initial rapport building tactic of showing respect works to your advantage.

To be clear, we are not advocating belief in or agreement with another's choice of actions when we use the word respect. We are advocating for respect for the human dynamic to achieve the objective of a safe and effective outcome in the situation you are managing. We are promoting understanding that the human condition is much more fragile and wrought with trauma than we usually consider. We are saying that your power position is stronger when you can empathize and first treat that human with respect. Finding common ground and building rapport gives you a powerful advantage in de-escalating a crisis. *"If we had to agree on everything before communicating well with someone, we would never get anything accomplished," observes Deirdre von Krauskopf.*

Too often our society promotes the false idea that you are either powerful or you are weak, you are a winner or a loser, you are the victor or the victim; therefore, you must choose a side. Interactions where one side has the "power" to dominate with authoritative control, perceived prestige and wealth makes the other side feel quite weak and disempowered. When one reacts from a disempowered state, often fear, pride or confusion leads the response. As we learned in the previous chapter, when negative and emotionalized triggers are in play, our reasoning and logic centers are not being utilized fully.

If that feeling of human suppression becomes a predominant thought, it becomes easier to understand the screams of defiance within groups, as well as why it quickly spreads. From a fear state, people can quickly escalate within themselves. Every negative, horrifying, devastating event seen or heard about gets piled on their emotional memory reaction. This triggers a fear-based response against those in the perceived power position; they react in whatever small way they can within their circle of control. This the birthplace of riots, criminal responses and life limiting actions. The same type of trigger for a perceived "play" for power and control is seen in bullies and abusers. They find someone or someway to exert power over others, so they feel less a victim, less a "loser," and less diminished in that moment.

As a public safety professional, knowing this gives you the opportunity to adjust your approach, if safe to do so. Shifting from a physical and verbal power-based authority to using powerful communications tactics allows you to meet people where they are and to seek common ground. When you interact with someone whose hackles are already up, they may already be triggered by the moment that caused your call. As you approach the scene, you are like a spark approaching an incendiary device. Your very presence can invoke fear, pride or confusion in others, due to their emotionally driven need to feel some power in the situation. Your body language, tone and choice of words is either priming them for escalation or allowing for a mutually respectful common ground. This also applies to our relationships with loved ones. Have you ever entered the conversation with the only goal of winning it? In those situations, your body language, tonality and choice of words were asking for a fight, and i is likely that you got exactly that.

A further advantage of using this tactic is self-preservation. If we can alter our perspective to recognize the aggressive antics of someone who is acting out as a 5-year old child, we can maintain power without flexing our outward muscles. We have the intelligence to understand we are the adult in the situation while others around us throw a temper tantrum. Everything can be captured in an instant, clipped for the most dramatic impact, and viral before proper context can be verified. There is a sense that facts are not relevant and the only thing that matters is the dramatic spin.

This emboldens individuals and groups to act out, expecting that you, "the authority," will be too afraid to react if you are being filmed. This entices many, especially youth, to exert above average aggression thinking that they are exempt from the consequences of their actions. Another motivator is the belief that actions give them "status" among their peer groups and the sense that they attain a power position, however momentary, for all to see online. Lastly, they come from a victim mindset, believing they will gain much sympathy, not because they pushed the boundaries too far, but due to the public perception of your reaction to them.

The saying "big dogs don't need to bark" is lost on the men and women who believe every interaction is a fight that needs to be won at all costs. It is much easier to escalate positional power based on the other person's interaction direction rather than as a starting point. Regardless of the capacity in which you serve, you can always escalate your authority. Starting with calm, safe confidence will make the other person's emotionalized response appear even more irrational. Therefore, if escalation is the answer it is very clear why it occurred.

When speaking to a group of middle- and upper-class university students, I was surprised at their unified explanation on how to handle perceived unfair interactions with law enforcement. One youth said that in order to stand up for his rights, he would rather fight till he lost, at all costs, than to lose face and back down to law enforcement who were, in his opinion, in the wrong. I asked for clarity, *"So, if you perceive an unfair stop or arrest, you are saying that you would not follow instructions and then utilize the legal system to win your fight? You believe the best course of action is to fight the officer until you are hurt, potentially fatally, or charged with worse offenses that would not as easily be resolved later? Charges that could impact your success for the rest of your life?"* His firm yes was echoed by nods around the room.

I continued, *"You are all well-educated and understand the law, If the officer remained calm and explained the logic behind the stop or arrest, why would you choose such an aggressive approach?"* Another student piped up, *"They are never calm! They are in your face! They are the aggressive ones. They harass us using stupid outdated laws and they want to hurt us to show us they're the boss."* When I asked how many times, he personally had an officer gets in his face aggressively, the answer was zero. In fact, no one in the room had ever had that sort of experience with law enforcement. At the same time, they absolutely believed what they viewed on YouTube was fact and they were emotionally primed for just such an encounter. This ego-centric mentality can only be countered with calm, safe confidence, that seeks to find mutual ground, and an approach that counters what their expectations are. If, however, each opposing side feels they MUST dominate aggressively from the start to win, then you have a recipe for disaster. According to Deepak Chopra, *"The ego is not who you are. Ego is your self-image, social mask; it's the role you're playing. Your social mask thrives on approval. It wants control; it is sustained by power because it lives in fear"*[xcv]

Have you seen the cartoon character with a little angel on one shoulder and a little devil on the other? Think about it this way. The angel side is your self-image, who you see yourself as, or who you want to be. It is not an outside voice; it is you wanting to be the best version of yourself. The cartoon depiction of the 'devil' that has been implanted in our head by TV portrays only the worst part of this "dark side." It should not be considered all bad because it is a mix of our self-preservation core, as well as our basic desires. It needs some moral and value-based controls, but it will never be completely eradicated.

Many have a belief that we must suppress the dark side completely, but that is unrealistic. Our basic survival emotions are necessary. And a distinction can be made between how we feel and how we choose to act. I am not advocating for actions that would harm self or others. I am proposing that what we may perceive as the dark side may also be there to protect us and ensure we are not taken advantage of. We all need our Ego. Managing it well is where we need to improve. When our Ego pushes us to give into weakness, we must remind ourselves that is not who we want to be, but instead that is our basic emotional desire trying to get the upper hand. It is our Ego that craves power and wants to win. This is a natural thinking process, and without control our Ego can be a self-centered, short-sighted, and shallow part of ourselves.

At its worst, the Ego can cause division. It separates us from community, family, spirituality, morals and values. An uncontrolled ego thrives in indifference. The more we are cut off from others, the more selfish and inward our thinking becomes. Pride rears its ugly head, always striving for prominence. Shutting out other people allows us to slip into a darker emotional place. We start justifying inappropriate behavior because the world sucks anyway, nobody cares, humanity is lost or "I have been hurt so it is okay to hurt others." When we start seeing most, or all, humans with indifference, apathy and disdain, it is much easier for addiction to take control.

This is not a natural state. Remember, our brain lights up at the sight of another human. We are designed to be part of a tribe, in community. A lack of community starts impacting our mindset. We move towards black and white thinking. We increase our judgement of the different values of people and begin labeling ourselves within the context of those varying values. One side becomes right and all others become wrong. Instead of trying to understand, it becomes easier to be the judge and jury.

Pride seeks the approval of those we perceive to be above us because we want to impress the popular, the powerful, the leaders, those we think are more valuable than us. For those we believe are less valuable than ourselves, we seek to control them, to gain power over them and make sure they know it. Finally, for those we think are at the same level as us, we tend to use them, ignore them, or treat them with indifference. They have nothing to teach us because we know it already. We see them in the context of competition, and we want to look better than them, often at any cost.

As public safety professionals consider the times you have seen a person escalate without instigation. Who was around? Who were they trying to impress? Whose attention appeared to be more critical than the uniformed authority standing in front of them. Now you can recognize them in their egoic state and realize that they are not aiming any particular angst at you. It is not personal. It is their egoic pride responding. Your interactions become much easier when you approach from a pre-escalation perspective. Prevention avoids any stroking of that pride ego state in the first place.

Another Ego instigator is insecurity because it provokes what we call 'lack' rather than abundance. Insecurity says, "There's only so much to go around, and I want it all," and, "I am not as curious about what I am going to get as I am about what you are going to get." It is a desperate need to make sure no one else wins because of the belief that, "if they win, then I must lose." This mindset is an emotional state of "fight" where, even if someone knows they are in the wrong, they fight for any win simply to stroke their ego.

The Ego also protects us when the world becomes too much. With the reality of stimulation and information overload, there is an increasing psychological need to withdraw. You may be interacting with someone who is shutting you out, and that can be frustrating. Know that this comes from an overpowering need to disconnect. Some of the strategies you gain in this book will gently ease open the gates move towards a better communication objective.

In a relationship as public safety professionals, there will be times when you have the kind of day that necessitates you shut down or release stress for wellness sake. Learn to create messages with your loved ones that help them know you need to withdraw or to take time for self-care, including no questions asked at times. My ex-husband would come home and say, *"There was a kid thing today; I need to zone out for a while."* He wasn't harming my senses with that insight; he was asking for what he needed to process what had happened that day. Our relationship was such at that time that he often did want to share and talk it out, and I had the background and experience to handle the details. If you want to protect your significant other from the ugliness, use agreed upon sentences that provide the unquestioned space needed for you to self-process. To protect your relationships and yourself from damage, find another person with whom you can safely share. Talking through traumatic experiences helps the hippocampus process into long-term memory and avoids the hamster in the wheel rethinking that can otherwise take hold and lead to PTSD symptoms.

Work with your significant other further to design wellness-based outlets. This could be physical exercise, blaring favorite music, a creative outlet or getting lost in TV (but not news as that stimulates emotional reactions). With my ex, one preset sentence told me all I needed to know to give him peace and quiet without my feelings being hurt or thinking he was shirking his family duties. Sometimes that meant cancelling plans with friends, going without him, or taking our son out for a while so he would have some quiet time to process his day. Other times he would come home jacked up and stressed and sending our son to the neighbor's or putting on a movie and locking the bedroom door for an hour was enough to refocus him. All of these scenarios help to transition from a bad place to a good one. Having a code system that gives them that needed time is a healthy addition to any intimate partnership.

Let's dive into a little more science behind the overload issues to help you meet people where they are with a more open and empathetic mindset. The first aspect is Information Fatigue Syndrome (IFS). This problem results from over-exposure to media, technology, and information. Our brain neurons get overloaded with all the input we are feeding it constantly and over time this can cause damage.

The overstimulation of our brains can create anxiety as we all have sensitivity limits. Instead of becoming smarter, our brain's ability to learn and engage in problem-solving and critical thinking will decrease. When overload hits a critical mark, we tend to shut down. When we refuse to shut down and instead push ourselves forward, our brain will do whatever it takes to retreat. This can include creating sickness to meet its needs by seeking out a virus to knock us on our butts. With repeated ignoring of the need for down time, our bodies can create more life altering illnesses. In "Information Overload: Causes, Symptoms, and Solutions," an article for the Harvard Graduate School of Education's Learning Innovations Laboratory (LILA), author Joseph Ruff states,

"Once capacity is surpassed, additional information becomes noise and results in a decrease in information processing and decision quality." Over time, information pollution or exposure to multiple environmental sources of data leads to the overstimulation of the brain. Consequently, a stressed and overloaded brain is at high risk of dementia and other neurodegenerative disorders (Parkinson's and Alzheimer's diseases)."[xcvi]

Dr. Larry Rosen, Professor of Psychology, describes your brain as a giant board with lights that spark with every concept crossing your mind. When there are too many competing inputs that require your attention, your brain needs to find ways to control and manage all the lights sparking up. It causes your brain to overload as it keeps juggling which concept needs priority and focused attention. To manage this, your brain uses a controller process that focuses attention while scanning all the other inputs for new priorities and adjusts to the latest most important area. It also keeps studying other areas in case they become important, resulting in difficulty maintaining attention on any one thing. Whatever interaction you are trying to influence, you are competing with everything else that person has in their head or is being stimulated by at the scene.

"The result is wandering attention, inability to stick to one task and frustration at the constant interruptions from new areas being lit up." [xcvii]

This is an important consideration in our personal lives too. There has been a significant rise to the diagnosis of ADHD in children (and adults) and the root of this may well be the result of information overload. Unfortunately, the rise of a diagnosis that recommends medication is closely followed by the "I'm bored" syndrome. Instead of limiting information inputs many parents who are overloaded themselves, turn to the electronic babysitter to ease the complaints instead of turning down or off the input's kids receive. Teaching mindfulness, learning patience and delayed gratification, exploring creativity, taking time to meditate are some of the healthiest actions we can learn and teach our loved ones as an antidote to overload.

Information overload is not a new concept; author Alvin Toffler raised the alarm over thirty years ago in his book Future Shock.[xcviii] His theory was that our brain has a limit to the amount it can process and absorb. He stated that overload instigates poor decision making and it leads to widespread mental disturbances that he labeled "future shock syndrome." With our earlier look at rising mental illness and spectrum disorders, including ADD, we are starting to see these influences, along with increases in mental health issues, poor social behavior and lack of respect for others.

As public safety professionals, you often require the cooperation of members of the public, or at the very least you need them to listen to your instructions. It can be frustrating when a person does not comply with seemingly simple directions.

Because of information overload, they are already inundated, and some may be close to a saturation point. Add in the noise and chaotic aspects of many scenes, including law enforcement, fire and ambulance sirens with lights blaring. and on top of the bustle of an accident scene or incident, you may find yourself dealing with people who have reached a saturation point in overload.

"Effects of noise on intrapersonal behavior suggest a variety of possible consequences for interpersonal functioning." The book, The Psychology of Safety,[xcix] by E. Scott Geller, references a study on human behavior and caring responses (Matthews and Canon 1975). Geller writes:

"In a noisy condition, only 15% of the potential helpers showed actively caring behavior … environmental stressors like noise and crowding usually have a negative impact on mood states, compared to 80% helpfulness without stressors…"leading to self-centeredness and lower awareness of another person's needs." If stimulus overload can affect people's attention to an emergency, it can certainly reduce attention to common everyday situations."[c]

He also concludes that this can impact workplace safety as stimulus overload may impact a person's ability to give focused attention to environmental hazards and demanding tasks. This is an essential factor for a public safety professional in situational awareness, safety protocols and self/peer care. Some agencies have even instituted policies to ban cell phones while on the job for the purpose of lessening the addictive distraction, removing the constant stimulus and eliminating the temptation to make a career limiting decision by taking inappropriate photos or video.

Overload is a definite problem in interactions and in human behavior decisions. Have you ever been with someone who stops talking to your mid-sentence to check the phone because it pinged? Have you been with someone who is regularly checking their phone feed while they are supposed to be engaged with you in an activity or conversation? They are in a zoned out auto-response to their electronic leash. This is why more and more experts are saying smartphones are addictive. this is one reason why it can be a challenge to get the attention you seek from those you are trying to engage. Often it is not intentional rudeness, but their brain trying to manage and order the stimulation and inputs. They have conditioned themselves to that 'ping' being the priority.

You may not be able to control others, but you can be aware of the sources that feed into our personal state within society. It can be summed up with this statement by James MacNeil, "The biggest problem with communication today is…we think that the biggest problem is outside of ourselves."

What does that mean? It means recognizing yourself as a participant in communication difficulties and learning how to better manage your own response. It means understanding how your actions and communication can impact others. It means choosing to break habits that are detrimental to good human interactions. It means we give ourselves and others some grace.

You will master how to break through, rise above, and create a safe environment for everyone to feel *"heard, understood, accepted, and respected."*[xci] I take ownership of myself and I choose to bring something new to my environment. I bring new tools in the mix and expand my capacity. This means gaining *"control of self, managing interactions, and influencing others"*[xcii] in a way that allows us to meet our conversational objectives in a powerful path to peace, as long as peace is an option.

"For some things, we control.
For some things, we can manage.
For some things, we can influence.
Then there is a world out there that we can't do anything about."
~James MacNeil

CHAPTER 13

"ME AFFECTS THEE"

You have power over your mind - not outside events.
Realize this, and you will find strength.
~ Marcus Aurelius

Combining enlightenment with strategy, allows us to shift from awareness to prevention. Here we learn to transform the ego to the ego-less self. In other words, we move from being egocentric to becoming a healthier version of "self … less," which ultimately serves better in communication. This will move you from a place self-focused separation which causes division in relationships towards a place of objective intentionality.

Martial arts practice has an underlying philosophy of perfecting the individual by integrating the mind, body, and spirit. This focuses on a psychological and physiological interconnectedness that leads to better outcomes due Similar training helps to make Special Forces operatives' elite, and public safety professionals able to think beyond themselves in a crisis in a manner that serves all involved.

Perhaps you have seen the meme which depicts an old Cherokee teaching his grandson that "the wolf you feed" determines your path of either goodness or darkness. However, the original version passed down through indigenous tribes is quite different from the abbreviated version we often see. Here is the complete story:

A boy comes to his old Grandfather and says; "a fight is going on inside me, it is a terrible fight; it is between two wolves;

One is evil; he is anger, envy, sorrow, regret, greed, arrogance, self-pity, guilt, resentment, inferiority, lies, false pride, superiority, and selfish ego.

The other is good; He is joy, peace, love, hope, serenity, humility, kindness, benevolence, empathy, generosity, truth, compassion, and faith.

The old Grandfather said; "Grandson, the same fight is going on inside of me and inside of every other person too.

The grandson thought about it for a minute and then asked his grandfather which wolf will win?

The wise Grandfather replied; "if you feed them right, they will both win."
He continued, "you see, if I only choose to feed the white wolf, the worst of the black one will be hiding around every corner waiting for me to become distracted or weak and jump to get the attention he craves. He will always be angry, and always be fighting the white wolf. However, if I acknowledge him, he is happy, and the white wolf is happy, and we all win.

For the black wolf also has many needed qualities, tenacity, courage, fearlessness, strong-willed, and self-preservation that I have need of at times and that the white wolf lacks but the white wolf has compassion, caring, strength and the ability to recognize what is in the best interest of all. You see; the white wolf needs the black wolf at his or her side. To feed only one would starve the other and they will soon become uncontrollable.

To feed and care for both means they will serve you well and do nothing that is not part of something more significant, something good, something about life. Feed them both, and there will be no more internal struggle for your attention, and when there is no battle inside, you can listen to the voices of more profound knowledge that will guide you in choosing what is right in every circumstance.

Peace, my son, is the mission in life.
A man or woman who is pulled apart by the war inside him or her has nothing. A man or woman who has peace inside has everything.

Many of us let our reactions to incoming stimuli control us and we do not give thought to why we react as we do. Where did the response take root as a perspective? Is it still serving you in a beneficial manner? Is it helping your relationship with yourself, with those you serve and work alongside, and with those most important to your heart?

Implementing these communication insights and strategies is a choice. You can choose to apply these to fully embrace an overall change to your outlook or you can incorporate them on a case by case basis. There will be other times that you choose not to use them at all. Sometimes the other person will be too much trouble to take the time with at that moment, sometimes you will have had enough of peopling and need some selfish time. Truth is, sometimes you will just want to pick a fight. You will choose to apply these tactics to build a relationship with someone, to avoid escalation and to create a bridge of communication that meets your objective. Where it gets tricky and disadvantageous is when our preconceived notions cause us to decide that the effort is not worth it, and we avoid relationship building before even giving it a chance.

"People fail to get along because they fear each other. They fear each other because they don't know each other. They don't know each other because they have not communicated. with each other."
~ Martin Luther King Jr.

Does the statement, "Sometimes you will just want to fight" surprise you given the rest of our teaching here? The reality for some of us is that this is just how we are hardwired. We will learn about our Ego States in the coming chapters. For some, the "angry child" Ego State is their go-to, especially when emotion is involved. We all have the Natural Child State with in us. This Natural Child is formed from birth to age three and is very self-protective. What we will share now is how you can fight in a way that leads to effective outcomes.

We advocate that you implement the way of Aikido, a Japanese Martial Art, for most of your interactions. James MacNeil wove this philosophy into his communications and emotional intelligence program over 20-years ago. His is not the only program that has woven martial arts into its lessons, but the distinction is that Aikido is not competitive, the goal is aggression avoidance. **The following section is taken from a licensed program where Sean is a licensed business partner and I am a global partner with licensed rights to use this content in these programs and books.*[ciii]

You may or may not have heard of the Japanese martial art, Aikido. The three symbols that create the name are:

- AI, which stands for harmony or flow.
- KI, which is all of the power, the universal energy. Energy permeates everything. It moves and flows around us. We are part of that energy, and it is considered "all powerful."
- DO, which means the path or "the way."

Have you ever had a moment in a conversation or while playing a sport where you just 'locked on?' Where you felt smarter, sharper than ever, and everything went seamlessly. Perhaps you know this feeling as being "in the zone." The Aikido philosophy would say you achieved Ki. When you put all three together, Aikido means: The powerful path to peace. For the public safety professional, we have adapted this to say, *"The powerful path to peace, when peace is an option."*

When practiced, this philosophy communicates to others that *"in my presence, we are safe. In my presence, we can handle anything. In my presence, we will not be striving for victor/victim outcome."* Aikido's principles focus on a centered response, utilization of energy, and nonresistant leading which have a great alignment to nonphysical conflict, verbal attacks, and interpersonal conflict. That is why Aikido is fundamentally distinct from the other martial arts.

Watching the Aikido Masters practice is not what you would expect for a fighting art. You will not see an adversarial battle between aggressor and defender. It is more like two people having a physical exchange where they are giving and receiving energy. With the swirling and flowing movement, it appears more like power dancing than combative posturing.

As an attack comes, the defender does not strike back or block the force of the attack. Instead, the defender accepts the incoming energy and shifts slightly from the line of attack with intent to unite with the attacker's power. Meeting the attacker where they are, the defender controls the direction of the connection and uses that momentum in their physical response. The underlying principle of Aikido does not resist an attack. Instead, those practiced in Aikido learn to blend, control, and redirect the incoming attack of their counterpart. In other words, as Morihei Ueshiba, Founder of Aikido is quoted in the book The Spirit of Aikido[civ] as saying; *"A good stance and posture reflect a proper state of mind."*

In our workshops we physically demonstrate the alignment between the various fighting arts and communications. It is fun, interactive, and it drives the point for the following lessons very well.

First, visualize two people of equal height, weight and strength, and who are fairly evenly matched from a skill perspective. Think about a bar fight scenario where these two evenly matched people are beating the crap out of each other. Would you agree that at the end it would likely be messy? Imagine the bar stools knocked over, bloody noses, the stuff strewn about. Even though someone would have 'won,' both would have gotten hurt. Someone could be declared the winner, but both would have lost something in the encounter.

Now, imagine that one of these two combatants have multiple black belts in Karate, Jiu-Jitsu, and Muay Thai with a championship belt to their name. This encounter would be between a fighting machine and a regular person with no specific fighting skills or training. Do you believe the experience and outcome would be different?

Most would say, yes! Of course, the outcome would be different! The fight would be over in seconds with the skilled fighter ending the confrontation quickly. In addition, a lot less hurt would happen in the process. Picture a punch thrown, an epic takedown, a smack on the ground and BOOM it's over sort of experience. Rather than a drawn-out fight with back and forth punches flying, the whole thing would be over in a moment. Although the fighter without the training would lose, the individual would actually be a lot less hurt than in the first scenario. Ultimately, the professional fighter's power means less hurt for the weaker fighter.

Let's take our imaginative scenario a step further. Imagine a 5-year-old child is sitting just outside the ring watching his favorite UFC fighter get defeated in a match. With a full-on rage-face, this kid decides to avenge his hero's defeat and challenge the victorious UFC fighter to a punching match. Picture a five-year-old coming at this massive man, swinging his little arms with furious intent to do harm.

What would you expect this professional UFC fighter to do in order to fend off the attack? The professional UFC fighter could choose to stop the child in his tracks and smack him down instantly, but the fighter would have no reason to do that. Clearly the fighter has all the power; he has no reason to be afraid. The child poses no threat and the fighter would have no reason to harm the child coming at him. Everyone present would recognize that there is no threat.

Is it more possible that we would see him putting his open hand on the kid's forehead to prevent forward movement and letting the kid swing away to get their pent-up energy out, while they talk to calm him down? That is how we wish you to see yourself at the end of this book. Equipped with the tactical and strategic ability to assess, mitigate and calm the moment when someone confronts you and tries to instigate you into a verbal bashing and potentially escalated fight. To recognize that most who are attempting to fight during a highly emotional or trauma infused moment are much like that 5-year-old child. Individuals who have lost emotional control in the moment facing off with you, the skilled champion with calm, safe confidence that will manage the interaction to the best possible outcome for all.

"Self-discipline begins with the mastery of your thoughts. If you do not control what you think, you will not have full control over what you do."
~Deirdre von Krauskopf

We will explore different fighting styles and how they relate to communications:

- *PUSH* - *PUSH*
- *PUSH* - *PULL*
- *PUSH* - *RESPECT the energy,*
  - *REDIRECT the energy and,*
  - *MAINTAIN balance.*[cv]

PUSH - PUSH: The first is the traditional fighting art of boxing, one with which we are all familiar. It uses assertive and defensive block and counter tactics. It means when a person attacks, the attack will attempt to be blocked or avoided, followed by a counterattack. This attack would continue back and forth with initiated force until a knockout or admitted defeat is attained for the win.

> In communications that would look like your typical shouting match. One voice trying to win, overpower, ignore incoming messages and counter with their own blows. However, PUSH-PUSH does not work when the combatant can overpower you with bullying, hateful words, low blows etc. It ends with a winner and a loser and hurt all around.

PUSH - PULL: This fighting style delivers blows but also uses a counterpart's energy, strength, and power against them and to your advantage. The goal is to deliver a higher level of pain than you received using multiple tactics. With the right counterattack, you flip, kick, attack weak points and wrestle them to keep them disadvantaged, and off-balance until a knock-out blow or defeat creates your win.

> In communications, this style is characterized by high emotion with intention to provoke escalation and countered with having something over another, a secret, threat, unfair punishment, embarrassment or digging up and hurling every past hurt, wrong, mistake the other person has inflicted with intent to cause the most pain possible to win. In lesser conflict it shows through passive-aggressive sniping, sarcastic emotional abuse, come-backs, silent treatment, and implied threats. The intention is winning by the other person giving up through guilt, shame, humiliation, hurt, complete relationship defeat, or fear.

PUSH - RESPECT the energy,
- REDIRECT the energy and,
- MAINTAIN balance.

In this fighting style, the one being attacked is coming from a position of superior strength; however, their intent to diffuse and calm the aggressor. This approach resolves the dispute and achieves the best possible outcome for both sides.

- You don't want to be in front of the energy,
- You don't want to go against the energy,
- You don't want any push or pull,
- You don't want to be in the way of this power,

- You want to get out of the way,
- You want to stop this and send them on their way,
- You want to stay balanced and grounded.

In communications this would show as a calm, safe confident presence. To meet them where they are at by acknowledging the aggressor's upset. Maintaining open body language (but readied for escalation if necessary). Empathetic listening and paraphrasing to ensure understanding. Using questioning techniques to redirect emotion to responses requiring logical thinking patterns. Maintaining a caring but focused attention on the outcome objective of the conversation. In a personal setting it may include setting the stage by finding agreement on timing for a difficult conversation. It also may include putting a halt to the moment and agreeing to a pause due to emotion taking over an effective outcome.

If you watch Aikido Masters, they are like a spinning top. When they are attacked, they spin to get out of the way of the initial attack but at the same time use a guided throw with minimal contact to move the attacker. The focus is on not getting in the way of the energy coming at them. The intention is to get out of the way of the attacker and let them run out of steam. With superior mental strength and physical strategy, Aikido Masters are able to achieve great success in any conflict. If necessary, they can escalate the physical response due to increased aggression, and if this happens, the aggressor will feel pain until they choose to stop fighting.

In your role of public safety professional, the same holds true, you can always escalate the response if necessary, but you want to remain in the superior position of calm, safe confidence for as long as the situation allows. If you search Aikido on YouTube, you will notice quickly that Aikido Masters always stand balanced, knees bent, feet spread out, one-foot forward, ready to move and pivot. Next, you'll notice, they do not make a fist, they always have their hands open in a body position of calm down. They do not aggressively pursue the fight, instead they show a calm, safe open-handed approach. This body language and physiology communicates that I'm safe

This body language does not flare the limbic system into a fear response. It does not automatically invoke a fear, pride or confusion ego response; it does not propel us in the direction of adversarial confrontation. You are saying with your hands that I want this to stop. I'm not fighting, but my hands are also not down by my side in a defenseless state. My hands are up, my palms visible. I'm ready; I'm prepared should different tactics be needed. For now, I'm not fighting … YOU are!

On the other hand, what does a closed hand mean? It is a fist, and we are fighting. How does this body language transfer into a communications tactic?

OPEN HANDS	=	OPEN MIND
CLOSED HANDS	=	CLOSED MIND ©[cvi]

From a communication perspective a closed mind appears when you enter into a conversation convinced that you already have all the answers or when your preconceived perspective is the only one worth considering. Even those of you who feel you have the stoic non-emotive face down pat. When you are internally emotionalized, with closed as your starting mindset, it is the equivalent of having closed fists ready to strike. If you are emotionally attached to the outcome, you are already imbalanced. If your perspective is so staunchly formed, you will be projecting in a manner that would be an emotional clenched-fist and your body language would show it and your energy would be felt subconsciously. Do you want to know why people fight you? Do you want to know why your teenagers talk back to you aggressively? Do you want to know why your significant other shuts down and will not speak to you? Most often, you started it. How we present ourselves is incredibly powerful, especially from a subconscious level.

If you show up with open physiology, relaxed (but ready) posture, hands opened and mind ready to hear information that may be opposite yours and say, "You seem upset, I'd like to understand?" Or, "You seem passionate about this topic, tell me about it." "It seems like we need to have a difficult conversation, is it okay with you that I am open, honest and direct and ask the same of you so we can come to a satisfactory solution together?" Then your body language and word choice show an openness to dialogue. You are then communicating, "I'm calm and ready for anything, talk to me." The other person will have a harder time having or maintaining an escalated arousal state because there is no perceived threat. They are more apt to communicate if they believe they will be heard, and a solution found.

When you enter a difficult conversation in a relationship saying, "'I know where I stand, but I don't know where you stand, and I want to understand and work this through." This posture communicates that we are here together and seeking to find a connection to define our interpersonal reality. This is the posture of Aikido. This is where effective conversation that lead to solutions in everyone's best possible outcome takes place.

If you walk into a room, you will never know who is an Aikidoka. Those individuals have no interest in drawing attention to their strength. In fact, what they project is the message that they want to live in peace. When practicing Aikido, the opposition is never referred to as an opponent, but as a partner. The ideology is that we are in this together, even in conflict with a desire to resolve that conflict in a manner that causes the least harm for all involved. The ideology of *'we're in this together, even in conflict,'* resonates with a no victim or victor philosophy.

Many of you reading this will fall into the A-type or Alpha categories. While this next quoted section speaks directly to men, many women in the Public safety professional fields are also A-type personalities. Please forgive the lack of unisex reference and recognize the relevant sentiment. This is a very direct and poignant insight from a top Alpha trainer, Navy Seal Sniper trainer, Eric Davis the author of Habits of Heroes. He writes:

> *"Too many men are caught in the unevolved "operating systems" of domineering masculinity that worked for their fathers and grandfathers. The widely accepted belief that manhood is synonymous with being "aggressive," "dominant," and "emotionally guarded" leaves those who subscribe to these stereotypes weak and isolated.*
>
> *You don't have to puff up your chest or be domineering, egotistical, or emotionally unavailable to be a man. That kind of BS comes from watching too much TV and is the kind of crap we pick up as kids. Holding onto those antiquated norms of manhood is regularly killing men and their families ...and most of them don't even realize it!*
>
> *In fact, things like aggression, pride, and independence are the very things that prevent superior levels of sustainable performance and consistent happiness. In sniper school, when guys just tried harder (aggression), their mistakes got bigger.*
>
> *When guys refused to hear what they needed to hear (pride) or thought they could use the "do it yourself" approach and ignore their coaches (independence), they just spun in circles, because they didn't have the knowledge, they needed to improve within themselves. Independence is the result of having gotten help to develop a skill or capacity. If we stick there, we never grow."*[xvii]

Learning to manage intense, emotionalized or uncertain moments starts with a focus on emotional intelligence, self-awareness and self-management. This leads to better social awareness and relationship management which earns you the right to influence others. You have control over your focused thoughts and are able to push yourself into "the zone" at will.

"Where focus goes, energy flows."
~ James MacNeil

It begins with an acute awareness of our unconscious, that wild emotional influence can direct us unknowingly based on feelings and experiences in our long-forgotten pasts. Left unchecked it can push us into living reactively, not attuned to how we are perceived and received in the world. When one is caught up in a reactionary emotion, a loss of focus on the elements of emotional intelligence occur. We now know that trauma and stress greatly impact our emotional intelligence. Countering this potential by building our resiliency is a means of adapting to the threats towards mental fitness. Otherwise we are letting our subconscious lead us into harm's way. Dr. Bessel van der Kolk, author of The Body Keeps Score notes that;

"The biggest issue for traumatized people is that they don't own themselves anymore. Any loud sound, anybody insulting them, hurting them, saying bad things, can hijack them away from themselves. And so, what we have learned is that what makes you resilient to trauma is to own yourself fully."[cviii]

We all have these moments where we are not consciously paying attention. An example we can all relate to is driving. When we first learn to drive, we are hyper-focused watching every little thing, talking ourselves through shifting gears, or watching our mirrors. As time goes on these things become more automatic. We may take more risks or have a close call that we recognize happened because we weren't paying attention. Hopefully the event reignites a more conscious state. My guess is that a significant number of traffic tickets are earned by people who are not in a conscious state while driving. They are ruminating some conversation in their head, grooving to some music a little too deeply, or have just gone blank at the end of a long day and are too exhausted to focus on anything. Have you ever arrived home to have that moment of realization that you cannot recall how you got there, what route you took, or what happened along the way? You were in a semitrance state. We all experience this auto-pilot state, and if this is not emotionalized negatively, it isn't necessarily going to cause any harm.

I am about to oversimplify a very complex brain that has levels of consciousness. As we explore communications and the emotionalized reactions you will come across in your professional and personal relationships, there are two states we will refer to primarily. These are known as unconscious and conscious states. We spend much time in conscious thought when we are working and concentrating on a task or when we are playing and focusing on the purpose of play. In the realm of consciousness, we are aware, but then too, in consciousness, we can start feeling the weight of the world. We start feeling the stress. We can become too laser-focused, too ruminating, too hypervigilant. The burden of consciousness can become too much, and we need to release from it and find a way to tone it down a little, if only for a little while.

There are two paths out of this overly conscious zone, up or down. Some people might enjoy a drink, or three, to take the edge off, deciding to slip out of that conscious engagement level into what might be perceived as a calmer state. However, alcohol induced numbness is not a real calm state, it is a cloudy state. It is not actually calmer; it just dulls your senses. The list of addictive behaviors that can take root is long: drugs, gambling, unhealthy sexual pursuits, other extremely risky behaviors that leave the real world behind while you are engaged at the moment.

Others may choose to ramp up and enter a superconscious state. Those who are extremely fitness minded and work out to a level where all thought is gone, or those who meditate and become consciously unaware are this type. Some may enter a deep level of prayer for the effect of transcending the noise of the conscious level. Some may take long walks in the woods and connect with nature, freeing their mind of conscious thought and being in the moment with something that grounds them. Some may work on a hobby or read a book with a hyper-focus that releases them from other thoughts.

There is another level of consciousness that becomes a near euphoric transcendence, commonly referred to as the zone. The zone is when we are not even consciously aware of what we are doing right, we're just doing it right and at such a speed and skill that it is beyond our measured thought. The zone happens during activities that create inner happiness, satisfaction, success and accomplishment through complete absorption in meaningful pursuit. Most of us have experienced flow, described by Mihaly Csikszentmihalyi, author of Flow: The Psychology of Optimal Experience as:

"An optimal mental state (Csiksgentmihalyi, 1990), flow is associated with optimal performance, as well as providing an optimal human experience. Given the psychological skills that are likely to influence flow, it is suggested that imagery may be useful for facilitating flow experiences."[xix]

Where would this be observed in the workplace? Consider a day or an hour that flew by productively, a conversation with a peer that seemed to happen in a blink of an eye and resulted in excellent outcomes, or a call where each attending service worked in tandem perfectly, everyone interacting effectively and efficiently with little input from commands. Remember an issue with another department that you had the perfect answer for and with a quick phone call and discussion, it was resolved. These are regular daily flow scenarios that happen when we are on point with our objectives and have the mindset and rapport to make it happen. We can train our brain to be more open and readied for flow experiences.

Deirdre first learned this mindset mastery from a marksmanship coach who introduced her to the teachings of Lanny Bassham when she first started out as a competitive shooter as a teenager in the early 80's. Lanny was a Silver Medalist in the 1972 Munich Olympic Games and was frustrated with his mental failure during the competition. He sought out training in mental mastery. Unable to find what he needed; he began interviewing Olympic Gold Medalists to learn what they did differently to win. His system, called Mental Management and author of

With Winning in Mind [cx], has since expanded to include programs for many sports, teachers, parents, and coaches (https://is.gd/mentalmgt). Deirdre has used the techniques for years, winning championships, medals, as an expert marksmanship in the Military, as a marksmanship coach for Police Army Cadets and as a leader, mentor, and coach.

Mental Management takes you through principles, goal setting and affirmations to develop the best version of you in whatever you wish to accomplish. This mindset mastery is very helpful when managing the impacts of a traumatic scene before the brain starts conjuring up narrow focused scenarios that do you harm in their repeated cycles. It would be extremely beneficial for lingering impacts of trauma as you move your framing towards more beneficial thinking practices. The overarching takeaways are:

- Conscious thoughts and mental pictures control our senses; what you think about, creates your reality.
- The subconscious creates the performance from input repetition.
- Your self-image and your performance are aligned; they are the total of your habits and attitudes.

Both our conscious and unconscious work with memory, habits, feelings, behaviors, and emotions. The magic is understanding that the unconscious is the source from which the conscious pulls, it is the accumulation of what it has been fed by the inputs received. Like the hard drive on the computer, it can be reprogrammed. The more traumatically ingrained or repeated the bad data is, the more time required to overwrite the existing data, but it can be done.

Many scientific studies have been done on athletes who achieve flow in their pursuit of Olympic achievements or superstardom. Sports psychologists are well paid to ensure the top athletes groom this ability. Describing flow at this level may seem out of reach for some. How can we focus on our everyday ability to manage self to achieve optimized wellness and objective based results?

Mihaly Csikszentmihalyi, author of Finding Flow: The Psychology of Engagement with Everyday Life, describes flow in a way that is easily understood. This part psychological study and part self-help book submits that flow is achievable by all and he backs his findings with a research study that is understandable to the average person. His conclusions fall in line with many great scholars and thinkers who say that happiness comes from within.

Csikszentmihalyi clarifies the many ways people have struggled to find happiness by assigning a certain power to concepts and things outside of themselves. His research confirms that genuine human satisfaction arrives in a state of consciousness called the flow. This state is where one feels alert, strong, in effortless control, unselfconscious, and achieving an optimal experience with the use of their unique abilities. He concludes that happiness is not a fixed state, rather it is developed with a focus on achieving flow in our lives. The primary ignitor of flow is self-control. When we work to achieve a flow-like state, we command the whirling mass of thoughts in our conscious and manage the inputs of our subconscious rather than letting those elements control us. Csikszentmihalyi writes, *"The best moments usually occur when a person's body or mind is stretched to its limits in a voluntary effort to accomplish something challenging and worthwhile. Optimal experience is thus something we make happen."*[cxi]

It does not have to relate to super achievements. Have you ever had conversations where you are so thoroughly engaged and, in the moment, that the hours fly by before you are almost startled into awareness of the time that had passed? Alternatively, you are doing an activity that so wholly engages you time seemed to have stopped awhile. This is what Csikszentmihalyi details, *"A state in which people are so involved in an activity that nothing else seems to matter; the experience is so enjoyable that people will continue to do it even at great cost, for the sheer sake of doing it."* He identifies many different elements involved in achieving flow:[cxii]

- There are clear goals every step of the way
- There is immediate feedback to one's actions
- There is a balance between challenges and skills
- Action and awareness are merged
- Distractions are excluded from consciousness
- There is no worry of failure
- Self-consciousness disappears
- The sense of time becomes distorted
- The activity becomes an end in itself

The achievement of flow is a self-directed halt to the interference of conscious and cognitive distractions. That requires a "letting go" element that needs your focused attention to achieve. This is not the focus of the beginning driver who is carefully thinking through each step of the process. This is when the activity is innate, coming from within, focused thought without unnecessary details on how to achieve the goal, it comes naturally.

Professional athletes do not think about their next move in a step by step manner, race car drivers do not think about every small technical detail of their driving, it becomes automated. Public safety professionals in the midst of action DO what they are trained to do as if on autopilot because their training kicks in and they are in flow to get the job done. Assessments, actions, re-assessments, actions, all occur in natural transition.

Absorption in activity at this level of consciousness means you have removed the egocentric self and have enmeshed your focused awareness into the action at hand while maintaining total control. As we consider communications and optimized interactions, this relates to how we gain the self-control to rise above the non-issue of perceived threats that are, in fact, merely emotionalized reactions and actions. People can choose to offend you without you choosing to be offended.

As Sean mentioned in an earlier chapter, this means having the mindset that can see and hear someone yelling and flailing around and yet you remain calm, strong, alert and asking;

> *"Am I safe?*
> *Are they safe?*
> *Is my partner/ teammate(s) safe?*
> *Is the environment safe?"*

If yes, then our response can be, 'Hey man, yell, get it off your chest if it releases that pent-up energy. I'm here, I'm listening, and I understand you need this venting release, and it is not harming me, you or anyone else right now."' This level of flow in emotionalized situations allows you to remain untouchable, fully engaged yet fully detached and not getting sucked into the emotional vortex. You remain attentive, ready to switch gears should the safety element change, but for now, you are watching it like a game being played. Your goal is not to manipulate, but to remain sufficiently detached as not to get sucked in.

This ego-less state also means you must trust in all your experience and training to take over should that safety factor change in an instant. It means having confidence in your skills and abilities to manage the interaction no matter which way it turns. While making the focused effort to talk in a calming manner, show body language that will create calm and visualizing the best outcome for the situation. You have your training, you have your experience, and at some point, you have to let go and know you've got this.

For this reason, we first want to challenge our subconscious inputs and train our cognitive functions to ensure what is being served up is relevant and helpful to the current moment and not some emotional influence from years gone by that no longer serves us. Once we have the subconscious flowing naturally through our neocortex and making proactive updates to old ways of thinking, we can become a powerhouse in thought and communications.

This practiced mindfulness gives us full awareness that we rarely have influence over an external locus of control; meaning we do not have much control in changing others or the environment. When we try to manipulate and control that which is outside of ourselves, we are often left frustrated, confused and fighting a sense of failure. When this is our primary thinking pattern, we can spiral ourselves into negative thinking patterns very fast. We weaken when we put our focus on those uncontrollable areas, all that "stuff … out there' with layers of factors we know nothing about. When we add in our beliefs, biases, perceptions, cultural inferences and our experiences, all that takes up more space in our mind and influences our behavior and actions. We find ourselves so overloaded with these images and our mind fills with unverified possibilities that we cannot clearly see the person right or situation in front of us. We cannot feel the vibe we are sharing with all those in our presence. We cannot speak in a manner that engages in open, honest, respectful and direct communication. Our objective will not be met because our emotionalized and reactive egocentric self is ruling the show.

Elevated emotions are contagious which is why escalation often occurs, whether at work or within your more personal relationships. It is why otherwise peaceful crowds turn ugly and riot. For public safety professionals, when your emotions are controlled, the others involved in the crisis will most often respond subconsciously to that calm, safe confidence. Many conflicts can be averted merely by managing our own emotions and thinking patterns. If we fail to do this, the interaction is no longer about the person you are dealing with and you. It becomes the person you are dealing with and ALL the potential threats your sub-conscious serves up. What follows is all our actions, body language, tonality, and words show that, triggering ALL their subconscious associations. Ladies and gentlemen, voila, we have escalation. When I can control what happens within me, my reaction to the world around me changes. I may not be able to control others, but I must control me.

CHAPTER 14

COMPLICATIONS IN COMMUNICATIONS

Who you are is speaking so loudly?
that I can't hear what you're saying.
~ Ralph Waldo Emerson

In this chapter, we will begin to add tools to our toolbox that help us build self-control and manage emotionalized interactions within ourselves and with others. You're going to understand more about the function of communication in gaining your objective, whether that is responding to a teenager's "whatever" comment or influencing someone to follow your directions for their safety or the safety of others. We will delve into self-talk and the impact our internal dialogue has on our wellness and how others read us in our body language, resonance, and speech. You will understand, as in other chapters, that this fantastic tactical information works in most cases. There will always be times where it is not the right tool and you will need to reach into that toolbox of training and experience for another option. One of the reasons we developed a 911 Relationship Retreat is for members who say, "my spouse needs this training too." To heal an existing relationship that is in poor communication health, both parties need to come to the same starting point to turn things around.

As you now know you can only control you, your responses, and actions. This section may resonate on a more personal level; however, the tactics are equally useful when approaching a member of public where you wish to avoid escalation. You will become far more mindful of your communications and more intentional in your objectives. You will learn to listen better, ask more questions, and then clarify for intent. You will learn to stimulate others interest so that the conversation you want to have has less risk and mystery surrounding it. Others will engage with you best when their mind can answer this one critical question, "What's in it for me?" If your escalated or difficult conversations have not gone well in the past, it may take a few attempts to share this information with those who are closest to you. This will allow them to feel safe and comfortable that you are leading with a new mindset now. Be patient with others. More importantly, be patient with yourself.

Communications can be such a challenge to understand because communication is limited in its capacity. Dr. Albert Mehrabian, Professor at UCLA[cxiii], conducted research in 1968 to try to understand the impacts of body language, vocal influences, and the words used when the message was inconsistent.

Consider how many times you say one thing and mean another. For example, consider sarcasm or innuendo, there is an incongruent message between the words, tone, and body language. This incongruence may raise a person's emotionalized ego by triggering pride, confusion, and potentially fear. Then of course, their response is coming from that emotionalized position.

Public safety professionals typically have what some may call dark or dry humor. It is often part of your coping mechanism and it is culturally ingrained. Therefore, as unlikely as it is to change, we would be remiss not to mention the impact of your choices when the outcome of the conversation is significant to you. Since the difference between Irony, Sarcasm, and Satire comes up as a regular question in workshops I will share general definitions here:

Sarcasm	The use of irony to mock or convey contempt
Irony	The expression of one's meaning by using language that tends to signify the opposite, typically for humorous or emphatic effect
Satire	The use of humor, irony, exaggeration, or ridicule to expose and criticize perceived stupidity or vices

What is important to understand is when your objective is to build a rapport bridge and open the lines of communication towards a mutually beneficial or safe communication, then this style of humor is not going to serve you well. It may be hilarious in the locker room or over a beer, but it is not so funny when you are working to avoid escalating someone's ego in a conversation. When sarcasm becomes the norm, it can be a warning sign between significant others. One of the key signs of impending relationship breakdown is having a feeling of contempt for your partner.

Where Mehrabian's work is also helpful to some public safety professional roles is when you need to be investigative in your duties and ask the public questions. You will observe the inconsistencies between body language, and words. It can be a powerful tool to probe or potentially raise the safety alert for you and other members on the scene. Lastly, with those most critical to your heart, having a little insight in this area can help you guide the conversation when you feel your communication counterpart is not being truthful, has a different agenda, or is avoiding the core of the issue.

Before we go further, the most important thing I can share about body language is that the baseline reading is as important as all the liar tells you may have heard about. This science is about inconsistencies, which implies you need a baseline to work from. When starting a new interaction, it is important to establish a baseline by building some rapport before asking the tougher questions like Forensic or Investigative Interviewers would. Our workshops can include a body language interactive segment should your teams need this training.

Deirdre's company, DvK Partner Group also teaches a Body Language for Professionals course aimed at sales, customer service, human services, and negotiations and we partner with agencies specializing in law enforcement training in this area as well. Often, these eager employees come to the course thinking they will be able to spot every lie a person tells them from that point on. They are disappointed to learn it isn't as easy Fox Broadcasting's "Lie to Me" TV show made it look with their instant reads on micro-expressions giving you the whole story. However, you will learn some basics that will help you guide, manage, and influence conversations. It starts with being curious and interested in your conversation flow, asking enough questions to establish a baseline and then looking for repeated inconsistencies.

Mehrabian's in this area work focused his formula on determining what was more powerful when communicating words, body language or vocal aspects. This was tested in face to face conversations where speakers were talking about their feelings or attitudes and said one thing while meaning another. The recipient had to inform observers what they interpreted as most important in determining the truth. Based on the speaker's words, vocal aspects of tone, pitch, pace, pause, and volume and body language the following results were discovered:

- 55% - Body Language or Visual Interpretation
- 38% - Vocal aspects of tone, pitch, pace, pause, and volume
- 7% - Words used[cxiv]

This does not mean words are unimportant. What we know is that people will prioritize what they trust in the physiology aspect. However, the entire message is based on the words, so the words matter. If you say something that is hurtful but say it in a pleasant voice, it only makes it more harmful and more insulting because you're trying to disguise the message. This is why irony, sarcasm, and satire do not work well in difficult conversations. What this research really tells us is that we should rely on more than the words. The words are powerful, but they're not everything. We also have to interpret those words, to listen where the emphasis sits, the tone, pitch volume of different parts of the speech, what their body language is saying and the word choices. Here is an example of the difference emphasis on words can make. Say the following sentence 7 times with the emphasis placed on each word differently.

1. I never said she stole my money.
2. I NEVER said she stole my money.

3. I never SAID she stole my money.
4. I never said SHE stole my money.
5. I never said she STOLE my money.
6. I never said she stole MY money.
7. I never said she stole my MONEY.

When we listen with curious intent to hear all the information provided, we can learn interesting insights. With every bit of intelligence, we can adapt our questions to gain further knowledge to aid our interactive objective. This is true of what you project as well, it is not about what you said it is about did you mean what you said? For congruency during face to face messaging we learn 7% is the message and 93% is lie detection.

If you want to make your points powerful, ensure you are congruent in your words, body language and vocal aspects. This is especially important when your objective is to improve relationships or build quick rapport. You want to say what you mean and mean what you say. From your nose to your toes. When the relationship is very important, you want your heart, soul, mind, beliefs, and philosophies to line up. When you do this, not only will the person you care for, never forget the words you uttered, they will feel your intent.

There is complexity to "communication channel capacity,"[cxv] as attempt to convey a large amount of information through an imperfect language.

"WORDS are LABELS that hide true meaning."
~James MacNeil

Every word is like a zip file. Can the person receiving your message unpack the zip files you are handing them and understand you? If someone asked you, "Do you know Sean Wyman or Deirdre von Krauskopf?" Perhaps you will now say, "Oh yeah, I read their book," or "I attended their workshop." You may have added us on social media and scrolled through learning a little more about us and feel you have a sense of who we are. Now that we have pointed this out, would you truly say that you have enough information to say you truly know us? What you know is our labels. Being able to identify me in a lineup does not mean you know me.

What if we had a few conversations over the course of training, or I mentored you over lunch? Now you might think, "yeah, now I really know her." There was some resonance, likability and trust built, so we may have rapport but to say we know someone with such a shallow dive on the relationship is far from true. The mystery of human life goes deeper than a label of vowels and consonants. We tend to attach profound meaning to certain labels or words without clarifying and ensuring we unpacked the meaning behind the zip file data that we received.

How many times have your words been misinterpreted? How many words do we share that people do not even try to unpack or do not unpack fully or do not unpack correctly? Yet, we throw words around saying "BUT I TOLD them!" Without creating an objective, you have to ask, was the goal really just telling them? Or was understanding supposed to be the goal? Was action from those words meant to happen? Was connection meant to happen? Words are only the tip of an iceberg of meaning. Language is limited, so we must be better at unpacking meaning. Not only hearing their words, but how they use those words. Understanding their body language and asking what your gut told you to help interpret data. This gives us more communication inputs to assess and helps to attach meaning to those words.

The scope of this communication complexity is best described by what we call the raging river.[cxvi] Within us we have a raging river of thoughts, feelings, biases, experiences that can never be adequately expressed by words. This tremendous meaning behind the words is wanting to be expressed, using an insufficient language further blocked by the available methods of communication. Then we add to this challenge of being face to face with someone who is influenced by social contagion, a science that was not considered in Albert Mehrabian's experiment. While the person receiving your message has the benefit of body language, vocal inflection and the words they also have the resonance of the room.

There one can be influenced by emotional contagion through social appraisal[cxvii], whereby a person scans the room or area for input into the emotional connection of the greater group. Facial mimicry happens subconsciously or can be portrayed through mirroring the emotions of another. It allows for quicker connection to the emotional 'vibe' of the situation. Why when you smile at someone, they tend to at minimum lift the corners of their mouth a little onward to a full smile back without any other established relationship. This fleeting facial mimicry is often an automatic and fast response, less than a second. It is also a source of science that creates understanding when the emotions of the group connect and align.[cxviii]

This Open Loop in the Limbic System means we can be vulnerable to the emotions of others. We get a feel, a sense, a vibe from those around us. When someone walks in the room and we get a feeling from their presence, often subconscious. I expect there are people you have met that you resonate with right away, there is something about them that makes you feel good, safe, engaged and interested. They have a good vibe while others you met make the hair on your neck raise for some unknown reason or just project a bad vibe that does not mesh with you. If you study this, you will be interested in watching the body language and vocal intonations of someone speaking when someone else walks in the room. Pending that person's sense of the individual who entered, they will often alter their speaking manner, however subtly. We have all heard the joke that certain individuals brighten a room just by leaving it. There is a science in this truth, we affect our environment and our environment affects us. This is why maintaining a calm, safe and confident demeanor can help those around you remain in a de-escalated state, you are offering an emotional contagion to follow, not only for the person you are interacting with but those in the immediate area.[cxix]

This adds to communication complexity because we have to consider our words, tone, pitch, pace, pause and volume, our body language and visual presentation and the 'vibe' or presence we are sending that provides 'a gut feeling.' The sender of the message has this raging river of thoughts, feelings, biases, experiences they are packing into their zip file of 'communication' and sending out. The receiver is trying to unzip this massive raging river and make sense of it, all within seconds. Add in trauma or depression and studies show this 'gut feeling' or emotional contagion is impaired. Their ability to attain the same level of emotional reasoning as someone not experiencing depression or trauma is also in poor functioning. Given emotions are part of our decision-making process this state will further hamper the ability to 'hear' the message being sent and make rational choices from the communication.[cxx]

So, consider, without any trauma the average communication exchange can be visualized as compacting our raging river and shoving it through a fire hose. We want to push our internal meaning as if it is a giant, massive body of water and the best we can hope for is what gets through a fire hose.

Then, we are not always in person and the next best thing would be a video call. They are on the screen so you can see and hear pitch, pace, pause and volume, but you lose the resonance or the vibe, the 'gut' feeling and any social contagion that adds to meaning. This massive raging river of meaning, thoughts, feelings, biases, experiences behind words can be visualized as coming through a garden hose. You likely have recognized a difference between in-person and other modes of communication, now you can break it down. Understand that this one small change means your message may not be interpreted as well as you intended. So, clarifying understanding becomes that much more important.

Now shrink it down some more and consider the phone, important for our communications folks. Now you only have audio to send and receive messages. The pace, pitch, tone and volume are more important now. The phone is a common communications tool, but it is not entirely effective when you intend to send any important meaning with your message. Visualize our raging river coming out through a straw. We open ourselves to more misinterpretation so clarifying and keeping calm, safe, confident verbal control becomes more important.

We must include the most popular mode of communication these days, the highly misinterpreted text option. We have lost the resonance, the body language and now even the tone, pitch, pace, volume and pause that tell us much. Emoticons try to fill some gaps, but it simply is not the same. We are now shoving a raging river of meaning through a syringe. And yet we still wonder, "Why don't they get me? I added a happy face, they should understand what I meant." Consider how many times you have wondered what a text meant or been challenged for ones that you have sent.

Understanding the importance of communication methods is in direct proportion to how important the conversation is. When you have a specific interactive objective, a difficult conversation or one important to your relationship, then it matters greatly. Think of how often you have stared at a text message wondering, "what do they mean by that?" How often do you text back, "I am not sure I am interpreting this message right would you give me a call so I can gain better clarity?" before you let your emotional reaction seep in? If we cannot understand the meaning it, is no surprise that we get that uncomfortable dead silence, staring at a screen wondering when they will answer. Alternately, you get a response that is way off the meaning you intended, and now you are in defensive mode trying to get back to where you started.

This experience can be like running through an unfamiliar house and the lights suddenly go off. You stop running and are still, a nervous or uncomfortable moment descends as your confidence waivers. Your ability to perceive meaning is challenged in this new awkwardness. It would be a game changer to simply state, "I think this is a better topic to discuss in person so we can hear each other with more clarity, add a little light to the situation." We hope this raises your awareness to the limitations of language and the challenge of communication. With our awareness heightened, we hopefully have some humility and a new desire to add intentionality to communicate more effectively.

Sharing this communication section with those closest to you will do wonders for your important relationships. When your circle of care understands the limits of language, the challenge of communication, the restrictiveness of method for understanding capacity, you are working together to improve your interactions. You can begin to bring more humility and intentionality to your messages. As Peter Drucker states, "The most important thing in communication is hearing what isn't said."

Let's take a moment to consider social contagion and your resonance or self-projection. The way we are treated is often based on how we project ourselves to be treated. There is some intelligence behind the "fake it till you make it" or "dress for the job you want not the job you have," style statements. While I would not advocate trying to be someone you are not, we often fail to consider what about us we want to project to the world and be remembered for. If you show up with a wrinkled, messy uniform, a sloppy appearance, a scowling face and expect to be respected because you are a person of authority, you should not be surprised if you do not get what you are looking for. Those who are disheveled on the outside often have trauma, issues or stress on the inside. When you are meeting a person for the first time, they are unconsciously judging you within microseconds. Your facial and body language might predispose them to the rest of your message before the words even come out. This teaches us that our message begins with our initial approach. A series of experiments by Princeton psychologists Janine Willis and Alexander Todorov reveal that all it takes is a tenth of a second to form an impression of a stranger from their face and that longer exposures don't significantly alter those impressions.[cxxi]

When it comes to your public interactions, we are in a culture of distrust that is heavily influenced by social media, however unverified and sensationalized. The onus to change those preconceived perceptions is on you. You have this insight now and you will have the skills to be a master communicator. Being consistent and congruent in your message from body language, vocalization, and the words used is the beginning of rapport building. When we are consistent and congruent, we are powerful communicators.

CHAPTER 15

OVERWHELMED WITH OVERWHELM

Everything you've ever done, every person you've ever met, every experience you've ever had is a part of who you are today, adding interesting layers to your being, and colorful depths to your soul. Everything needed to be as it was, so you could grow as you did and do.
~ Karen Salmansohn

One of the challenges you face as public safety professionals is that humans as a whole are already overwhelmed. You may come across individuals whose cups are overflowing. There is an ancient parable that helps us understand this concept.

> *Once, a long time ago, there was a wise Zen master. People from far and near would seek his counsel and ask for his wisdom. Many would come and ask him to teach them, enlighten them. He seldom turned any away.*
>
> *One day an important man, a man used to command and expecting obedience came to visit the master. "I have come today to ask you to teach me to open my mind to enlightenment." The tone of the important man's voice was one used to getting his own way.*
>
> *The Zen master smiled and said that they should discuss the matter over a cup of tea. When the tea was served, the master poured his visitor a cup. He poured, and he poured, and the tea rose to the rim and began to spill over the table and finally spilled onto the clothes of the wealthy man.*
>
> *The visitor jumped up and shouted, "Enough. You are spilling the tea all over. Can't you see the cup is full?"*
>
> *The master stopped pouring and smiled at his guest. "You are like this teacup, so full that nothing more can be added. Come back to me when the cup is empty. Come back to me with an empty mind."*[cxxii]

When we want to convey a challenging or difficult message, we want to set our objective, stimulate their interest, and ensure we have created a safe environment for the discussion. You may even have practiced what you want to say in your mind and yet you still face the biggest problem in communications today. You have to be able to get your ideas out and the person you are sitting with is just there looking at you with a full cup, a blank stare, or a non-responsive manner. What we learn from this is until a person is ready to hear, you may be asking yourself, "*why am I even talking?*" Until they feel "heard, understood, accepted, respected,"[cxxiii] and until we have stimulated their interest, the chances of them receiving your message as intended is very low. No wonder there are such communication challenges and quick escalations occurring! You may see this in your personal relationships quite easily, but not as sure how it relates to your career.

Remember Sean's story about the Veteran who was venting and raving on? The man needed to release what was in his cup before he could 'hear' Sean's offer to help him. There may be times when you are trying to direct someone out of a building, give someone direction in a medical situation, get an address so you can send help, or write a ticket to someone who was on their last nerve before you came along and lit them up. Their cup is overflowing and if it is a safety or emergent situation, you will not have the time to let it drain and you will need to reach for another body of knowledge to manage them. However, as Sean detailed, when it was safe for all involved, letting the man yell and swear and swing his arms in the air to empty his cup allowed for an intervention that avoided more pain and trauma in his life. It avoided the potential harm to the man and potentially to Sean and his partner should he have grown violent with a hands-on approach. It avoided the lengthy paperwork process of a mandatory psychiatric assessment. It also avoided taking Sean off the road for a significant amount of time to manage that escalated situation.

Do you see the potential benefit to you? For your time, effort, and to get your message through as intended, does allowing someone to empty their cup makes sense? Building rapport in these moments becomes very strategic and intentional. We are going to engage people in the conversation by making sure their cup is emptied so we can stimulate their interest. Then we will present ourselves in such a way that they will 'get it' and we will be able to confirm we are on the same page moving forward. By the end of this book, you will have questions that help you move these challenging conversations forward. Viktor Frankl, author of Man's Search for Meaning,[cxxiv] psychologist and Holocaust survivor says,

"Between stimulus and response, there is a space. In that space is our power to choose our response. In our response lies our growth and freedom."

Let's come back to you for a minute because it just so happens that there are times that your cup is full and the next person who walks into the room may be the unlucky soul that steps on your last nerve. Your overflowing cup has you yelling at your kids for minor things, dropping a sarcasm line on your loved one, and kicking the cat out of the way. For those significant interactions, you will need to make a focused effort of controlling yourself and emptying your cup before you get home. Crank your music and sing, hit the gym first, listen to a motivational recording or book on tape to switch gears so you are ready for the next call, or ready to go home.

The most obvious indicator that a discussion is not going to go well is the way it begins. When a discussion leads off with criticism and/or sarcasm, a form of contempt, it has begun with a harsh startup. John Gottman, author of What Predicts Divorce?[cxxv] reports,

"Statistics tell the story: 96 percent of the time you can predict the outcome of a conversation based on the first three minutes of the fifteen-minute interaction!"

Understand that if you do not control yourself, you are a threat. If you are not in a good mental space, you will not be showing up at all because you are already sucked into an emotionalized and reactionary headspace. Alternatively, if you are showing up and know you are not fully present and think that is okay, remember you are only somewhat present. In addition, your ego is also present and prepared to be fully engaged in a triggered moment. That is not the moment you want to have a serious conversation with someone you care for because if you do it will escalate quickly. They may freak out, shut down and even pretend to remain in the conversation. How many have seen this in conversations? "Sure," "Yep," 'Un-huh," "Whatever." When you hear these phrases, you know they are not engaged. They have shut down and no verbal message is getting through, only the emotion. They just want it to end.

Have you had an argument with a one-word wonder? This tends to be more common in men, but in the public safety professional fields we hear it is fairly balanced across gender. So, replace he and she as you see fit. Statistically though, it is quoted in a Psychology Today article, *"He won't talk to me," or, "I can't get him to open up. No matter what I do, I don't get anything more than a one-word response," or, "I'm so frustrated, I could scream." 85% of conversations between marital couples that deal with differences or difficulties are initiated by women. A high percentage of those conversations do not leave either party feeling satisfied. When conversations leave one or both partners feeling frustrated, disappointed, hurt, or angry, not only is there a feeling of incompletion, but a diminished willingness to re-engage at a future time. The accumulation of these "incompletions" diminishes optimism and lets feelings of hopelessness and resentment set in."*[cxxvi]

There are also times you know you are not getting through to someone, yet you still go on talking. Not for their sake or the interactive objective, but because we want to get the emotion off our chest, even knowing it is not being received on the other side. For us to have a worthwhile communication interaction you first control self. Therefore, I am not triggering them by engaging a negative ego state that is showing up to fight.

We do another demonstration in our workshop that is quite effective; I will attempt to provide a visually impactful written version. Imagine holding a full cup of water in your hand. Look at it as someone comes by and grabs you by the elbow and shakes your arm. What happened to the cup? The cup was agitated, and water spilled out. The water came out because that is what was inside the cup. When someone agitates you, what comes out of you is not what he or she put inside you. The interaction triggers what your subconscious already has at the ready from a lifetime of built up stuff. If you don't like what's coming out, face that fact first. Instead of accusing the agitator, admit they hit a trigger and wonder why you have that trigger in the first place. To manage your agitated cup, consider where and when it got planted and how it was so quickly retrieved from your subconscious for that knee-jerk reaction. Then ask yourself, does that triggered reaction still serve you presently?

I am compelled to share a story of a father and a daughter I watched who are very similar in personality and mannerisms. They have this ability with one sentence, one tonality, or inflection to set the other one off in mere seconds of seeing each other. At first, it was incredible to watch as an observer, quickly relating it to this agitation lesson in my head. One time, after observing their escalation and internally dissecting the agitation points, I was considering talking to the dad and sharing what I had learned about avoiding their quick escalations. I am cautious when noting things in others as I am well aware that I have a way to go to perfect it within myself. That lesson was driven home a few days later when after a bad day my son and I were together, and he agitated me so quickly my critical parent kicked in and a sharp retort flew out of my mouth. He was even more triggered and angrily replied before I caught it happening, visualized a STOP sign, took a couple of deep breaths, adopted the Aikido body language, and apologized for instigating a snipping war, asking if we could start over. My son, who has attended the corporate and personal development version of this course, knew what I was doing. He has worked for me enough times to see I was trying to change the agitation factor. He too changed his stance, took a couple of breaths and agreed that we had both let our ego states flare and then we got through the challenging conversation together.

I realized that, like the father and daughter, my son and I are very similar and have the same triggers and emotional ego state defaults. The years of advice from my calm, quiet strength ex rushed into my brain about not letting my son "get to me" replayed at high speed. With most people, I am incredibly calm, and it takes a lot, an awful lot, to provoke me. With my son it was zero to sixty in seconds. As married partners and after separation, as co-parents, we usually had the difficult conversations with our son together. My ex could keep the conversational flow calm with his experience dealing with domestic and agitated situations, he added authority when required and I had the psychological questioning and probing element down pat. I believe the term is, 'like a dog on a bone,' is apt, and this skill ensured we got to the core of the issue quickly. Between the two of us, as a team, we could get to the root of the problem without too much heightened emotion and define a reasonable solution, punishment or negotiated end.

Later, after we separated, and I was alone with my son more and I tended to become emotionalized when having challenging conversations with him. It was as if I was missing a calming factor that I had not built within myself when dealing with Adam because my ex had that part covered. I needed to own control and manage myself better with him. Otherwise I would continue to have these emotional, often ineffective, conversations that needed an intervention by my ex to resolve. Since learning this information, we have not had another battle of wills. I was able to own my reactions, catch my triggers, stop them and come at the situation with a different perspective. My son was able to catch himself better as well, and we both agreed to call each other out if self-control was not apparent. We still disagree on some things, and I am still a parent and he a child under my roof when he is home from University, but our difficult conversations are not as difficult anymore.

As individuals, we own much more of our communicative experience and responsibility for our relationships then we tend to accept. We are a key part of the story, and in difficult conversations we are very often the instigator. We tend to give ourselves more grace than we give to others. Sometimes I'm the one pushing the button, and sometimes I am on the receiving end and have control over whether I allow the reaction to happen or not. Ideally, if it is a meaningful relationship, I want to remove my buttons and I want to stop pushing theirs. I want to end that game. I want to manage me, so I'm no longer part of the problem. I want to control myself, so I am not caught up in an emotionalized response that is no longer serving me well.

Shifting our focus to emotional management, we will provide enough information to understand the critical impact your emotional intelligence has on your enjoyment and wellness in life. We will share how to remove the ego and the "smaller self" from the equation, so the higher self is the one other people are dealing with regularly. You want to extract yourself from unhealthy emotionalized reactions that do not serve your objectives. You need to be the one who brings the calm, safe strength to a situation and exude self-mastery. When we are centered, balanced and happy within, we do not have to win over another's loss. It starts with recognizing that wellness is vital to strong emotional intelligence. This does not imply we do not have battle scars from life, simply that we are achieving maximum health in all areas we have control over.
Bruce Lee observes, "Notice that the stiffest tree is most easily cracked, while the bamboo or willow survives by bending the wind." This is a very philosophical statement from a man known as one of the world's best fighters. This statement implies a strength

and physical capability while also embraces an intellectual view of staying above it all as much as possible. As far back as the 5th century, there are variations of the following parable. We will share this version titled, Mighty Oak and the Bamboo Tree:

> *Imagine a huge, bulky, stiff and unyielding Oak tree in conversation with a young growing Bamboo Tree.*
>
> *As the mighty Oak watches the Bamboo sway and shake in the wind each day, he can't help but mock; "Oh look at you, bowing to the power. You are a weakling; you're a wuss, you are an embarrassment to horticulture, you are an embarrassment to all plant life."*
>
> *The Bamboo would merely give in to the wind and go with the flow and the mighty Oak would say "look at me, I don't budge, I don't take that crap, I'm big and strong."*
>
> *The Bamboo would just continue to move with the wind as he grew taller and stronger each day, flowing in the wind.*
>
> *The mighty Oak would scoff; "I don't bend to anyone, no one pushes me around!"*
>
> *Then, one night, a massive storm comes, and the winds are vicious and later the next day; guess which is still standing?*
>
> *The bamboo; because the bamboo can bend all the way down, touch the ground and stand back-up.*
>
> *The oak lay broken up; it cracked under the weight of strong power, it lay in pieces in the ground; it has powerful root system, so it will likely continue to grow, but it will never be the same.*
>
> *The Bamboo, after hearing time and again how its ability to bend to the ground and bounce back up was a weakness, discovered that flexibility was the key to success. And the Oak, being so stiff, so formidable, so rigidi only understood in terms of win or lose. The lack of flexibility was the mighty Oak's downfall in the end.*

This story is an important metaphor for the public safety professional fields where that stigma to remain unyielding, stoic, quiet in the face of trauma can, with the right storm, uproot or break you. That direct, indirect or cumulative trauma incident creates a significant injury to your roots and your way of life. Does it make more sense to seek out numerous ways to win and be strong? Would it be healthier to develop a mindset that says, "I am going to find a way to move forward to make the best of this situation?" There is a mighty strength in flexibility, so let us open our minds, our hearts, and ourselves to a conversation that can take us to some transformational mental fitness.

There is an additional insight in this parable that offers insight in the public safety realm. In Louisiana, landscapers have discovered if you plant oak trees close enough together, their roots intertwine, and they are a formable force against weather. This is an important consideration if you feel you are not quite ready to adopt the flexibility of a bamboo tree. You can still lock arms within your ranks from a trauma informed perspective and weather any storm together.

Part of the bamboo's success is its deep root system. Much of the early life of a bamboo tree takes place under the soil, building the roots healthy and deep. Our training is like the bamboo, it will take time to cultivate the strength from practice. You plant a bamboo seed and water it and fertilize it and nothing will show for two years. Suddenly it shoots up so fast you can watch the growth right before your eyes as it spurts dozens of feet into the sky seemingly overnight. How did it happen? Well, it has been working on developing a strong root for years below the ground, away from our eyes. This is important for those who may need to take the time to build or rebuild their root system by maintaining consistent care and attention even if the results are not immediate. We want our root system to feed our mental fitness as we grow into the most powerful version of ourselves. One that is flexible, strong, and able to withstand the nastiest of storms. This strength does not make us scary; this type of strength makes us safe.

"Well people tend to communicate well. Hurt people tend to hurt people," says James MacNeil. Strength is not fearful unless in the hands of individuals with questionable character. We want to have controlled power. We want a power that is used to serve a purpose bigger than ourselves. Safe, calm confidence, good character, and competency are all things we want to have to benefit others. A humble strength that aims to improve relationships and better every interaction is power under control, and this comes from a place of wellness. How do we create this optimum wellness and well-managed root system that we actively take care of and nourish consistently? We start by identifying what our root system consists of, which will be different for each of us by way of priorities and favorites. Although root systems are personal, most include some elements of; love, family, relationships, peace, contentment, self-discipline, fitness, friends, confidence, financial stability, good health, acceptance, nourishment, spirituality, or your faith journey, social elements, relaxation or hobbies to name a few.

Make a list that resonates with you and put a scale of 1-10 next to it. Where do you fall in the areas that help your strength building system? What areas are falling below acceptable and causing you stress that strains your wellness? Do you have plans to take care of those low-end ones? Are there other root structures that you can build to bypass one area that is not currently doing well? For example, you may be in the midst of a family break down, so love and family are a little weak. Building up fitness, social groups, hobbies, faith options can help carry and strengthen you while you adjust and adapt to the weakness in the family and love root fractures.

As Theodore Roosevelt observed, *"It is hard to fail, but it is worse never to have tried to succeed."* Too often we choose to mask and cloud our stress with coping options not realizing that we first need to invest in our roots for optimum wellness. Some people will manage the more significant stressors in life with increased agitation, biting people's heads off over nothing. Some increase drinking, solitude, or risky behavior. If you watch closely, you will also note an impairment in their ability to have well controlled and managed conversations if any amount of emotional input is part of the discussion.

With your peers this can increase safety risks. Having someone on edge puts everyone on edge and emotions are contagious. It can be a simple word or motion that escalates an interaction to fighting or worse very quickly. True peer to peer support means asking the awkward question and offering support. If that is uncomfortable, you may consider planning a group activity in a more informal setting where they may open up and ask for help. What you may find out if they are only getting 2-3 hours of sleep a night, waking up with copious amounts of caffeine, and falling asleep with scotch/beer/wine or whatever their preferred poison is. They are a trigger waiting to be pulled. Anything can explode that last nerve and you are the potential gateway to help them, either personally or by offering options and resources that can. You may even save their life.

This could even be you. Do you rely on caffeine and sugar, working hard to make it through the day until you can decompress with spirits or pain pills at night? When the body and brain are not getting enough rest and you are not getting the right nutrients needed to survive, let alone thrive, then you are that walking nerve. Do you want to put others at risk by not addressing the source of your trauma or stress? Is pride so important that you would allow one bad day or cumulative stress to build up to a moment you may regret for the rest of your life? Deirdre says, *"The truly brave face their demons with determined ferocity and vigor for only in ignorance can weakness allow self to defeat self."*

All life forms want to grow big and strong and to live as long and be as fruitful as they can. We humans like to complicate this known fact. We are all over the map asking, "Why am I here?" and, "What is my purpose?" and, "Why should I go on?" and, "Why should I engage?" With that complexity of thought, we may fail to see opportunity. Instead we often find ourselves paralyzed and indecisive in life. This is not just about a life vision; we are talking about your next meaningful conversation. When I pick up the phone what is my objective ? Am I calling to book an appointment, wanting to argue with a family member, or am I calling to impress someone? When I walk in the room, am I building a relationship, opening the lines of communication, seeking a peaceful conclusion, closing the deal or do I need more analysis? When I arrive on a scene, am I hoping for a fight to release pent-up frustration or do I want things to go smoothly, so there is less paperwork? On the truck, do I want to poke my Captain and start an argument, or do I want to get to our call and back to the house in peace? When I call my ex, do I want to inflict some damage with a sarcastic insult, or do I want to take my kid to the ball game on an off weekend?

Because we are often unclear what the conversation is for, we rarely accomplish what we want. We show up mentally unprepared, without a plan or an objective. You may have experienced being in a meeting that seems to go nowhere and took forever to get there. Internally you are screaming, 'just shoot me, why am I here?' This happens in difficult and emotionalized conversations as well, they start with one purpose and then a lifetime of angst gets yanked out of your subconscious and the battle ensues.

The reality is we might be the problem in other people's lives for some of these moments. If you don't have a clear objective for every important conversation, people might wonder why they are talking to you. They may be checking out of the conversation because the disorganized litany of complaints is too long to contemplate.

Having an objective is not a requirement for every conversation. Many of our daily interactions do not require structured purpose, they are transactional, everyday discussions. This training is aimed at every conversation where the outcome has a meaning for you. Whether it is the expectation of a smooth call or it is a difficult conversation that has to happen with a peer or superior or it is a more personal, heartfelt discussion that need an appropriate element of care, for all of these it is best to start with a plan. Clarity of objective takes precedence so let us review the three lessons from the flexibility of the bamboo tree:

- Number one is flexibility; because the flexible, survive.
- Number two is wellness; it gives us strength and vigor to thrive under duress.
- Number three is having a clear objective. I want to survive whatever comes my way

When you master these lessons and integrate this thinking process into the moments that matter most you will find a significant lessening of stressful events and challenging interactions.

CHAPTER 16

EMOTIONAL INTELLIGENCE: ME FACTOR

"Our police service culture has embraced emotional intelligence and communications as essential training. We often manage social and emotional interactions and how they may trigger us from our own past gives an advantage often taking years of experience to learn. Most Police agencies aren't used to thinking, 'you have to have strategic communications and emotional intelligence,' in order to create a level playing field with the public, and with the media."
~ Mark Saunders, Chief of Police, Toronto Police Service

When the terms emotional intelligence (EI) or emotional quotient (EQ) first appeared to the masses, they served as the missing link in a peculiar finding: people with average IQs outperform those with the highest IQs 70% of the time. This anomaly threw a massive wrench into the broadly held assumption that IQ was the sole source of intelligence and success. Decades of research now point to emotional intelligence as being the critical factor that sets star performers apart from the rest of the pack. The connection is so strong that 90% of top performers have high emotional intelligence. Emotional Intelligence, a psychological theory, was developed by Peter Salovey and John Mayer from social-emotional research conducted from the 1960's onward they described EI in this way, *"Emotional intelligence is the ability to perceive emotions, to access and generate emotions so as to assist thought, to understand emotions and emotional knowledge, and to reflectively regulate emotions so as to promote emotional and intellectual growth."*[cxxvii]

Emotional intelligence can sometimes appear as a soft skill in the minds of those who value tampering down their feelings. It is not soft though; it is a strategic skill for self-control. There are four quadrants to understand: self-awareness, self-management, social awareness and relationship management. These summarized areas were popularized by Daniel Goleman when he studied all the medical research and summarized and simplified it for common understanding. Since his book Emotional Intelligence[cxxviii] was published, EI awareness has exploded in the private and public sectors as a critical element for hiring, managing and developing success behaviors. Brent Gleeson, Ret. Navy SEAL, says it well;

"Emotional intelligence is widely known to be a key component of effective leadership. The ability to be perceptively in tune with yourself and your emotions, as well as having sound situational awareness can be a powerful tool for leading a team. The act of knowing, understanding, and responding to emotions, overcoming stress in the moment, and being aware of how your words and actions affect others, is described as emotional intelligence. Emotional intelligence for leadership can consist of these five attributes: self-awareness, self-management, empathy, relationship management, and effective communication."

Emotional Intelligence is not only a leadership competency, it can have a positive or negative influence on organizational culture and individual decision-making. You have experienced or heard of the person who is technically superb in their role, but just doesn't seem to be able to communicate effectively with their team members. Alternatively, you have seen a leader who uses one style of leading or managing which seems to squeeze the life out of a team. These examples describe people who have low emotional or social intelligence. They can do a large part of their job, but the crucial aspects of self-awareness and interpersonal effectiveness are missing. Emotional Intelligence (EI) and Social Intelligence (SI) make you aware of and help you to skillfully use your emotions for your development and for influencing and leading others. Developing your emotional quotient (EQ) means that you will be able to increase your ability to influence and inspire others while self-managing more effectively.

SELF-AWARENESS

"If you don't understand your own motivations and behaviors, it's nearly impossible to develop an understanding of others. A lack of self-awareness can also thwart your ability to think rationally and apply technical capabilities."
~ Laura Wilcox, Director of Management Programs, Harvard

Self-Awareness reflects the following aspects of Emotional Intelligence:

1. Reflection and understanding of your emotions and recognizing the impact they have on others.
2. Accurate self-assessment: identifying, understanding and developing your strengths and weaknesses.
3. Self-confidence: a reasonable reflection of your self-worth and capabilities.

Our brain's limbic system (emotional center) and our neocortex (logic and reasoning center) are in a fight for control with the emotional side being the first to show up. To have expertise in managing in a continually adapting environment, like the public safety field, having all available skills and tactics works in your favor. These include developing a strategy, improving a complicated process, setting priorities, understanding consequences, and gleaning keen insights from inputs. That means strengthening the emotional controls to allow your reasoning and logic to come into play quickly.

The amygdala triggers fight, flight and freeze, and if it has not been trained to seek the input of the neocortex when the situation is not life threatening, then it can become quite the quick trigger. This is often called an amygdala hijack. As the part of our brain concerned with our survival, it responds faster than the neocortex. Such responsiveness is particularly useful when confronted by a potentially life-ending moment. However, when quick trigger turns to hair trigger because our stress and wellness have lessened our overall self-control, it can become the cause of some of our worst life moments. It is not only clear and present danger threats that trigger this response, either. Both real and perceived threats can trigger the amygdala. We can fall into the trap of imagining the worst before we have all the facts. How many of us, when hearing or perceiving the worst possible outcome, can feel our temperature rising, our heartbeat getting faster and our jaws clenching? When we allow ourselves to envision the worst-case scenario, before we have all the facts, we can react in ways that harm our wellbeing, our livelihood, and our most precious interactions.

Beyond our wellbeing and improved interactions, healthy self-esteem and self-control impact our ability to manage the stress and trauma that is an unavoidable element of the public safety professional career. A study done on the relationship between EI and PTSD by Khatuna Martskvishvili revealed, *"The EI score is predictor for PTSD. The trait of self-control factor has predictive value for PTSD. Trait EI facets, specifically self-esteem and emotion regulation, are also PTSD predictors."*[cxxix]

Knowing we can help avoid potential trauma by developing our EI is great, but how easy is it to do? Consider your first year in your field. There were likely some moments where your flight, fight or freeze reaction came into play. Your training and peer mentorship kicked in and you took control of your emotions to get the job done. Public safety professional fields provide extensive training to face your fears and enter situations and locations of danger that the average person would be scared of and avoid. It eventually evolves from a forced effort to meet those moments to second-hand nature.

The same applies to training to control and to manage our internal reactions to emotional stressors. With practice you develop the ability to regulate issues that trigger you or escalate your emotionalized responses. I am not speaking of suppression, but a process of weighing possibilities with an open, adaptable mindset to change as the situation unfolds. Often, with the more stoic among us, there is a thinking and responding mindset that manifests as abrupt speaking and black or white thinking. This is fed from a win or lose mindset or a definitive right or wrong bias. It does not always 'show' as outward emotion, but it is still an emotionalized reaction, one of suppression which is not healthy in the long term.

Triggers are different for everyone. We all have our childhood and life experiences that feed into how we perceive and react to the world around us. We all have triggers. If you do not think you do, consider the family or person in your life that irritates you more often and faster than anyone else. They are pushing your buttons! Often, we do not even know why someone triggers us; the emotional reaction is fed into our response by the subconscious without context.

Unless we take the time to analyze our response and figure it out, it will continue to have a hold over us. Do you have the self-awareness to know what kind of interpersonal communications can hook you more than the rest? It can be difficult to control one's actions when we do not realize what exactly pushes our buttons. Taking the time to list the behaviors, tones, attitudes and mannerisms that hook you is a great exercise in self-awareness. Do an investigative look at why each one does. When did it start? Who was the initial person that irritated you? Does that irritation serve your best interest today?

Another aspect of emotional self-development comes from our ability to empathize with those with whom we interact. There is a disenchantment with humanity common to public safety professionals. With repeated interactions with people at their worst, we may lose our empathy strength when it comes to connecting with other people. Humans are a community-based species biologically, viewing most with apathy and disregard is not a natural state. If we attempt to deny we care or are impacted by challenging people or disturbing scenes, we are building up accrued stress and trauma in our memory center. You cannot un-see the tragic situations you face shift after shift, it does not just go away. It's no wonder there's a traumatic breaking point. You do care deep inside and trying to bury it causes psychological conflict.

Emotional well-being means you still have curiosity and interest in others. It is natural to be at least somewhat curious about most people. The reason why sitcoms, reality TV and dramas are so popular is because we get engaged with other people's stories. At times, it is the emotional high of watching a happy ending. Other times it is comparing your life to the story and feeling good that yours is not that bad. There will be exceptions of course; however, for the most part, you want to allow your empathy skills into important conversations. That way the last person or last hundred people do not impact your communication strength and power with the next interaction. That curiosity should extend to yourself with inner reflection and self-development. We want to understand our strengths and weaknesses and accept that we can evolve our perceptions, beliefs, and knowledge. That which groomed us in our first 18-years of life may not prove very relevant today. Be open to developing your weaknesses to aid your personal and professional life is a wise choice. A mindset of "that's just who I am" does not cut it if you are consistently damaging your wellness root system and your relationships in the process. Ignoring that which hurts your long-term health and happiness does not fall on any intelligence spectrum.

When it comes to healthy self-esteem, we should also build our capacity and comfort with the value of saying NO. Research shows that the more difficulty you have with saying no, the more likely you are to experience stress, burnout, and even depression. The ability to comfortably say no is a critical self-control aspect that can be a challenge for many of us. One of the ways to build this skill is to work on our phraseology. When it's time to say no, avoid phrases such as:

I don't think I can	I'm not certain
Maybe	I'm not sure right now

These phrases mean "no ... for now" and can often be the start of feeling guilty. You do not want to do the thing asked but you are not comfortable with an outright no, it leaves the situation in limbo. Saying no can also be a challenge for those who have rescuer or pleasing mentalities as they often feel obligated or guilted into helping, even when they are strongly opposed to doing so. They internally gripe about saying yes, and at times can also feel the person asking is taking advantage of them.

An excellent tactic comes from Mike Mandel, a hypnotist and handwriting expert who works with law enforcement on challenging cases. His Counter Intimidation Strategy is part of his Brain Software Program.[cxxx] He writes, *"The counter guilt or counter peer pressure strategy has the purpose of providing a means to successfully and effortlessly defeat attempts to manipulate you verbally. Often, the person who can heap the most verbal pressure such as guilt on the other person usually wins."* For example:

> Partner: "Could you please write this report for me, I am crunched for time, and you are so much better at it?" (Appeal to Ego/Rescuer)
>
> You: "Can't you do it yourself? I'm swamped." (Guilt trip: You are cutting into my time with your request).
>
> Partner: "I have to go to the airport and pick up my invalid mother." (Guilt trip: How can you be so callous as to try to stop me helping my mother?)
>
> You: "I promised my wife I'd be home on time tonight. I can't afford to be home late again." (Guilt trip: You are endangering my marriage.)
>
> Partner: "I'd write it myself, but the Captain said one more bad report, and I'm being sent to remedial training..." (Guilt trip: Your selfishness may kill me.)
>
> You: (reluctantly) "Well...I guess I can do it then..."
>
> Partner: "Thanks. (Feels the win) Make sure you print three copies, deliver it to the desk Sergeant and file it before 6 pm online."

We can see in this dramatized example that often the person that piles on the most guilt, wins. It could have been anything: an appeal for taking a questionable shortcut, an argument about what to do on the weekend, ask to help someone move, or even a hard pitch from a salesperson. Piling on guilt can be very effective; however, it is the mark of a poor communicator. To be a master communicator, you must learn to purge the guilt script and response method and address the actual issues in question. Two simple techniques will deactivate guilt and psychological pressure while clearly stating your purpose. Mike Mandel shares:

- First: Agree in principle with whatever the other person says.
- Second: Clearly state your purpose.
- Then: Repeat ... as many times as necessary.

Note: Agreeing in principle does not require you to repeat back everything they say to you.

Friend:	"I need you to go to Atlanta with me because my grandmother is seriously ill."
You:	"I know you want me to go to Atlanta with you, and I realize your grandmother is seriously ill, but I can't make it."

Alternatively:

Friend:	"I need you to go to Atlanta because my grandmother is seriously ill."
NEW You:	"I know how you feel (agreement), but I can't make it."

The best response phrases agree in principle, are quite general and can be used repeatedly:

- I know how you feel...
- You're probably right...
- That's quite true...
- I see your point...
- I don't doubt it...

"How many times do you repeat this?" The answer is simple: One more time than they do. Note that this works just as well if the person is overwhelming you with "reasons" to do something instead of guilt," advises Mike Mandel. I have used this tactic many times to strengthen my no position when the simple no thank you was countered with

reasons or guilt plays from friends and acquaintances. Often one or two back and forth sentences can stop the line of demand coming at you.

Saying no to a new commitment honors your existing list of obligations and provides you time to pursue things that add to your self-wellness pursuits. Over-committing and saying yes to things you honestly do not want to do adds to your stress. You will eventually feel used or resentful for having done the thing. Alternately, you may gradually resent the person who repeatedly guilts you into doing something which is not healthy for that relationship.

SOCIAL-AWARENESS

"Anyone can become angry -- that is easy, but to be angry with the right person, to the right degree, at the right time, for the right purpose, and in the right way -- this is not easy."
~ Greek philosopher Aristotle

Social awareness competencies rally around the ability to carefully consider the needs of others and interact in a way that meets those needs. It also creates understanding on how your presence and actions impact others. These competencies are useful for any position that requires you to garner support, to provide information, to give direction, to build quick rapport and to build stronger, more enduring relationships. Emotional intelligence is not merely controlling your emotions, it has to do with knowing how, when and to what degree to express emotion in differing environments. The social awareness competency indicators consist of:

Empathy	Sensing others' emotions, effort in understanding their perspective, and taking a curious interest in their concern
Service Mindset	Anticipating, recognizing and meeting the needs and expectations of those you serve professionally
Organizational and Group Awareness	Recognizing the dynamics within the political, environmental, social, technological, ego states and potential legalities (for Public Safety Professionals) and make effective use of these relationships in achieving your interaction objective

Dr. John Gottman, an expert on marital stability and divorce prediction, notes, *"While empathy is only one part of emotional intelligence, it can enable us to be less preoccupied with our well-being and more concerned with mutual well-being."* Empathy is the one element of EI that public safety professionals in our training over the past years report can become challenging for them. It seems to lessen as they become tenured on the job. For some it grows to the extreme of compassion fatigue. Vicarious traumatization or emotional stress from helping others through traumatic events may even lead to apathy. Another way to think of this is being without feeling or becoming numb. Over time this unrecognized tension and attitude of indifference, detachment, and dispassion often seeps into personal relationships. Over time it can also morph into acute stress disorder.

When considering tactics to help you empathize, listening is key. Removing your natural preconceived response and taking in the words, emotions and body language of the individual you are fully engaged with can provide you with incredible intelligence. You are not compelled to agree with what the person is saying, only to empathize with their perspective and position. This allows them to feel heard, understood, and their point of view accepted. In our workshops, we teach and practice a STOP, DROP and ROLL tactic created by Tammy Stanley, one of our training partners, to keep it memorable.

STOP when you find your attention waning, your mind jumping to conclusions, your next response or internal eye roll forming this is helping to create apathy towards the person or moment. Recognize this as an emotion that isn't serving you if you want to build rapport, control your ego state, maintain a de-escalated state with the other party or build relationships. Visualize a big red stop sign that dictates to your conscious mind the need to get this budding emotion out of the way. This will allow you to remain in the moment and think clearly. As a bonus this will also provide you an internal self-control trigger.

DROP the emotion that is hooking you in the moment. Whether it is their attitude, whining, rudeness, or it is your bias against them or their life situation, drop the perception that has you hooked and take a moment to step into their shoes. Hear what they are saying from that perspective and meet them where they are. How do we drop what may be deeply ingrained responses? We ask questions that challenge our thoughts.

- Where is the perception coming from?
- What could be affective their behavior?
- What happened to them that brought them to this moment?
- Could there be anything else going on here that I'm not aware of?
- Is there any chance that I understood the intent wrong?
- Is there a possibility I am missing something or misunderstood?

These types of questions change the tone of the input our brain is recording. It removes the power from preconceived notions and bias and allows for an empathic consideration. If you are safe, your partner and peers are safe, and the person is safe, then continue to run these questions in your mind. Internally keep on challenging yourself until you cannot jump to that conclusion or make that preconceived assumption anymore. This is a communication tactic that is especially powerful in personal relationships, when faced with disappointment with others or conflict conversations.

Stop, Drop and then ask yourself "how could we revisit this in a way that might be more effective?" Identifying what is the added value in getting triggered or pulled into an emotional response can save many disagreements. You now have the power to shake the attachment to the years of hidden emotional inputs that may no longer be serving your interactive objective. You will start to feel you are being triggered is when your subconscious feeds you these questions:

- "They should have …
- "They were supposed to …
- "How dare they say that …
- "That's not right (I don't "like" their choices) …

Further challenging questions can also include:

- Could I look at this differently?
- What is the body language of the person and those around them telling me?
- How will this interaction help my objective?
- Are their words inviting me to dig deeper with questions?
- What's the added value in getting my emotions engaged?
- How important is a peaceful outcome to me?
- Does it really matter that they think differently from me?
- Is there anything else I could do to make me happy here?
- Am I addressing the concerns and feelings of this person as a priority, so they feel heard, understood and accepted?
- Is my body language, words and tonality enticing openness in this communication or am I being judged by my actions, not my words?

It is a tactical questioning technique that may not solve every issue presented, but it will stop the emotional trigger from taking the conversation somewhere that does not serve you or them well. It will ensure your brain stays in a more rational and reasoning state, and it avoids letting a perception hook you into an emotionalized response. Separating the emotions coming at you from the situation that needs an appropriate outcome. Recall the UFC fighter against the five-year-old little kid. You want the safe, calm, confidence to know you can handle this interaction while maintaining control and balance.

Time to ROLL out a new plan now that you have freedom from preconceived perceptions and emotional triggers. You want to set your interactive objective.

What do you really, really want out of this situation? When you want to ensure the best possible outcome for all involved, maintain an empathetic, respectful and accepting manner to garner the best possible interaction. This includes any peripheral people that may aid your interactive objective.

This strategy will ideally include acknowledging what you think you heard or witnessed by paraphrasing their message back to the person. A great way to ensure accurate understanding, especially if the person is highly emotionalized, is to understand that you are likely hearing not only their current issue, but a lifetime of emotional reactions fed to them from their subconscious. Often a simple "you sound really upset by this," or "this is clearly frustrating you," can allow them to feel heard and open the pathway to more in-depth questioning. The follow-up strategy should also ensure you are withholding judgment in your response or next question.

While a temptation may exist to criticize, dismiss or challenge the feelings or opinions of your counterpart, none of these are empathetic positions. It will not create an environment for the best possible interactive outcome. It may even invoke fear, pride or confusion and escalate their emotional and physical response unnecessarily, adding to your stress.

Much of emotional intelligence comes down to social awareness. It focuses on the ability to read other people, to be curious about their motivations and drivers and to consider what they are going through at the moment. Over time, this skill makes you an exceptional judge of character. You develop an understanding of their underlying influencers and motivations. You become difficult to offend as you build a firm understanding of who you are with strong self-control and other-person awareness. Other's opinions and viewpoints do not trigger you, which creates more open-mindedness along with a reasonably thick skin. This is exceptionally helpful to strengthen self-esteem. We live in a society where we tend to be more interested in other people's opinion of us than our own cultivated self-concept.

"We are not thinking machines.
We are feeling machines that think."
~ Antonio Damasio, Neuroscientist

CHAPTER 17

COMMUNICATION POWER TACTICS

Words are powerful and we choose to use them constructively with words of positive encouragement, or destructively using words of negativity and despair. Words can help, hinder or hurt relationships. The more we have control over what flows out of our mouths, the better our relationships will become.
~ Deirdre von Krauskopf

This chapter falls more in line with the context of established relationships and the tactical advantage we describe will build safety and security into your conflict conversations. Dr. Stephen Proges, a leading expert on the autonomic nervous system, states that we have an imperative for safety deeply wired into our minds and bodies. For great communication to occur our partner must feel safe to express themselves freely. Porges's Polyvagal Theory describes how our autonomic nervous system mediates safety, trust, and intimacy through a subsystem he calls the social engagement system. Our brain is continuously detecting through our senses whether we are in a situation that is safe, dangerous, or life-threatening. *"When our body and mind experience safety, our social engagement system enables us to collaborate, listen, empathize, and connect, as well as be creative, innovative, and bold in our thinking and ideas leading to improved relationships. Most couples are not dealing with life-threatening situations. Instead, they are navigating chronic disconnections with understanding each other, building tension, defensiveness, or irritability that signals danger to their senses, which ultimately takes a toll on their relationship."* [cxxxi]

Some of you will naturally have an open, safe and empathetic manner. Others will need to develop or re-develop these skills if you want great relationships at work, at home, in society. Like developing any habit or building any muscle, it takes practice, grace and more practice to perfect.

The greatest tactic you can develop in social awareness is to hone your intuition, meaning your ability to read your own emotions and to understand how you are affected by others. It is a fundamental survival skill. The open-loop limbic system describes the way others affect us. Our emotions can be altered by a person or groups emotional state. An excellent example of this is any championship sporting event where the crowds create a vibe of excitement and competitiveness. Another example would be a rally where groupthink can ignite and maintain united chanting, even turning ugly when protesters lose all sense of decency and decorum. We can also recognize this when someone walks into a room with a certain presence or attitude that impacts your state. Your conscious mind will pick up the change in milliseconds, calculating what change in the environment occurred and inputs a reaction to it based on your emotional history. When that infecting person enters the room, shifting the vibe and instigating the change, we tend to point to them as the issue. However, in this situation, you did not read their emotions, you read your emotional response to them. Stop/Drop/Roll can help here as you reflect, analyze and then consciously determine where your response came from, and whether it is serving you at the moment. Intuition is not reading them; it is reading you and assigning a reaction with the current knowledge you have unless you challenge it. Just using this shift in understanding you will notice how you allow your environment and the people in it to affect you. This self-awareness will significantly enhance your social awareness.

Now that you have a better understanding of you, it becomes easier to relate to others when they are coming at you from a less than ideal place. By maintaining self-control, listening with an empathetic framing and challenging your perceptions you are in a better position to manage the interactions and earn the right to influence.

The last aspect to consider is tactics to facilitate deepening conversations. If you ask psychologists and psychotherapists, they will say everything that is said is said for a reason. So, if somebody says something, not only is it technically on the table, it is intentionally on the table, even if subconsciously. There may be some exceptions, but this is generally a scientifically validated way to look at it. In addition to the words, the means of conveying the message have been offered from a body language, tone, pitch, pace and volume standpoint. If I ask, "How are you doing?" and you reply, "Fine," in a manner that raises my eyebrows, I have been offered the opportunity to say, "Well I heard the word 'fine,' but I'm not feeling that from you, would you like to talk?" The door to communication had been cracked, and if our rapport is good, you may choose to open up further.

The strategy is useful in pre-escalation when dealing with the public; however, it is absolutely gold when used in your personal relationships. You can wait for that simmering hint of discontent to become more overt, or you can choose to jump on the hint you were offered and tackle the emotion before it grows. When we consider these moments in a manner where we respect the invitation to dive deeper and use the moment to serve the relationship, we have learned the secrets of receptivity.

Think of every word, the person's body language and tonality as the tip of an iceberg. All of these are invitations to deepen an interaction. Be prepared when you take the next step; you want both of you to be able and willing to invest in the time that may come next. By diving deeper, we may find something that would be very valuable to our conversation or our overall relationship. It could resolve a meaningful objective or work towards a stronger rapport.

Our next master communicator tactic comes from a slightly subtle tell people tend to have. Imagine that every word is a door. Some doors are wide open, some are locked, and some are squeaky. Most doors are wide open, since almost everything spoken is said for a reason. Once it is on the table, it is fair play. Some words are like squeaky doors. This is when a subtle sound emits after a word and it draws out a little. Let's say you ask your significant other to go to a movie and mention the one you want to see. They reply, "I guessssss, if youuu want to." This is when someone puts something on the table, but they are not fully comfortable with it. They are seeking safety and comfort before they trust enough to open up. They are putting feelers out to see if you will treat their next words with respect. We can say, "I sensed a little more than what you said there, would you help me understand what you hinted at?" Depending the rapport between us and their feeling of safety, you may hear, "Okay, well the truth is…" and they begin to open up that they hate that type of movie.

Because we are focusing on public safety fields, there is truth to the perception that many of us have a tendency to come on strong. Those who work in fields of authority over people, who are regularly influencing the course of action others must take, are more accustomed to getting through doors. Therefore, you may push on a locked door. You might come on too strong, too soon, and do so in a way that causes the other person to be uncomfortable. It is possible that you may lose an opportunity to build instant rapport or to deepen a relationship.

This may also impact those relationships that help you get your job done, the support and administrative personnel who serve your needs behind the scenes. They may be hesitant to share an insight or ask questions that would be helpful because they are not comfortable with your approach, your questioning or your brisk manner. There is an opportunity to discover this when people regularly use squeaky doors with you; they are testing your ability to hear their truth. Some of us come on too strong and some of us do not come on strong enough, and some are comfortable enough to probe deeper when confronted with an open door or squeaky door. We suggest you may wish to adjust as appropriate. You want to master your skills at listening to whether the door is open, squeaky or closed. If you are not comfortable with this, you may hesitate and not push on that door, missing out on valuable insights. Most often people appreciate someone deepening the conversation, probing and showing genuine interest in the interaction. If you notice squeaky doors are a pattern with a particular individual, that is a sign there is some distrust with how you handle their truth, or they lack comfort and security in sharing deeper meaning with you. It is in your hands to adjust your approach and work to build your safe strength in that relationship.

There are those few occasions when the door is locked, and individuals do not want to share anything more. It may be a one-time thing. They may have told you everything that they want to tell you. They may have been triggered and want to pull back and lock their vault. In that case we want to be respectful. Closed doors are most often a result of wrong time, wrong place or uncertainty in a person's ability to articulate their truth to you.

Questions are powerful because they engage our subconscious mind, not only for the response but in seeking or imagining things related to that question. The stimulus of a question demands a response, some may hold back their answer, but the brain has already moved to neocortex to review possible responses and decide how they want to proceed. When brain is stimulated with a question it can force us to order or list in a logical fashion to properly respond which is helpful when wanting to move someone from an overly emotional place to one where they are using rational and logical thinking. How we ask is equally important. When the question triggers another's motivation to find an answer then it is a positive outcome. However, if fear about the response is triggered, we may heighten the emotions in another which makes it more challenging to gain the objective of our questions.

Therefore, we want to ensure we have built rapport, are engaged in active listening and using inquisitive body language to provoke a motivated stimulus and response and avoid a fight or flight fear centered response. One of the ways we can do this is to confuse the brain slightly to lower its defenses. Here are a few power questioning tactics that will aid deepening a conversation. These can be a little dangerous if you are not in rapport, so that should always be your starting point. They also can be considered manipulative and controlling without good intention. If used inappropriately you will be caught in time; your body language, resonance, tone, pitch, and volume will not be congruent. When you are caught, you will have violated the authenticity factor which is the most repulsive thing you can do in communication, and the other person will shut down and it will affect the relationship. We strongly suggest that you only use these questioning techniques when appropriate, which is when you are genuinely in rapport and you are genuinely interested.

1. "How do you mean?"

This has been called by workshop participants for many, many years the ultimate truth serum. They say, "Once I ask that question people just open up to me; they tell me what they haven't told me before." It is grammatically flawed so there are some English majors likely flinching right now. It is supposed to be, "What do you mean?" but by changing to the odd-sounding "How do you mean?" you tend to bypass the critical factor.

Techniques to bypass the critical factor are used in psychology and hypnotic inductions. It is the part of the brain that provides a barrier between the conscious and subconscious mind. Neuroscience identifies the location of the critical factor in the anterior cingulate gyrus, starting at the front of the brain under the forehead and above the eyes. It runs along the corpus callosum, which separates the two hemispheres of the brain It is the valley connecting the two sides that you see when looking at a brain picture. The accepted theory is that all information gets passed through this region during the process of receiving communication. There are ways to bypass the critical factor to gain access to the subconscious. The easiest is to spark the imagination (which is why "I'm curious" works well, our subconscious likes solving for unknowns). Our imagination and creativity reside in the subconscious, so it engages a bypass quickly. In therapy, the technique called revivification is used. Revivification is the act of recalling a memory. When we remember something, we must re-experience it at a certain level by accessing our long-term memory and visualization in our hippocampus. Shock, momentary confusion or surprise can also be effective, as can abrupt physical movements that affect the loss of equilibrium. They are all techniques used in hypnosis and therapy.

Your curiosity is awakened by the odd choice of wording in the question "How do you mean?" It makes the brain open up. When we hear a squeaky door, or someone admits they are uncomfortable with a topic and you say, "How do you mean?" The brain is confused and more likely to open up and share a truth or reveal why they are uncomfortable or hesitant to talk about a topic. There's something about this question that just encourages a person to open up. There is another shorter version of the same concept and this is saying, "How so?" You can use them in conjunction when you are really trying to dive deeper into the conversation. As an example:

THEM:	I'm not really comfortable to talk about that.
YOU:	How do you mean?
THEM:	Ummm, last time we talked about this your face was unhappy looking.
YOU:	How so?
THEM:	Well, it was scrunched up and you rolled your eyes, I don't think you are receptive to my needs in this.
YOU:	How do you mean?
THEM:	Well, ummm when we ... and the story pours out.

At times you need to provoke the person to continue peeling the onion for themselves by guiding the conversation and remaining fully engaged while fully detached. Keep your hands open and your body language receptive. Their subconscious will be alert to your physiology changing and showing judgement. The truth generally comes out three or four layers deep, so continue asking good questions, probing when necessary to move towards the core issue or core concern.

2. Last Word

The next technique is the psychological use of repeating the last word or few words that the person said. This is also common in interrogation and professional interviewing. When repeating only the last word(s) you invite the other person to explain further. In therapy it is called Parroting. There are dual goals with this technique. First, you ensure you heard what was said correctly, and second, you encourage your counterpart to expand or clarify their thoughts. It is important not to go too far with parroting. Only repeat the last word or a few words over an entire sentence. It is also important to note that too much of this technique can become annoying and feel manipulative in excess. When used correctly, parroting may encourage your counterpart to talk through varying aspects of an issue and potentially even come to their own logical conclusion.

You can add this into your tactical pattern of questioning to move towards your objective. You can see how these techniques will be able to help the other person feel heard because you're asking them to help you understand where they are coming from. As they are peeling their onion and revealing their thoughts, feelings and needs with more clarity, they feel heard, understood, accepted and respected, and often we get to the core issue in minutes without the added drama.

This is how to master receptivity. We suggest you share this with those closest to you and practice on each other to remove any awkwardness or discomfort. We are not suggesting you use it as a game or a trick but make it a part of your natural curiosity when engaging another human in conversation. In time you will find you use these questioning techniques unconsciously; they will surface naturally when the time is right to deepen a conversation, especially a difficult one. The only thing that changes is the unique variation of questions you will use based on the interaction and objective of the moment.

3. Most

Lastly, we want to reiterate that asking information seeking questions will engage the rational mind. When the rational mind has to take over, the emotional mind must step aside. When you add the word most, or any kind of ranking word, most, least, biggest, tallest, last whatever, then the person's subconscious feeds every possible answer that could be on the list and then the conscious mind will rank them until they come up with the answer.

If you have somebody ranting and raving then after establishing some basic rapport, being mindful of your physiology and active listening for a bit interject a "most" question.

- "What do you hate most about this situation?"
- "Of all the frustrations you mentioned, which one irritates you the most?"
- "You sound really unhappy right now; I want to understand so tell me which issue is the most important to deal with first?"

They might say, "My girlfriend broke my TV set in the fight," and to come up with that answer, they have to think about everything they hated about the whole fight and rank them. By the time that is done, they are much more rational, the emotions have subsided somewhat, and you can begin to use more tactics to move them towards your objective which is the best possible solution for all involved.

Depending on how emotional someone is, you may need to repeat these tactics several times to move them into a consistently rational state. Others will have so much trauma and emotion build up that they will not be capable of being moved to a rational state. You will only achieve short spurts of logic-based conversation.

CHAPTER 18

EMOTIONAL INTELLIGENCE CONTROL

You will never have a greater or lesser dominion than that over yourself.
~ Leonardo da Vinci

Our brains are intensely complex machines processing billions of bits of data simultaneously. Our brains do not come with an owner's manual and no two are the same. These truths can cause some issues over the course of a lifetime as command and control is a learned experience unique to every single person. Understanding some basic mechanics can go a long way to avoiding challenges along the way. The Reticular Activating System (RAS) is nerve bundles in our brainstem, the reptilian part of the brain. It controls our sleep/wake cycle and has the onerous job of filtering every single thing we see, hear, smell, touch, taste, think and intuit, and correlating these against every known experience and emotion we have in our hippocampus, and deciding what gets popped into the subconscious directly and what gets elevated to our conscious thought. Consider that a moment, every single input, whether direct or indirect, the RAS goes through that process in microseconds and decide if something is a threat, important or useful to us.

Ever buy a new car and then suddenly you see your car everywhere? Ever been in deep conversation in a loud environment when someone calls your name and you instantly turn your head? Ever hear a new phrase suddenly it is popping up everywhere you look and listen? The RAS knows what's important to you and filters incoming stimuli to bring these new interests to the top of the mind. Whatever it is has not actually changed, just your attention to it has. Like adding a filter to a spreadsheet, your RAS has now re-prioritized what it thinks you want to know about.

Conversely, the RAS is not programmed with your best intentions in mind. If you are craving a cheeseburger it will highlight every burger joint you pass, even if you are recovering from a triple bypass. Without us taking some control on what filters WE deem important, it runs amok, trying to make us happy. It is constantly seeking ways to validate your beliefs. If you think people are horrible, it will prioritize all the negative news, highlight stupid people moments and completely toss the good deed you observed and the feel-good news story you skimmed, tossing it to the deep subconscious as unimportant. When you think you are inept and clumsy, it will gladly find things to fumble over to help you validate that important thought you had.

Your beliefs, perceptions, biases and self-concept all provide filters to the RAS to create a reality that validates it for you. It will influence your actions and attention and create a self-fulfilling prophecy. The more you control the parameters to prioritize your filters, the more you will gain opportunities, meet people and gain information that moves you towards you desired objectives. This management of the RAS will go a long way to helping you tame the subconscious from sending you outdated and unhelpful emotions. Let's dig into where it can also be useful for emotional intelligence.

SELF MANAGEMENT

Daniel Goleman, in his book, Emotional Intelligence,[cxxxii] it states, "Self-management is handling our emotions so that they facilitate rather than interfere; delaying gratification to pursue goals; recovering well from emotional distress; deploying our deepest preferences to take the initiative, improve and persevere. Some aspects are:

1. Self-control
2. Trustworthiness
3. Conscientiousness
4. Adaptability
5. Achievement orientation
6. Initiative"

Your strength of self-control can be probed by answering the questions:

- Am I a victim of how I feel?
- Am I a victim of my tendencies? Temptations? Strengths and weaknesses?

Questioning why we respond the way we do allows an inner reflection and understanding that you can choose how you feel about something. You can choose to build resistance to your temptations. You can choose to build on your strengths and take measures to improve your weaknesses. Will reading this once or taking our class magically change you overnight? No, it will not, but you have the tactics to now build these skills with practice.

An illustration of this comes from Geoffrey Tumlin, author of Stop Talking, Start Communicating.[cxxxiii] He describes the limbic system brain in a modern communications context. *"Long ago, our Neanderthal ancestors needed a quick-thinking, reflexive brain to navigate a world filled with saber-toothed tigers and club-swinging neighbors, and much of that brain is still with us. But over time, a more modern brain evolved as well, which was capable of reasoning, reflection, and restraint. The Neanderthal and modern parts of our brains often operate in tension. When something triggers a negative emotion, the*

Neanderthal part prefers to club the source of the emotional trigger first and ask questions later, while the modern part suggests that perhaps we should think things through before taking a swing.

When a gratifying impulse or urge presents itself—like an urge to say something sarcastic or insulting—our Neanderthal brain will lunge for it, while our modern brain will calculate whether resisting the feeling might be prudent. Impulsive and unfiltered communication usually costs our relationships dearly. Saying what we want, when we want isn't modern at all—it's Neanderthal. It's ironic that our modern devices facilitate the kind of communication that bypasses our modern, reflective brains. Quick communication pushes the act-first, think-later buttons of our Neanderthal brain, but it was the ability to do the exact opposite that helped us out of the cave in the first place. Restraint—the ability to not say something, even when you really want to—is what distinguishes civilized communication from Neanderthal communication. Restraint also safeguards a thin but vital blanket of civility and politeness that protects most human interactions."

Another aspect of emotionally intelligent people is a willingness and acceptance to embrace change. This mindset is where your adaptability, flexibility and situational awareness fall in. The only constant *is* change! Our mental fitness is stronger when we can understand and embrace this. As a certified Change Management Expert, I often ask in workshops, *"What are some of the reasons you do not like … the particular change we are discussing?"* Inevitably, the highest response comes back as lack of control over the change. However, you do have control, a lot of control over how you prepare and embrace the change.

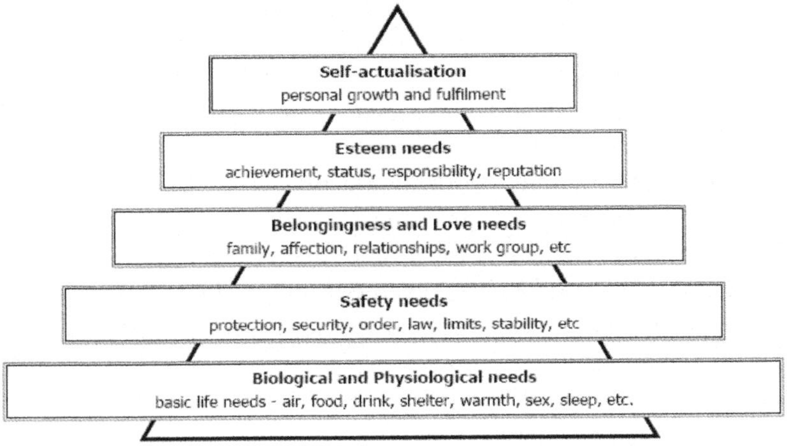

cxxxiv

It is very human to want to control your environment and outcomes. Psychologist Abraham Maslow's hierarchy of needs pyramid identifies our most basic needs in order of priority. We can move up and down this pyramid based on our current life status.

The foundational needs are the physiological ones; these are biological requirements for human survival, including; air, water, food, shelter, health, reproduction and sleep. If these needs are not satisfied, the human body and mind cannot function optimally. All the other needs lessen in importance until these basic needs are met. Safety comes next with a motivation to seek protection from the elements, life stability, law, civil order, security, and some may add freedom from fear.

Love and belonging feed into our being a social species with a natural want to be part of a community. These are our social connections and feelings of belonging. This desire for interpersonal relationships motivates behavior including familial, intimate, friendships, building trust and acceptance and the giving and receiving of affection. When someone grows up in an abusive or dysfunctional home, this is where you will see the draw towards gang affiliation, it becomes a surrogate family. It also influences an attraction towards the brotherhood and sisterhood within paramilitary organizations.

Our esteem needs are broken down by Maslow into two categories: Esteem for oneself (self-love, dignity, achievement, mastery, independence) and Desire for reputation or respect from others (popularity, status, prestige). Maslow wrote that the desire for reputation or respect in children and adolescents overshadows real self-love, dignity or even self-esteem. That overpowering mindset is an important fact for public safety professionals to understand when communicating with youth. Psychologically when you show that open, respectful manner, it will gain further headway than with an authoritative approach. Maslow wrote that the desire for reputation or respect in children and adolescents overshadows real self-love, dignity or even self-esteem. That overpowering mindset is an important fact for public safety professionals to understand when communicating with youth. Psychologically when you show that open, respectful manner, it will gain further headway than with an authoritative approach. Maslow wrote that the desire for reputation or respect in children and adolescents overshadows real self-love, dignity or even self-esteem. That overpowering mindset is an important fact for public safety professionals to understand when communicating with youth. Psychologically when you show that open, respectful manner, it will gain further headway than with an authoritative approach.

Lastly, Self-Actualization, is the desire to be all you can be. It is often developed with maturity when one strives to realize their full potential, seeks self-fulfillment and personal growth experiences. This is the stage we often work towards perfecting the process of living and enjoying the moment.

Maslow teaches that although generally pictured in a pyramid to show what needs to come first, it is not a rigid model. We all have known of the child prodigy in sports, music, arts, and other expertise areas. Those kids that seek their championship level from a very young age and who often bypass a need to be part of a group in order to chase their passion. This insight helps us to understand where most humans need to exert control in their lives. When it is not happening, they may become more emotionalized and easily triggered when faced with more control being taken from them. Any hit to a person's hierarchy of needs can set them off, especially when in front of peers. This is also common with anyone experiencing a loss or perceived loss of love through accident or domestic situations. Knowing these triggers allows you to maintain self-control and a calm, safe, confident presence.

For personal development, it is also beneficial to understand our own need for control. Psychologists share that our sense of control comes from two sources. The first is an internal locus of control, which is the belief that our thinking and personal actions have the power to impact and change any given situation. This is an empowering perspective. The second is an external locus of control, which is the belief that we are at the mercy of others and external forces have control over us. This is the "it is what it is" mindset versus. the more empowering, "it is what you make it" perspective. Whichever it is, that thought process is deeply ingrained and influences our self-esteem, our self-control and our well-being. Those with internal locus of control are more apt to be confident, be adaptable, have lower levels of stress, and be healthier, finding it easier to maintain focus on self and what can be controlled.

SELF-DISCIPLINE

Like a muscle, these emotional intelligence tactics take time and grace to develop. This is where self-discipline comes in. Self-discipline is the ability to give yourself a command and to obey it. I first heard the "*Captain your Ship*" speech from Ret. State Senator, Brain Nieves[cxxxv] with whom I have spoken on tour and facilitated trainings several times. He shares with audiences the psychology of self-discipline when it comes to managing our mind and in a leadership capacity. Visualize your brain as a ship (Starship Enterprise or Pirate ship, you choose). We know a ship has a captain and there is a crew. A captain's job is to give orders, and the crew's responsibility is to follow them.

The captain is our conscious brain, and the crew is our subconscious brain. When our emotional intelligence is low, we let the crew members run our ship. They take control and feed our conscious with whatever memories, emotions, and reactions they feel relevant based on the RAS input of priority, including inputs like that time on the playground in elementary school where you got bullied. It does this without strategic thought, without thinking how it will help or harm us currently as we navigate through life. These minions are often controlling our reactions. If you have watched any minion movies, that should terrify you a little. Directing the priority to both our subconscious and RAS systems builds a strong self-directed emotional intelligence that improves our intentionality and outcomes in life.

Self-discipline is leading your thinking process using the captain of your ship. You give the orders to yourself after taking into consideration the inputs from your most valued crew members. Then feeding the orders back down to the crew to follow. In our brain, that means we do not act without consideration to our rational and reasonable neocortex. Are we always going to be able to do that? Likely not. Sometimes the crew will throw so much information at you that you will have analysis paralysis and not be able to make a decision. Other times you may feel weak, or so tired that you let a secondary crew take control and give rash, impulsive and emotive commands that don't serve your navigational goals. Sometimes you are simply good with having a glorious battle, even if you lose. Only you, as captain, can choose to reflect on those situations where the crew took charge and take a corrective course to get you back on track. A more advanced and mindful exploration of this concept is rooted in the Laws of Attraction.

SELF-ESTEEM

Self-esteem is a buzzword of the self-help industry, and for good reason If we are not well adjusted with our inner selves, it impacts our relationships and interactions. When we have low self-regard, it may lead to depression, or inhibit our potential. Some psychology articles will even state that low self-esteem can raise the tolerance of emotionally and physically abusive relationships, for both men and women. Conversely, excessive self-regard feeds into the mindset of entitlement, and may lead to narcissistic tendencies. Either way, when our self-esteem is not balanced, it can influence the ability to learn from failures.

Think of the bamboo tree with its extensive root system. Our root system feeds our wellness and stability, so we want to grow it deep and wide to provide us great stability in times of stress. Imagine that our bamboo tree has one large, thicker and more powerful root than the others and call it your self-esteem. It is at the core of your emotional awareness and peace. It feeds your reactivity or nonreactivity and influences your ability to take something seriously, but not personally, even when insulted. Ideally, we want to see that insult as a cry for attention. We want our wellness to be so solid that we can plainly see that this is a hurt person lashing out and hoping you will be triggered into their familiar scripted exchange that soothes their hurt by bringing you down with them. You want to see them as that angry little child taking a swing at you while you remain safe, secure and balanced, knowing your communication strength. Often, we allow ourselves to remain part of a group that does not treat us well because we know no different. Only we can choose to break free of what pulls us down. "The Crab Story" illustrates this,

"On one sunny afternoon, a man was walking along the beach and saw another man fishing in the surf with a bait bucket beside him. As he drew closer, he saw that the bait bucket had no lid and had live crabs inside. "Why don't you cover your bait-bucket, so the crabs won't escape?" he asked. "You don't understand." the man replied, "If there is one crab in the bucket it would surely crawl out very quickly. However, when there are many crabs in the bucket, if one tries to crawl up the side, the others will grab hold of it and pull it back down so that it will share the same fate as the rest of them."

When we do not feel compelled to fight back from a place of hurt and weakness, we can communicate better. When someone lashes out at us, especially those we are close to, we can feel sad for them instead of offended. We have the option to change the usual defensive based retort by saying; "I am sorry you feel that way, what was it specifically that upset you? Or, "it seems I have offended you, that wasn't my intent, what can we do about this." At that point, you have now opened the door for a different ending and invited the other person to communicate any real issues that are impacting them. The objective is an effective relationship or communication exchange. Healthy self-esteem allows us to move away from a victim or survival mindset.

Lastly, I will touch on how we can allow others to create our self-esteem. When we give the power to an external locus of control, we may allow our RAS to feed into the inputs we hear. If you are regularly told you are sloppy, clumsy, disheveled and rude, then question where that identity came from and challenge whether you want the initial instigator to still control your self-esteem. I witnessed this firsthand with someone I cared for. I watched close friends and family put him down when all he needed to do was take control and change the perception, starting with his own belief in himself. Anyone can change how they dress, act and present in the world. That is self-projection, it would only take a short time to prove those long-ingrained beliefs as ridiculous.

There is confusion for some in understanding about the distinctions and the offshoots of self-esteem. Let's break it down.

- Self-esteem is how I feel about me.
- Self-image is how I see myself.
- Self-projection is the image that we project or convey to others.
- Self-ideal is the person you perceive you should be or could be if you were the best version of yourself, that is our self-ideal. How we see our potential.

With that clarity, we will come back to self-esteem as it is the fundamental one. As discussed in our agitated cup example, how you feel about yourself is what comes out of you. It is the core of your presence in every single moment and every single interaction. When someone is acting out or reacting, our self-esteem asks us, "Am I threatened or not?" Our RAS triggers inputs as threatening more easily when we are over stressed or not feeling well, recognizing we are in a weakened state.

When our self-esteem is healthy, we are more confident and kinder within ourselves. If someone we value, respect or care for doesn't like something we do, we don't put the same weight on their disapproval as we do when we have low self-esteem or are highly stressed. When the words we hear become the last straw, it is because we are at an emotional low and are more sensitive. Do you see the distinction? When we are well, with good self-esteem intact, others don't have the same influence. Their opinion is just that, an opinion. Also, there isn't the same threat of loss to our family or social bonds. It is about them not liking the situation, behavior or that thing done to them. Their perception does not have the power to do the same level of damage to how you feel about yourself, it is merely an opinion and can perhaps be considered a valid point. The danger is when we are at an emotional low, and we place too much value on someone else's opinion or their insult. It becomes much larger and more hurtful and damaging than it needs to be.

The most effective way to change low self-esteem is to improve our belief system. Understanding what we are good at, what we are okay at and what we need to develop gives us the realistic perspective that most of us are not great at everything, and that's okay. We want to grow what we ARE good at and build upon what is weaker if that is important to us. At times, it also means accepting some areas require more effort than you have to give so it can move to a lower priority, as long as it is not impacting your wellness and meaningful relationships. If you have no idea where to begin, you may ask the people you care for the most to help you develop a list of your greatest traits, and the ones you could focus more on, and BELIEVE them. Other self-esteem boosters are:

- Don't judge yourself against anyone but yourself.
- Keep your word with yourself.
- Honor yourself like you would someone else you care for deeply.
- Stop being your own worst judge, ask yourself "what can I learn from this" instead.

- Catch yourself in the act of the person you wish you were. Whenever you see your ideal self-projection make a big deal of it internally. Recognize and savor what that looks like, feels like and lock it in.

- Be more of a doer than a talker, we can often say what we think our inner self or others want to hear but when our actions do not match our words, it has a damaging impact to our inherent self-value and our relationships.

- Nourish your body, making healthy choices cognitively and then recognizing and thanking yourself in the act of treating yourself with respect. "Garbage in, garbage out" is a truth we like to ignore.
- Don't own your imperfections, you may have made a mess, but it does not mean you label yourself a pig. There's a difference between guilt and shame. Guilt is I feel bad about what I did; shame is I feel bad about who I am. Guilt may be helpful if it propels you to change poor behavior. Ongoing shame is merely destructive. Recognize what you did and make a commitment to yourself to choose differently in the future, forgive yourself and move forward.

- Start with little wins. Behavior scientists have proven that the grades of children that make their beds are consistently and dramatically higher than kids who don't make their own bed. At the beginning of their day, the child knows that bed looks better now because they accomplished the task. The first task of the day is out of the way, and the brain is now primed for task-oriented accomplishments. They built up their self-esteem with that small little discipline.

    - "I made my bed."
        - "I feel good."
            - "I can make other things happen too."

If you are thinking, "how can such a small thing have a big impact on my self-esteem?" Let's view it from the perspective of one of the toughest men on earth. Admiral William H. McRaven while Commander, United States Special Operations Command author of; Make Your Bed: Little Things That Can Change Your Life... and Maybe the World where he shares the ten life lessons of US Navy basic SEAL Training, the first being;

"Lesson #1: If you make your bed in the morning you have accomplished the first task of the day. It will give you a small sense of pride, and it will encourage you to do another task, and another, and another. And by the end of the day, that one task completed will have led to many tasks being completed over the course of the day. Making your bed will also reinforce in life that it's the little things that matter. If you can't do the little things right, you'll never be able to do

the big things right. And if by chance you have a miserable day, you will come home to a bed that is made. That you made it and it will give you encouragement that tomorrow will be better. So, if you want to change the world, start off with making your bed."[cxxxvi]

Lastly, many articles, journals, books and programs share these next words of wisdom. One of the greatest gifts you can give to your inner self is to forgive yourself and others. Grace and forgiveness restore our humanity and remove the ugly cloud swirling around inside our hippocampus (memory storage) waiting for the moment it can hurl the hurt, anger, and grief into our thinking system. It serves no purpose but to continue to hurt you! Forgiveness does not mean you need to become best friends with someone who hurt you, only that you don't allow them to keep hurting you through your recurring memories. This framing helps us manage interactions with people who do hurtful things, as the saying goes "love the sinner, hate the sin." Do not paint the whole person with a particular behavior or action, instead question what made them act that way. It allows your heart to heal and to accept that some people's actions may not be worthy of your attention and thoughts anymore.

If we can separate the activity from the individual, we can keep an appropriate intensity in a conversation without making it personal. Think about it in a context of speaking to a child. Instead of saying "you are a bad person," replace it with, "who you are is far too great for that kind of behavior." Alternatively, "that behavior is unbecoming for whom I know you to be," or, "what happened to you that this was the choice you made?" are also appropriate ways to address undesired behavior. Consider this: The scent of the rose lingers on the one who casts it. The more compliments you throw, the more compliments stick on you. Be the person who builds up others and forgives, restores and encourages people and you will find it easier to turn the same grace on yourself.

At our workshops, attendees often ask how to manage the people closest to them who are negative and destructive. We ask them to visualize a roundtable with marbles circling in larger and larger circles. When you keep adding positive people and talking about positive moments to the middle, those good thoughts will slowly push the negative away from you. Sooner than later you will begin to notice the more negative influences in your life simple fade away and drop off the edges. Those filled with anger and hate do not want to be around their positive counterparts; they tend to leave and distance themselves on their own. It aids your self-esteem by maintaining the ideology that you are not going to be pulled into someone else's storm, instead, you will pull them into your peace. As Will Smith encourages, *"Stop letting people who do so little for you control so much of your mind, feelings and emotions."*

Emotional Intelligence and Resilience

To build you skills we have added this app link. "The skills and storylines are based on current psychology using psycho-education, elements of Cognitive Behavioral Therapy, also called CBT, Positive Psychology, EQ, gamification and AI to take you on an adventure that supersedes the game. You will find yourself equipped with emotional intelligence skills that will get you ahead in all your relationships. eQuoo was successfully tested in a 5-week 3-arm RCT (randomized controlled trial) using the mental health and wellbeing metrics 1) resilience, 2) personal development, 3) interpersonal relationship skills and 4) anxiety proving that playing a level a week supercharges your mental well-being – don't trust just us, trust the science! eQuoo is a product of PsycApps Limited.

Link to Download the app: ***https://equoogame.app.link/EQWebsite***

CHAPTER 19

PERSONALITY AND EGO STATES

Every person has three personalities, that which we exhibit,
that which he has and that which he thinks he has.
~ Unknown

Most of us are aware there are different personality profiling programs we can use for career and self-development, team building or simply understanding people better. There are easy to understand programs, like the birds in D.O.P.E. (Dove, Owl, Peacock, Eagle), cartoon characters, or even a Poker style assessment. Deeper meaning and interactive insight come from longer more in-depth programs like Myers-Briggs and DISC assessments. Personality testing can be helpful in understanding your strengths, weaknesses and communication styles. Usually, unless you are in a larger company that uses one of these tools for team and leadership development, many of us are not aware of the dynamics of our base personalities in interactions. Situational Analysis and Transactional Analysis take this psychology a step further by delving into what happens when our emotions are triggered. Emotions contain inputs from our subconscious which are routed up to our conscious reactions from events as early as birth and some say even in utero. This is important because someone's basic personality may change dramatically when they become emotionalized. Their reactions are then influenced not only by nature (basic personality), but with the added aspects of the environment they were nurtured in. In addition to these two inputs, any trauma associated with their early years or as they develop will influence that emotionalized reaction.

We will provide a quick introduction into personality assessments before taking a deeper dive into Ego States. This will provide you the difference between basic personality profiling and the emotionalized states you will more often deal with as public safety professionals. For those who have never explored any of this, most personality assessment will categorize you into one of four basic groups:

- Bold, outgoing, and a natural leader.
- Shy, quiet and prone to introspection.
- Analytical and drawn to facts and logic.
- Attention-seeking, outgoing and a little flamboyant.

Each general personality type has typical strengths and weaknesses. Each will have a preferred way to receive information based on their unique style. How we communicate with each other can be impacted by understanding how we best receive information and sharing your general personality type with those who regularly communicate with you can aid them in their approach to you. It also helps us discover and relate information in a manner that other styles will best receive to gain our interactive objective.

Our Ego States go a little deeper. They are formed in the first couple of years and are heavily influenced by the environment we are exposed to. These egoic states are where our natural personalities lean when emotions are triggered. It is this cross section of nature and nurture that truly defines how we act and react in the world. We are often not aware of why some triggers instigate higher reactions than others and the science behind this explains the reason why. Therefore, understanding personalities is helpful but it only takes us so far when avoiding escalation or wanting to de-escalate someone. As public safety professionals, you are often dealing with people in a heightened emotionalized state. Therefore, we will spend the majority of our teaching on understanding, managing and using tactics to avoid escalation of a person's Ego State. This is key in our pre-escalation strategy.

EGO STATES

Many psychological and sociological theories attempt to explain the complexities of human behavior. Dr. Eric Berne[cxxxvii] (Ret. Major), a Canadian who immigrated to America, finished his education and started working at Yale University. After becoming a psychiatrist, he also served in the US Medical Corps Unit during WWII. In 1958 he introduced a new psychotherapeutic approach that broke behavior reactions into Ego States and named it Structural Analysis which detailed how our Ego States develop. Later his work included Transactional Analysis in Psychotherapy, which is how our Ego States interact. He further added to his work with Games People Play and Life Scripts. These identify how we default to specific patterns of communication, based on our life experiences and internal thinking. Two prominent Ph.D. students expanded on his therapeutic approach by identifying Drama Triangles [cxxxviii](Dr. Stephen Karpman) and I'm OK, You're Okay[cxxxix] (Dr. Thomas Harris). Their work further simplified, expanded on, and popularized Berne's work at a non-therapist level.

Before Berne's work, the most frequently cited and known psychotherapeutic theory was the work of Sigmund Freud in the early Twentieth Century. Freud theorized that personality consisted of three components working together to create our complex behaviors and reactions. They were called the Id, the Ego, and the Superego. Freud believed that all three aspects were required for us to be mentally well and stable. Freud stated the following:

- The Id comprises the irrational and emotional part of the mind,

- The Ego comprises the rational part of the mind, and
- The Superego comprises the moral part of the mind. Culturally developed from parental and societal values and norms.

Dr. Eric Berne's theories began with building blocks and investigated how our childhood impacts our current personality and emotional reactions. From his findings, he created Transactional Analysis. His work focuses on the present state of our behavior and actions. The here and now versus only analyzing one's childhood like Freud and others more traditional psychoanalysts. He began to develop his work by observing patients where he noted clear behavioral changes in their tonality, gesturing, facial and body expressions and even how they structure their sentences at changing intervals. He found it intriguing that his patients seemed to be influenced by different personality states based on the direction of the conversation. He later identified these as Parent, Child, and Adult "Ego States." Berne taught that these are unconscious drives or motivators fed by our emotional state in any particular moment in time. More importantly, we have the capability of recognizing and altering our conscious choice of reaction with training. His student, Dr. Karpman, shares in an article entitled "Intimacy Analysis Today,"

"Berne's main focus was that the goal of Transactional Analysis treatment was to 'cure patients faster' by using measurable contracts and new theory. Trimmed to the basics by using 'Occam's Razor,' (the law of parsimony, the problem-solving principle that states the simplest solution tends to be the correct one,) written in layperson's language for easier understanding.

However, perhaps Freud's greatest contribution (and the one that influenced Berne) was the fact that the human personality is multi-faceted. Regardless of the classification or name given to a particular area of personality (id, ego, superego) each individual possesses factions that frequently collide with each other. Moreover, it is these collisions and interactions between these personality factions that manifest themselves as an individual's thoughts, feelings, and behaviors."[cxl]

Using his technique to observe communication cues will help public safety professionals identify which Ego State is dominating in your communications. This allows better problem identification and also enables you to manage the interaction wisely and influence the best possible outcome. We will learn to come from an adult state that does not get sucked into the emotional dominance of your own default ego driven state. This aspect of self-awareness and interactive management is what Berne called Transactional Analysis. These intellectual insights provide you power and influence in how you relate to others with your communications. Berne's work can be broken down into four areas:

1. Structural Analysis: Individual Ego States

- The personality and emotional reactive identity which provides a perspective from which to explain thinking, feeling, and behaving. They are labeled Parent, Adult, and Child Ego States.

- Through this process, we can study personality by observing here-and-now indicators such as the person's voice, gestures, and vocabulary. These readily observable criteria provide a quick insight to infer a person's history and for predicting future reactions.

2. Transactional Analysis: Interactive communication styles and social behavior

- The communication that occurs in social interactions whether verbal or non-verbal, as well as common and expected and uncommon or unexpected exchanges between Ego States. Psychologically Berne called these exchanges "strokes."

- This knowledge allows us to see patterns in communication exchanges and the ability to stop, start or change our communicative approach to gain better results in our interaction objective.

3. Game Analysis: The psychological games people play

- The learned behavior patterns that one can recognize from predictable outcomes. The same arguments that occur year after year at a family event is a good example.

- Understanding the games played by those closest to us and with others trying to suck us into a particular communication exchange allows us to stop, listen, think and respond in a way that improves our communication outcomes. This takes time to master as games and scripts are quite ingrained in us.

4. Script Analysis: A complex set of transactions people act out compulsively

- The notion that everybody has a script or life plan which determines their actions and behavior choices. Analyzing our internal scripts moves primarily unconscious motivations into our conscious awareness so we can decide if they continue to serve our well-being and relationships, or not.

- This area gets more into the therapeutic area of practice. However, understanding the basics can help us identify unhealthy patterns of communication and relationships that do not serve our mental wellness or personal growth.

Freud and other researchers have stated that the human brain records memories like a tape recorder. Psychologists currently have the perspective that memory is not reproductive but reconstructive, meaning it does not mirror exactly what we experienced but is often a recollection of events influenced by our own beliefs, needs, biases, and emotions. This is why two people at the same scene can recall the event differently. Our memory is more accurately described as "an ever-changing mechanism with an amazing ability to create morphing narratives of our past and present experiences. A fact critical to our wellness and interactive success is our memory's imprint the emotion caused by those memories. That feeling is what is recalled from the subconscious whenever we are triggered.

Later in life, something happens and the subconscious feeds our conscious this emotional imprint as a factual response to our current reactive state. Often those old emotional memories were created at a time in childhood when you did not have the power or control to change the impact of the moment that left an emotional wound. When someone triggers a similar emotion, your reaction is layered with the current moment along with that imprinted "feeling" that was fed to your conscious action, all within milliseconds.

Typically, we are not trained to review these emotional reactions to question and determine whether they serve us well in the present day or not. This is an important consideration when analyzing why certain verbal and non-verbal communications trigger us. It also gives us insight as to why trauma can become so destructive when replayed in our brains. The hippocampus brings all that emotion front and center when we think about stress or emotional impact of that traumatic moment.

Lastly, all the research on this subject explains why we seem to have the same arguments with the same people or type of people over and over again. This knowledge allows us a tactical advantage in communications. We may not be able to control our every emotional response, but we can at least revisit it and analyze why we reacted in a certain way. We can grow our emotional intelligence by delving into whether triggered reactions serve or hinder our mental fitness. From this point, we can begin controlled measures using the tactics we share in this book to change what does not aid our communication objectives in future interactions. You will find that once you have some insight on your own life script, you will view your interactions with others differently.

Our behavioral and communication styles consist of three Ego States; the Parent (P), the Adult (A) and the Child (C). These states are further split into sub-categories called the Nurturing Parent and the Critical Parent. The Adult State is not split. Then we have the Natural Child, or Free Child as it is sometimes called, and the Adaptive Child. Adaptive grows from our young childhood influences as we learn to appease or to challenge the adults that have influence and control over us.

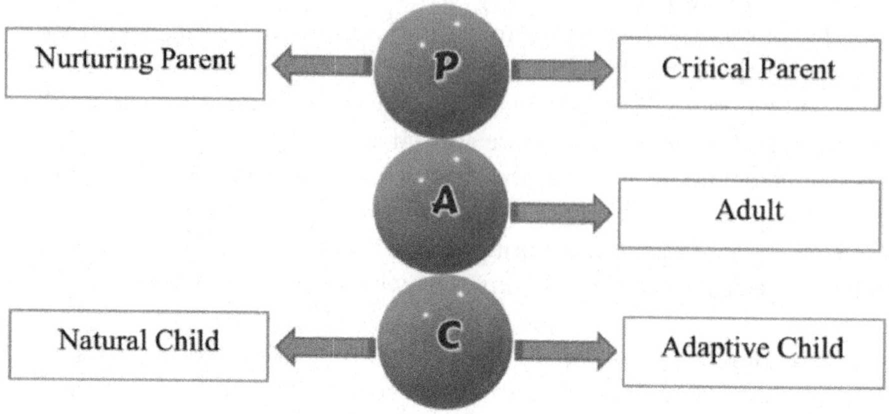

PARENT EGO STATE

The Parent Ego State represents the mass of data recorded in the brain from external events experienced from approximately 0-5 years of age. It imprints the lessons, thoughts, feelings, mannerisms, culture and behaviors that are learned by the primary adult caregivers.

It is the TAUGHT input. A majority of it recorded and imprinted before we can talk, express ourselves, or have any control over our environment. It details our cultural values and norms. It imprints a way of communicating and treating others from observation. It is our learned behavior from matching and mirroring those in authority over us. There is no understanding of how to filter or edit the memory and emotional data as it comes in. A child does not yet know how to analyze and create their perspective. Therefore, all information is imposed upon the brain as fact.
Some of the Parent imprinting can be very helpful in guiding our emotional well-being, and some is not at all helpful. If you ever found yourself sounding like one of your parents in a way that made you inwardly cringe you have discovered an unhealthy portion that you may want to focus on changing. If you find yourself overly self-critical, this is the state that influences our healthy limits for self-love and inner talk.

The Parent Ego State is divided into two areas, the Nurturing Parent and the Critical Parent. The nurturing Parent influences our caring, empathy, loving, protective, permissiveness, openness, kindness, supportiveness, consideration, protectiveness, forgiving and helpful traits. The Critical Parent influences our morals, values, judgements, punishment, restrictions, rules, strong opinions, assertiveness, rigidity, decisiveness and discipline.

CHILD EGO STATE

The Child Ego State represents the brain recordings of internalized events and base nature reactions to the external events we are exposed to from approximately 0-3 years of age. This is referred to as the FELT input. The child ego state is the core of emotions, thoughts, feelings and behaviors natural to us before we can speak. These are recorded purely as emotion and it the real, raw, natural aspect of ourselves. It includes everything from how we have fun, play, gain joy to how we react when upset. This is why two or more siblings can have very different basic personalities even within the same environment.

At some point, a traumatic childhood experience may impact a child's natural state, as will any form of abuse. It is the child inside that offer's up feelings from a distorted view of emotional undertones we often don't know are there. This may restrict our more adult side from seeing things accurately from a logical, reasonable and measured perspective. The more we are triggered or emotionalized as an adult the more the child state takes over our reactions. The Child Ego State is also broken into two broad areas, and from within a therapeutic environment, it is broken down further to better described the adapted states.

The Natural Child can split have two different nuances: The Free Child and the Little Professor. Home to our spontaneous feelings and most unaltered behaviors, t is the part of us that experiences inputs in a direct or immediate manner. It is our nature and base personality that is creative, curious, playful, expressive, competitive, authentic, affectionate, and emotional. Our natural self-soothing ability and resilience resides here. Our child state may aid or hurt intimate relationships. When we are not in-touch with our inner natural child it can have serious impacts on our intimate bonds. This is due to adaptations forced upon us before we had control over our lives.

The Adapted Child is the part of us that was learned in order to comply with the parental and authoritative messages we were given growing up. We adapt to stay safe, to receive strokes, and to seek attention, good attention when that is offered and bad attention when we are not given enough good. If we grew up in a critical, restrictive household, we may have chosen a rebellious versus a compliant adaptation. Different adult influences and expectations will mold variations to a child adaptation strategy, and it remains with us through life. This is why a child may act differently with one parent or adult than another.

THE ADULT EGO STATE

The Adult Ego State forms from when we start to speak until our first exposure to a broader world, like preschool. Usually around 1-2 years of age, children begin to gain some control over their body, choices, and interactions. Most of us are familiar with the terrible twos. It is the emerging adult ego that grows from new social and external stimuli. The brain starts to assess the new data received and validates what is different from what they are told, what they observe, and what they feel about it. This is the part of ourselves that learns to problem solve, compare and challenge the inputs we receive with new information and grow a self-identity that is not simply a replication of the parental or caregiver inputs we have mimicked thus far.

Berne describes the Adult as being "principally concerned with transforming stimuli into pieces of information, and processing and filing that information on the basis of previous experience." The other states impact the development of the Adult State. This is the one we want to get good at using on demand when we are triggered into an emotionalized response. Like all things it needs to be used in moderation; too much Adult and we lose the emotional capacity to build strong relationships.

Dr. Harris, a Ph.D. student of Dr. Berne's, created an easy summary that allows us quick understanding. In Dr. Harris's book, I'm OK, You're OK[cxli] he described the adult state as "a data-processing computer, which grinds out decisions after computing the information from three sources: The Parent, the Child, and the data which the Adult has gathered and is assessing." He also formed the alignment of Ego States to their core influence with Child being a FELT concept, Parent being a TAUGHT concept and the Adult being a THOUGHT concept. Each of these States has an appropriate, insufficient and excessive component that, through understanding gives us a quick read on a person when they are communicating with us.

EGO STATE	AGE	CONCEPT
NATURAL ADAPATIVE	Birth – 5 but shows up by 2 years old "terrible twos" first move away from total reliance on 'parental figure'	FELT: How we feel and internalize the world around us from a feelings-perspective. This is our most natural emotional state
PARENT	Birth – 5 Imprints on how to act, speak to others, care as narrow source of	TAUGHT: How we internalize all the stimuli from parental & authority figures around us. Cultural norms are imprinted

	information at this stage.	here.
ADULT	3 or when new socialization occurs, and one questions the inputs and applies personal reasoning based on new information from broader sources.	THOUGHT: How we internalize our learned inputs to date with new views influenced by new adults, media, peers and community to develop our own unique opinion and thoughts

We often get asked what happens during adolescence, which is a whole other level of science where the fusion of brain development and hormones take things to an entirely different place. We will share a short introduction into this developmental phase. Pamela Levin, who studied with Berne, wrote an interesting article called "Ego States and Emotional Development in Adolescence."[cxlii] She gives us a great summarized insight:

"A great deal more is going on emotionally and psychologically during adolescence. There are essential events that need to take place during this time for the person to become a psychological adult instead of a child. The process through which this takes place is brought to light with the lens of ego states."

When Berne first shared his research on Ego States he was doing so from a psychologist's perspective while treating patients. He inferred that we are not born with three wholly functioning Ego States, instead they develop within our environment and experiences and all three begin to show by around age 12. There is still the process of adolescence before a child morphs into an adult. Pamela Levin's research stated: *"To evolve into a mature adult, the adolescent needs to update old patterns and form a unifying 'skin' around the three major ego states formed in childhood. This is accomplished through an adolescent developmental process that both repeat and revisits prior stages but at new levels of sophistication. Levin lists seven primary growth tasks that the adolescent goes through in order to emerge as a psychological adult:*

1. Unifying parts of their personality into one cohesive whole
2. Revisiting earlier development and experiences, which are readily available, and updating any patterns as necessary
3. Developing and integrating sexuality, including recalibrating self-image to match physical changes
4. Engaging in preflight behavior (facing fear, testing consequences)
5. Separating from the authority of parents or mentors and replacing it with their own.
6. Pulling up their emotional root from parent or mentor relationships that have sustained growth until now.
7. Building a bridge between the world of childhood to adulthood."[cxliii]

As typical in all psychological therapy, the understanding is that our adult selves are heavily influenced by our early life experiences. The Ego State theory is the easiest way for a layperson to understand the immense influence our childhood beginnings have on how we see and interact in the world. The good news is we can challenge those recordings and inputs, and reprogram beliefs that do not serve us well, similar to the transformation from adolescence to full adulthood. This is also how healing can begin in adults who had adverse childhood experiences.

Our brain's neural plasticity allows for constant growth and learning. Sadly, we are not taught this so many people live with the influence of subconsciously fed memories from early childhood scars in our daily communications and interactions. Add in experiences through adolescence, and we may not enter adulthood with a healthy self-concept. This is why in Trauma-Informed care, we seek to change the question from "What's wrong with you?" to "What happened to you?"

For personal wellness, our emotional control and self- management will not likely change without questioning why we currently feel and react the way we do. This, along with introspective thinking on whether our Ego States are helping us or hindering us in our relationships and life successes. Ego State therapy has been found to be particularly beneficial for trauma victims, and PTSD sufferers. This approach promotes our ability and capacity to challenge and change our perspectives from self-defeating behavior to healthier and more balanced mental fitness.

How do we recognize our Ego States and those of others we are interacting with? Pay attention to body language, gestures, choice of words, the tone of voice, inflection, and emotional cues. We all have each of the parent, child and adult ego states within our personality at various intensities. When it comes to balance and wellness, we want to lean towards having an appropriate amount of each. The following charts will show how to identify each and what is an appropriate, insufficient or excessive amount.

CRITICAL PARENT CUES:

Body Language	Finger wag, Finger pointing at you or jabbing into surface Could be fist pump into palm or air or the military karate chop with more formidable stance More direct and authoritative giving instructions Arms crossed or hands on hips Assessing or Judgmental facial cues (lips pursing, brows scrunching, eyes narrowing)
Words Phrasing	Instructional or authoritative in tone, pitch, volume, pace "You should, must, need to" … "I think you …."

	"I will show you how to …" "This is the way you do it" Judgmental/Condemning when displeased "that's rude." "How dare you speak to me that way" Putting you in your place Heavy sighs, tongue clicking, audible signs of annoyance
Culture	Morals, values, cultural norms are important and will weave into conversations, as will explicit or implicit bias and prejudices.
Telling	They will "tell you" about insert behavior they don't like in others, what they see as 'wrong' with the situation' and how you should act, fix it, be more like them. Set in their opinions/views/morals

CRITICAL PARENT: JUST RIGHT - TOO LITTLE - TOO MUCH

Appropriate CP	Insufficient CP	Excessive CP
Sets boundaries; sets values; hold accountable self & those under their charge within reasonable parameters; follows rules & norms for appropriate social & cultural behavior; teaches right from wrong, promotes good morals, stands up for others in community	Does not set any rules, boundaries and has little accountability for one's own actions or calling out others bad behavior. Self-interest over values or morals. Neglectful, has a do not care mindset; apathy & disinterest in being part of or promoting community	Aggressive; bullying; angry with the world; extremely intolerant and judgmental; close minded; prejudiced; explicitly biased; regular state of disapproval; physically or emotionally abusive. My way or the highway; ignorant towards community outside of self-interest

NURTURING PARENT CUES

Body Language	Hands are palm down in calming movement Active listening, leaning in, nodding If consoling, would rub shoulder, arm, pat a person May self-sooth by rubbing own arms, stroking in comfort Hugging oneself or may show minor rocking motion Facial cue would mimic or mirror easier, happiness, or show signs of empathy … pinching when sad, feeling bad May shudder or reflex bad in distaste or horror
Words Phrasing	Coaxing, questioning, suggesting, empathetic Assertive, coaching, guiding, helping others "what have you considered?" "Let me see how you do it and I will coach you." "do you mind if I share …" "I'd like to help you …" Let's do this together" Will try to calm others "it's going to be okay." "we'll get through this." "I'm here for you"

	Will show disappointment, upset, in choice of words "I'm so disappointed in …" "I expected better of you" Sad sighs, 'oh dear' phrasing, gentle admonishment
Culture	More open to values and beliefs of others while maintaining own. Swaying opinion over rigid stance Defending other's rights, protective of weaker (kids, animals)
Guiding	They will guide and coach you with mindset of caring for something bigger than self

NURTURING PARENT: JUST RIGHT/TOO LITTLE/TOO MUCH

Appropriate NP	Insufficient NP	Excessive NP
Accepts your problems as yours and supports but does not take on your pain, grief, responsibilities, problems as their own. Empathetic. Caring beyond self. Protective of those perceived weaker or in need. Teaches how to treat others and self well.	Unemotive. Uncaring. Neglects feelings of others. Indifferent to pain and suffering. No empathy or suitable sympathy.	Fretful. Takes on others grief, responsibilities, problems as if their own. Hovering. Fearful. High drama. Nervous. Highly compassionate … takes on the world's issues and frets on it.

NATURAL CHILD CUES

Body Language	Carefree, relaxed, comfortable in their skin Friendly demeanor, approachable looking Spontaneous, energetic, curious, loving Open stance, active hand movements, open hands In creative or competitive scenarios will look very focused, determined, self-activating Quick and natural facial expressions to reflect self and group vibe
Words Phrasing	Words are authentic and inclusive "in the moment" Expressive whether for fun, excitement, rallying the group, intent on their pursuit. Tends to be the helper in the crowd Will work to lift other's moods with cheering up words, Positive comfort, humor Emotive reactions to positive or negative stimuli If introverted they will be quiet but facial expressions will mirror the people around them Can be quick to anger "all about me" "Hey, let's do this!", "Take a load off and chill." "How about we..." "Hey everyone, over here, look." "I'm just trying to have some fun here." "Let's move the party to …" "Wouldn't it be great to …."

Culture	Enjoyment of life. Active and engaged with friends, family, community. Balanced in outward and inward self-care.
Rallying	They will rally, gather, cheer, incite, get caught up in emotion

NATURAL CHILD: JUST RIGHT - TOO LITTLE - TOO MUCH

Appropriate NC	Insufficient NC	Excessive NC
Views the fun and good around them. Understands time & place for fun. Has good self & social awareness. Treats others as they wish to be treated. Able to self-reflect. Able to relax and take time for self. Has curiosity. Driven.	Unable to relax. Stiff Rigidness. Robotic. Low self and social awareness. Awkward. Little sense of humor. Not driven or curious about the world. Possibly on spectrum	Highly spontaneous. Does not think before acting or speaking. Risky behavior. Takes few things seriously. Does not care about other's inputs. Embarrasses others. Self-absorbed. Overly competitive w/o care for fair play. Possibly ADHD

ADAPTED CHILD CUES

Body Language	Little Professor/Withdrawn: Reactive to external demands with compliant but sulky or avoidant behavior (minimal eye contact) Body language is more controlled, inhibited or muted May be sneaky, manipulative, maneuvering for advantage Behaviors showing, guilt, fear, depression, anxiety Pleaser in mannerisms and words May squirm, shift around, seem uncomfortable in own skin Tendency for more negative expressions and words May be overtly pacifying people around them, anxious May be whiny, pouty, overly emotional, frustrated Angry Child: Eye may be restless, roaming, assessing, perceiving judgment of them or threats around them May be bossy, trying to step in and solve things, take over, control the situation. May hesitate and procrastinate … draw out their answers May show unnecessary aggravation, envy, or jealousy May be overtly bullying, cruel, aggressive … pushing for a fight, quick to anger
Words Phrasing	Both tend towards manipulative expressions, trying to get what they want. For little professor the goal is "I want things to remain controlled and moving in a direction I am comfortable with." For Angry Child the goal is "I want what I want" and often makes

	excuses when things don't go their way.
Culture	Self-centered, my needs usually supersede others
Self-absorbed	Wary and calculating always aiming to move towards personal wants and needs.

ADAPTED CHILD: JUST RIGHT - TOO LITTLE - TOO MUCH

Appropriate AC	Insufficient AC	Excessive AC
Self-aware of childhood traumas and taken steps to self-develop emotional intelligence. Understands time and place. Considers social impact of actions and words. Weights pros and cons of actions. Reflective. Has enough angry child that they are not a doormat or easily bullied.	Presents as victim. Usually seeking a Persecutor to confirm their low self-image, or Rescuer to save them (see Drama Triangles). Very little self-awareness or social awareness on how their behavior impacts others.	Little Professor: Highly inhibited, scared of everything. Anxiety issues. Overly pleasing. Adapts to stronger personality's will. Angry Child: Has adult temper tantrums. Minimal care how others see them. Bully, abuser, attacker.

ADULT CUES

Body Language	Confident, calm, safe Relaxed and comfortable with self In the 'here and now' when communicating Highly curious, strong drive to learn and develop Ask questions, clarifies information Engages to gain mutual understanding Great listening indicators, nodding, leaning in, vocal encouragement, open positive body language Uses logic and reasoning to make points Considers responses carefully, does not use aggressive, sarcastic or hurtful tones or words Non-movement indicates they have tuned out to inner thoughts Normal everyday conversation (no emotional overtone) falls into this category. Will allow the curious and inventive aspects of child to show Coachable Adaptable
Words Phrasing	"In my opinion…" "Let me see if I heard you right …." "Have you considered…" "Who … what … where … when … why … how?" "I would like to see the … facts, evidence, information … that

	supports that …" "How would you go about it?"
Culture	Assessing both sides of a situation before making decisions. Fair and impartial. Open to new ideas, knowledge and experiences.
Logical	Balances logic, reason and personal emotion to make decisions.

ADULT: JUST RIGHT - TOO LITTLE - TOO MUCH

Appropriate A	Insufficient A	Excessive A
Healthy mix of reasoning, logic, and reflective consideration. Able to accept, change and adapt to new ideas, inputs and knowledge. Appreciates the need for appropriate self-reflection and development. Not prone to emotional hijacks but comfortable with their emotions. Accepts responsibility for actions and words. Weighs pros and cons and then takes decisive action in reasonable time.	Highly reactive and emotional. Makes quick decisions based on feelings. Doesn't value new ideas, inputs or knowledge and relies on 'gut' feelings. Does not make good decisions when logic or reason is an essential input.	Robotic and unemotional. No sense or care for social awareness or social cues. Analysis paralysis …challenged making decisions as decisions require emotional input. Appears cold and unfriendly, rigid. Tends to have high cognitive bias and fits facts and information that already align to preconceived notions into considerations

TRANSACTIONAL ANALYSIS

"The unit of social intercourse is called a transaction. When two or more people encounter each other sooner or later one of them will speak or give some other indication of acknowledging the presence of the others. This is called the transactional stimulus. Another person will then say or do something which is in some way related to the stimulus, and that is called the transactional response."[cxliv] This statement from Eric Berne sets the stage for us to discuss Transactional Analysis. Now that we understand the Ego States, we can begin to watch for patterns in others and analyze how they begin or respond to communication exchanges. As public safety professionals, being able to assess the Ego State you are faced with can aid your ability to manage your own reactions. You will also learn to avoid being triggered and redirect the conversation using the tactics we will share as you seek to move people to an Adult Ego State. We will share the predictable patterns of exchange, as well as the unpredictable ones. For each, how we initiate the communication has great

bearing on how people respond. These Ego State responses are easy to hear when we pay attention. James MacNeil has a great acronym for this called:

E.A.G.E.R. ©
"The Ego-state Addressed is Generally the Ego-state that Responds"[cxlv]

Predictable responses are when we choose a certain phrase, tone, body stance expecting that we are subconsciously invoking a likely response from the other person.

PREDICTABLE	*PREDICTABLE*	*PREDICTABLE*
EGO STATE TO STATE	**PARENT TO CHILD**	**CHILD TO PARENT**

PREDICTABLE EGO TO EGO

When a parent ego state speaks about something or other people, they generally get a parent response. Depending on your predominant parent state, that could be on the nurturing or critical side.

Parent #1: "Oh that poor kid, he just wiped out on his bike!" (Nurturing)
Parent #2: "Oh no, poor little guy!" (Nurturing Parent response)
OR
Parent #1: "Oh that poor kid, he just wiped out on his bike!" (Nurturing)
Parent #2: "Well, you could see it coming, that kid takes too many risks!" (Critical Parent response)

The same holds true for Adult to Adult or Child to Child States:

Adult #1: "Hey do you know what time it is?" (Adult stimulus)
Adult #2: "Yes, it's 1630. (Adult response)
Child #1: "Hey the boss is away today, let's take a long lunch." (Child stimulus)
Child #2: "Yes, let's do it!" (Natural Child State response)

OR
Child #3: "Oh no, I am worried I would get in trouble." (Adaptive Child response)

PREDICTABLE PARENT TO CHILD

Now if we are talking directly to someone and we use the tone of either type of parent, then we are predictably invoking a child response. Ever wonder why some people act like children when they talk? You are likely talking to them from a parent ego state.

Parent: "Why are you in such a crappy mood all the time?"? (Critical Parent stimulus).
Child: "Because you're always on my back about crap!" (Adaptive Child response)
OR
Child: "I'm sorry, I am really upset about …." (Natural Child, Little Professor)

PREDICTABLE CHILD TO PARENT

The same holds true when we approach someone from a Child State as we are asking for a Parent State to respond. Ever wonder why someone is always talking down to you? Check your tone, pitch, words and body language as you are likely asking for them to talk to you that way.

Child Ego: "Can you help me with my photocopying, I don't know how to do it?" (Child stimulus).
Parent: "Oh you always need help, very well let me save you again!" (Nurturing Parent State response) or,
OR
Parent: "What am I, your secretary? Figure it out!" (Critical Parent State).

Transactions are not always predictable; however, and there are pros and cons to these scenarios. In a crossed transaction, the ego state stimulated is not the ego state that responds. There could be exchanges with unexpected responses or intentional negativity associated with them.

CROSSED TRANSACTIONS		
Attempt: Adult to Adult:	**Attempt: Parent to Parent:**	**Attempt: Adult to Adult:**

EGO seeks dominance so response is Critical Parent to Child.	Response avoids emotional commitment and response is given in Adult Ego State.	EGO seeks logic but receives emotionalized response from either a Parent or Child EGO State

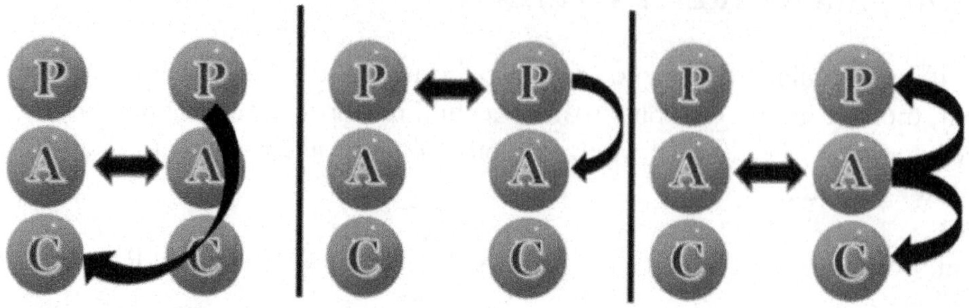

These exchanges are crossed transactions and not considered a healthy way to communicate. Crossed transactions are an opportunity for you to use your calm, safe, confidence power position to change the focus of an intended stimulation. You can choose to ignore the emotionalized trigger that the person wants to lead you towards when you reply with an adult state. This allows you to interrupt their game script and take control of the stimulus/response interplay.

Questions to analyze the Ego State

To figure out which Ego States are in play during a communication transaction, you can ask yourself these four questions to aid your analysis and action:

1. What Ego State am I communicating from?
2. What Ego State is the other person communicating from?
3. Which Ego State is the most effective to use with this particular person in this situation?
4. What tactics will I deploy to influence the other's Ego State to an Adult State to seek my objective?

To develop your skills in this area, study the conversations you have and those happening around you. When analyzing transactions, you want to pay attention to WHAT is being said and also HOW the words are spoken. What emphasis, tone, pitch, and volume are used in conveying the message? Then consider the body language and facial expressions. These non-verbal signs are what Dr. Berne taught as being critical to understanding what Ego State is being used.

Once you practice this, you will find it becomes second nature to identify the Ego State coming at you, as well as noting the state you are coming from when talking to others. If you do not like the way someone speaks back to you, you can analyze how you stimulated his or her response and change your communication approach.

CHAPTER 20

TAKE THE DRAMA OUT OF TRAUMA

So many people prefer to live in drama because it is what they are accustomed to and comfortable with. It's like someone staying in a bad marriage or relationship - it's actually easier to stay because they know what to expect every day, versus leaving and not knowing what to expect.
~ Ellen DeGeneres

Now that we have a good understanding of how emotions impact our communication, we will go a little deeper into how our childhood roots can impact these Ego States and our interactive success. Often by understanding this we can start to manage patterned exchanges that trigger us and seem to loop us into unhealthy relationships or repeated arguments with certain people or personalities.

The Parent Ego State causes the most fluctuation and confusion, both within us and in our conversations because of contradictions in what we observed and learned. This comes from our experiences with all the authority figures our young selves witnessed and how we choose to manage ourselves as we mature. We have all experienced the "do what I say not what I do" phenomenon. Perhaps you were told not to lie, and then watched one of both parent's fib and outright lie in front of you. Perhaps you were lectured to not drink and drive while remembering your younger self riding home in the back seat of the car being driven by a drunk parent. The contradiction could be played out in any number of great speeches about being positive, following your religion, treating others well, and then watching a parent behave in a manner completely opposite of what they told you.

There are recorded memories of the good parent and the bad parent moments, both the loving cuddles and the harsh lectures. Maybe your recordings are of an abusive or alcoholic parent who was the very definition of contradiction and uncertainty. These situations can cause an inner conflict and mess with your values and belief system. Your self-image is of being a good, kind, decent human being to others, and yet inwardly you are constantly beating yourself up and bullying yourself with self-defeating emotional abuse. The other people you interact with are having similar struggles, as well. If you pay attention, you can observe the behavior changes as they happen when they are triggered by certain words, bodily gestures or even a perceived tone.

When schooling and socialization begin to expand, our Adult Ego State starts to cultivate the data received from parents, caregivers and key adults and then tests the validity of their impressions with other inputs. Our adult is our reasoning center. The more we allow children to figure things out for themselves and question life through their natural curiosity. the more astute the adult becomes. The Adult state evaluates the inputs demonstrated and taught to them based on how they want things to go or even how they may imagine them to be from a child or emotional perspective. From there, the Adult learns to balance wishes with reality as the that Ego matures. When this comparison and validation process is dysfunctional, a child may feel like they are not okay, and those inputted recordings can have an impact throughout life.

This eventual Adult phase is further impacted by the Natural Child and Adaptive Child impacts. Those earliest memories have a huge influence, even those heard and felt in utero. If a child is not nurtured in a loving, consistent environment, or is confused by mixed parental messages, then challenges or delays to a well-functioning Adult State are more likely. The great news is that these impacts can be altered, and new life positions formed. Lastly, the experience of adolescents further morphs our Adult Ego State as peers take over the predominant role from authority figures in our life.

Dr. Thomas Harris, a student of Eric Berne and author of, I'm OK; You're OK[cxlvi], describes this process as the four life positions.

> *"One of the clearest statements on the development of positions is made by Dr. Lawrence Kubie,[cxlvii] who stated early in life, sometimes within the earliest months and sometimes later, a central emotional position is frequently established ... it becomes the primary position to which that individual will tend to return automatically for the rest of his or her days. This, in turn, may constitute either the primary safeguard or the major vulnerability of his or her life. In fact, the establishment of a central emotional position may turn out to be one of the earliest among the universals in the evolution of the human neurotic process, since it may start even in the pre-verbal and largely pre-symbolic days of infancy. Whenever the central emotional position is painful ... the individual may spend his whole life defending himself against it, again using conscious, preconscious, and unconscious devices whose aim it is to avoid this pain-filled central position. Kubie then raises the question as to whether or not these positions are alterable later in life. I believe they are. Although the early experiences which culminated in the position cannot be erased, I believe the early positions can be changed. What was once decided can be undecided."*

THE FOUR LIFE POSITIONS

Harris theorizes that our personalities are influenced by the four following positions

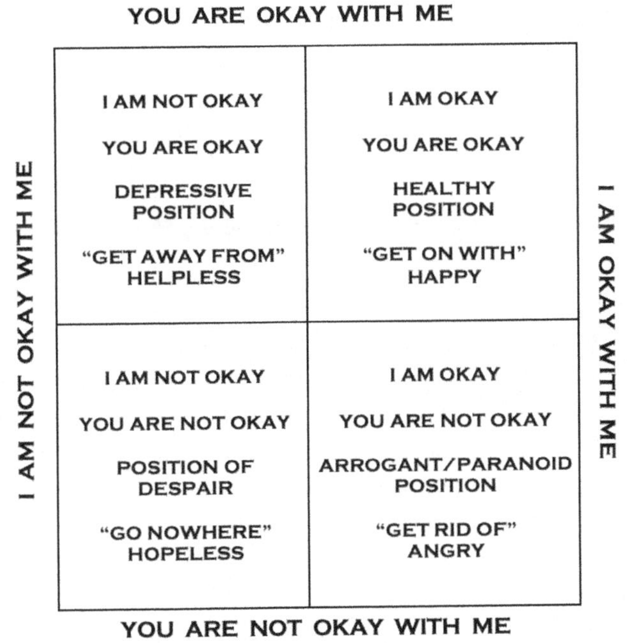
YOU ARE OKAY WITH ME
I AM NOT OKAY
YOU ARE OKAY
DEPRESSIVE POSITION
"GET AWAY FROM" HELPLESS
I AM OKAY
YOU ARE OKAY
HEALTHY POSITION
"GET ON WITH" HAPPY
I AM NOT OKAY
YOU ARE NOT OKAY
POSITION OF DESPAIR
"GO NOWHERE" HOPELESS
I AM OKAY
YOU ARE NOT OKAY
ARROGANT/PARANOID POSITION
"GET RID OF" ANGRY
I AM NOT OKAY WITH ME
I AM OKAY WITH ME
YOU ARE NOT OKAY WITH ME

From very early in life, a person can adopt a particular philosophy about themselves in the world. The first three positions are primarily developed by the circumstances of our upbringing, and by the age of three most have adopted a general belief of position one, "I am not okay, You are okay" as we are under a barrage of "wrong" and "no" from our parental influences.

Sadly, the second and third positions "I'm not okay, you're not okay" and "I'm okay, you're not okay" come from abusive, highly restrictive or traumatic experiences where loving parental strokes are missing or unhealthy. While the first three are largely unconscious imprints from our environments and based on our feelings and emotional inputs, the fourth position "I'm okay, you're okay" is one of choices and developed conscious beliefs and actions grown from our emotional intelligence. As we develop our Adult Ego State, gain independence and self-regard from new accomplishments and receive strokes from new sources many shift to position four, "I'm okay, you're okay." For some, this may not happen until further independence occurs in adulthood, for others the shift is never made.

Children who develop with a positive sense of self-worth and a respectful view of the self-worth of others will usually stay in the "I'm OK, You're OK" realm. For the many who develop with an "I'm not OK, You're OK" mindset tend to use games to attempt to control or handle those people. Games are learned interaction and behavior patterns, and the outcomes are quite predictable. Games are played with different people with various intensities. Most games are not intent on positive relationship outcomes. An example for children would be the mine is better than yours game. Different degrees of games intensify until they become entirely irrational, damaging and toxic to relationships. This happens at a societal level, as well. Politicians play games at levels that involve the movement of communities, societies, and countries. Games most often come from a Critical Parent to Child Ego State and avoid the equality and reasonableness of the Adult.

As public safety professionals responding to neighborhoods in high crime and high poverty areas, you will come across a higher percentage of youth and adults that have been emotionally impaired due to their perceived life position from environmental, generational, and societal cues or from a lack of positive stroking. We can correlate this to the impact of solitary confinement. The most harmful thing we can do to another human is deny them human interaction and attention (zero stroking).

Related to this extreme is the common neglect and abuse that comes from overwhelmed, highly stressed, or addicted parents who do not have the emotional capacity to provide self-esteem building love and positive strokes to their children. The link between criminal behavior and low stroking home environments can be seen clearly among those in prison. When Laura Bates interviewed death row inmates for her book, Shakespeare Saved my Life,[cxlviii] she asked the question, "What do you feel your parents think about your death sentence?" The majority response was, "I am exactly where they told me I would be."

In our personal lives, it is important to understand the power we have with our children as well as our loved ones when it comes to positive and negative stroking. When children do not get enough positive strokes, they will push boundaries until they get negative ones because that is better than no strokes at all. The kind of stroking patterns we tend to develop come from how we were raised. Those raised by critical or abusive parents are comfortable seeking negative stroking patterns as adults, as seen in the hard-nosed father who carries on the tradition of keeping his kids tough and prepared for the harsh reality of life. And the entitled adult who grew up with overly nurturing parents will tend to be soft and not discipline their own children.

Stroking patterns tend to support our base existential life position and reflect our self-esteem and how we feel about ourselves in relation to others in our life.

Babies who develop in an environment with unconditional love and positive stroking will thrive over babies who develop in a strict, conditional, low stroke environment. Conditional love is where someone will only give positive strokes if another does precisely as he or she says and acts within the narrow parameters set out for them. This does not mean that children do not need values, morals, boundaries, and discipline. It means there is a difference between saying to a child "YOU are bad, YOU never do anything right, YOU are useless" and, "Your behavior is unacceptable," "You have been shown how to do that so show me the proper way," or "I expect better from you when you do …" A good summary of this perspective is "Hate the sin, love the sinner."

Conditional strokes can be motivating when actions are rewarded with positive strokes. You may be complimenting a behavior, skill, intelligence that you want to see more of. It can cause harm if you only stoke the areas you relate to or appreciate (i.e. sports) when there are differences between siblings (one is creative or technically inclined) or even individually if, over time, a child loses the strokes they grew accustomed to from you. For example, one child is talented in baseball and gets the most of a father's praise and attention. While another child looks on, failing to be appreciated for their talent in music, art or building things because those are not the father's area of interest.

A child loves to follow their parents around when they are young and is very interested in or mimics a love of a hobby, perhaps fishing, certain sports, fixing cars, sewing, curling up together with a good book. Then puberty hits and they have no interest anymore, their friends and social networks become a priority. If all your positive strokes were conditional and based on that aligned activity and togetherness, your strokes will fade, and your disappointment will show. As those conditional strokes fade, the child often turns to seeking negative strokes to regain the attention lost by acting out, arguing or misbehaving. When parents focus on the underlying traits and behaviors that make someone excel at any particular talent and provide strokes based on these, then it is easier to transition your strokes as interests morph. Change this one simple way of stroking and you will enhance your child's self-esteem considerably.

An unconditional negative stroke is the most harmful kind of stroke as it expresses that we are not okay. There is no condition around it, we are just not good enough, not lovable and the very core of us is flawed. Enough unconditional negative stroking in early life can damage self-image, self-concept and even a desire to live. As an adult, we can continue to self-talk ourselves into these beliefs and feelings inside our head, regardless of the face we show to the public. With recurring replays of these negative strokes from parents when we believed we did not do enough, act soon enough, or save the day in a manner acceptable, we later become our own critical parent. This internal self-abuse can also lead to a downward spiral that may move someone to feel life is not worth living or that the world would be better without them and no one will see it coming.

In our adult relationships, this can have an impact as well. When relationships are new, there is a phenomenon that we call looking at someone with rose-colored glasses, or the honeymoon phase of a relationship. This is the period when we are learning about each other and everything is new and exciting. In his book The Five Love Languages ~ The secret to Love that Lasts,[cxlix] Gary Chapman concludes that there are five emotional love languages. A love language is the way that people speak, seek and understand emotional love. Interestingly, Chapman comments that, in the initial phases of a relationship, we often display all five languages to each other, yet over time our need for our primary stroking takes precedence. These are the five love languages Chapman describes in his book:

1. Words of affirmation
2. Quality time
3. Receiving gifts
4. Acts of service
5. Physical touch

Once that honeymoon stage starts to dissipate, we will feel less fulfilled if we are not receiving our primary stroking preference. Another interesting insight is that we often give love in the manner we prefer to receive it, and therein lies the problem for many couples. Some may happen to have the same preference and carry on blissfully fulfilled after the period when you are giving all five. More often, however, when the honeymoon phase passes, you will settle down and give the one language that you prefer without taking the time to explore whether that particular stroking is the one your partner wants to receive. Your preference may be physical touch, while theirs is acts of service. It will not take long for a disconnect to grow and a feeling that you are not appreciated, loved or fulfilled the way you used to be. The key to a healthy relationship, according to Chapman, is to learn your partner's primary (and secondary) love language and to make efforts to give what they want to receive. They, in turn, learn your love languages and reciprocate by giving you the strokes you desire for ultimate fulfillment. This is a task best accomplished when you have open and honest communication between you.

Even if you do not buy the book and learn this particular version of stroking, you can work towards communicating better ways to learn, give and receive the strokes you need to feel fulfilled and increase your happiness. Pay attention to the kind of strokes you like and grow your comfort level to ask for them. Learn the type of strokes your partner longs to receive or ask them what they want more of. It is entirely rational and reasonable to ask for positive strokes. Having the self-awareness to ask for what fulfills you does not diminish the value of the stroke you will get! As with most things, typically the more you give, the more you receive!

John F. Twomey, Ed.D. shares an interesting study of the practice of transactional analysis from a body language perspective. He shares that, "*often the Parent is in control of the upper body as the person is transacting, while the Child is kicking away with his feet at the bottom. The hands and other parts of the body often hold "secrets" for the Child, while the Parent is in the executive.*"[xl]

If you have confusion over which Ego State you are interacting with you can watch for movement and "tells" from the upper and lower body, which may help you determine their state. As public safety professionals you will want to move people away from their more emotionalized Parent and Child Ego States and influence an Adult exchange. This lessens the escalation factor considerably and there are two basic strategies to maintain or move people to an Adult State.

The first tactic is asking information seeking questions from an empathetic stance. When someone is highly emotionalized, they are not able to think rationally or logically. Asking information seeking questions forces someone to leave their emotional center and assess how they wish to respond. The more upset they are the more you want to layer questions with multiple choices, so they have to list, prioritize in their head and then choose the best response. It keeps them in their neocortex executive center longer. Beginning from a non-threatening, safe perspective, you start with meeting them where they are and showing empathy:

- "You seem really upset right now" (meet them where they are)
- "I understand this is an upsetting situation and I do not wish to upset you further." (show of empathy)
- "Would you be okay if I asked you a question so I can better understand the situation?" (seek permission to engage … primes the neocortex for incoming question)
- "Would you list the top three things that are upsetting you right now?" (forces listing and prioritizing)
- "Would you share the most upsetting aspect of this situation?" (forces them to think of details and prioritize their upset)
- "Would you provide me the order of events right before ____ happened?" (back to functional aspects, they have to list and prioritize in their headfirst … calming the emotion).

Sean's favorite, C.H.O.R.D.©[cli] has worked really well. "I believe in communicating honestly, openly, respectfully, and directly with everyone I come in contact with.

Is it okay if I do that with you?" In a non-threatening manner, Sean disables people's defensive nature and opens them up to a difficult dialogue.

Open ended questions direct people to move from their emotional center to engage their neocortex. Getting someone's executive center involved can sometimes be all that it takes to start to calm someone down. Meeting them where they are and showing empathy allows them to feel heard, understood and to have their emotions respected. Psychologically, this allows their reasoning center to step in. Asking information seeking questions that require them to categorize their response demands that their neocortex (logic center) take the time to think through the situation and order their response. This keeps the logical aspect of their brain in play long enough that their emotional stress response can begin to calm. This may or may not work to keep them calm, and repeated use of this technique may be required to keep redirecting someone from their emotional triggers.

A second tactic is the use of a more assertive adult to adult strategy called giving I-messages. When we use I-messages, we are accepting responsibility for our own perceptions, thoughts, and feelings. We are not interpreting how others feel about what we are saying. The receiver of I-messages usually does not feel threatened or attacked when this tactic is used to convey how we feel.

Realize that if someone is too emotionally attached to their own Ego State, they may not be able to hear you yet. You will need to give them time to be heard, understood, accepted and respected first. While some may feel they are communicating from an Adult Ego State, if they are not able to exchange I-message statements, they are likely coming from a different state. Commonly, an excessive Critical Parent will view themselves as reasonable and logical, if you agree with their opinion. I-message statements can convey how you feel without challenging their perceived authority.

There is an expectation that most communicators will choose to come from Adult States as reason and logic are powerful persuaders. I-messages can create calm and focus on the subject at hand versus the emotion behind the issue. Avoiding you-messages, which may inflame fear, pride or confusion, keeps escalations from happening in the first place.

- I feel that ...
- If I heard you correctly ...
- I believe another course of action could be worth considering ...
- I would like ...

ANALYZING TRANSACTIONS

Dr. Eric Berne give insight on how to analyze transactions, *"When two people communicate, one person initiates a transaction with the transactional stimulus. The person at whom the stimulus is directed will respond with the transactional response. Simple Transactional Analysis involves identifying which ego state directed the stimulus and which ego state in the other person executed the response."* Transactional analysis can help you understand yourself better and how some conversations go wonderfully while others fail miserably. It helps you clearly see how you approach and interact with others is quite controllable. Transactional Analysis Therapy has also proven incredibly successful for PTSD and Acute Stress Disorders. It also reconciles the traumatic impacts adverse childhood experiences have on your current wellness and happiness.

What sets this therapy apart from other treatments is resiliency, the root belief that each of us is responsible for our own future, regardless of what may have happened to us in the past. You may feel after reading this book and researching some of these topics further that you would be well served by changing certain internal and external communication behaviors. Those that do not serve your wellness or happiness anymore. If this describes you, Transactional Analysis Therapy is a therapeutic approach that may work for you. For those who like to work things out for themselves, you may start with paying attention to and deciding to challenge some of your communication approaches, deciding what Ego State you want to use to gain the best objective in your interactions. This includes how you talk to yourself. For those whose experiences have carved a deeper wound in your soul, we have recommendations to put you on the path of healing.

While touring and researching treatment centers in order to have a solid recommendation list for you, we came across an outstanding and highly unique PTSD and addiction healing center called The Guest House. This location is co-founded by leading trauma expert, Judy Crane and her partner John West. Their in-house treatments are triple the normal time frame allotted for addiction recovery. While interviewing her we learned a startling fact, those she treated from the military, especially command and special forces, often required eight months (a tour of duty) to heal from PTSD. For the numerous public safety professionals, she has healed, it was three months of intensive in-house sessions with several months of out-patient work. We highly recommend The Guest House for severe trauma and addiction healing. As Judy says, *"We are not bad people trying to be good, we are wounded people trying to heal."*

STROKES, GAMES AND THE DRAMA TRIANGLE

For our communications positioning you will find that most of your typical day to day interactions are in an Adult Ego State where there is no triggered emotion interjecting into the moment. This is our baseline state where we are at our most reasonable for assessing the transaction stimulus and responding with ease. Every communication interaction provides stroking, the recognition of another human, and if stroking is exchanged that is called a transaction. Strokes come through verbal and non-verbal means, including recognition, communication, hugging, touching, kisses. Any strokes are preferable to the absence of any. As we inferred earlier, this is why solitary confinement is so powerful as a punishment. However, so is ignoring someone close to you. Giving the silent treatment is the relational equivalent of solitary confinement.

It is helpful to our self-awareness and self-management development to recognize our most common Ego State defaults when we get upset about something. This can help us catch ourselves and choose to rephrase our speech to get better results.

It is also helpful to learn what triggers us when we play life position games or run scripts with certain people or types of people. Self-development and Ego State therapy can be hugely beneficial to trauma infused challenges in our transactions. We can then learn to change the way we communicate, seek healthy recognition and approval and to mend harmful self-talk.

We will not spend much time on games people play or the drama triangle but will touch on it quickly to help in your personal relationships. We delve into this more during our workshop and 911 Relationship Retreat. Games include those guilt statements we may have heard from a member of our family to get people to do something for us. Dr. Berne described games like this, "Games are defined as sets of often repetitive transactions with hidden or ulterior motives that result in predictable, well-defined outcomes." Some of the more common games played are adapted from the website, Changing Minds.[clii]

GAME	DESCRIPTION	PERCEIVED BENEFIT
Stop me if you can	Damaging activity, i.e., using drugs, alcohol	Gets attention, avoids responsibility
Blemish	Finding fault with others, nitpicking	Distracts attention from self
Courtroom	Describing how they are right, and others are wrong "logically"	Get support, sympathy and absolution

If it weren't for you	Blaming others for their lack of achievements	Absolution of guilt
I'm only trying to help	Offering help then complaining if it is not accepted	Gains self-status by controlling others
Look how hard I've tried	Put in lots of effort that intentionally fails	Absolves oneself from responsibility
Now I've got you! (You S.O.B.)	Vents rage on someone with high blaming	Displaces anger. Absolves responsibility
Poor me	Displays themselves as helpless and unlucky	Gaining sympathy and support
See what you made me do	Blaming others for own damaging actions	Absolution of responsibility, instilling guilt

Dr. Stephen Karpman, another student of Dr. Berne, has developed the highly insightful aspect of games we play in his acclaimed work with Drama Triangles.[cliii] He allows us to understand, view and manage ourselves from the starting point and ongoing play of games. He purports that whenever we play games, we consciously or unconsciously step into one of three script roles: Persecutor, Rescuer or Victim. Like Ego States, we can move from position to position as the conversation progresses.

For those of you challenged with personal lives charged with an uncomfortable amount of drama and stress, this would be an excellent subject to study further. As much as you want to believe you can escape or ignore any possible dysfunctional interaction, we all carry drama and burdens. When one of these moments is triggered in the right way or by the right person, we jump on the Drama Triangle at some base point with varying levels of intensity.

If we cannot understand this fundamental truth, we miss out on an opportunity to learn from our past actions, catch ourselves in unhealthy patterns, and change those moments that are not serving us well. If you are working to move beyond a traumatic past that doesn't serve you well, then it becomes even more vital to embrace a transformation in your self-mastery and work to achieve goals you once thought outside your reach. It starts with a conscious awareness of what goes on in our subconscious minds. Denial is merely a defense mechanism that hides the hurt that drives your emotional reactions and leaves you unable to see the impact of your communications.

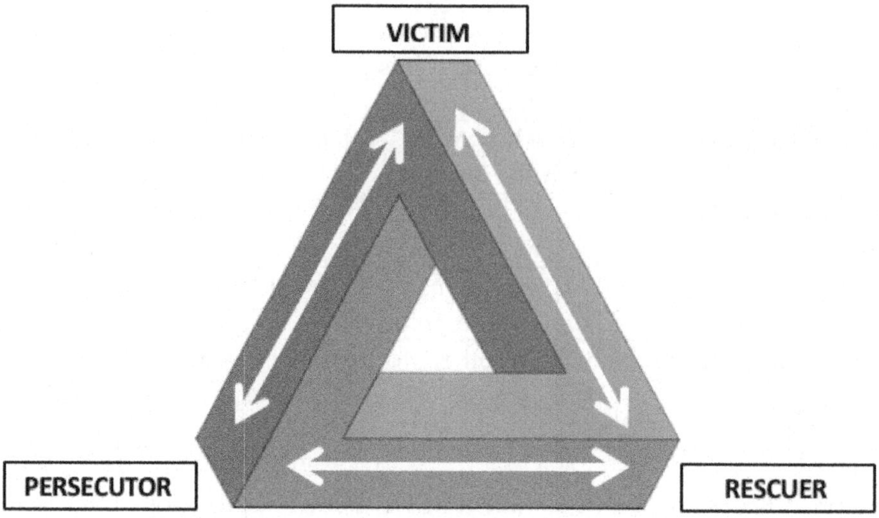

DRAMA TRIANGLE

Dr. Stephen Karpman

Like the Ego States, we tend to gravitate towards an initial role in the Drama Triangle. This is in response to our hot button or whatever has hooked us. Often it would be the role we chose as a child to deal with any family dysfunctions. It doesn't mean we will stay in that role; you can rotate around the triangle pending the script or game being played with either the established or any new relationship games. Depending on the exchange you are reacting to, you can change roles several times a day, being the victim to your spouse, the persecutor to your employee and the rescuer to your child. Alternatively, a mix of starting as the Rescuer to a sibling only to have the conversation go off the rails and you switch mid-conversation to persecutor. Each one of the roles entails discounting someone to some extent.

For those who do not believe they enter the Drama Triangle, I have one word: denial! Those who say, "I'm not like that," "I don't have any drama," are operating from the position that "I am right, and you and your drama are wrong." That is a persecutor role. Those who say, "I'm always looking out for others," or, "I don't cause or participate in the drama," are saying they are the rescuer in this situation. Those who say, "I always get the short end of the stick" or sigh with a heavy "It is what it is," when they are unsatisfied are coming from a victim role. If you are resistant and stubborn with this assessment, you are missing out on an opportunity to heal a cyclical conversation pattern with one or more people in your life. A pattern that likely does not serve you well and leaves you frustrated.

PERSECUTOR	VICTIM	RESCUER
I am better than you I discount you I blame you I put you down	I can't… I am no good Self-pitying Poor me … I have no idea	You need me You can't without me I know better than you You're lacking but I got you
	DESCRIBED AS	
Aggressive Angers easily Judgmental	Helpless Complaints of unmet needs Downtrodden	Over-helpful A fixer Self-sacrificing Needs to be needed for fulfillment
	TYPES OF STATEMENTS HEARD	
It's your fault What were you thinking? Why did you do that? (with anger) What's your problem? Can't you do anything right?	I'm not responsible! I didn't know! Why is this happening to me? No one likes me! Please help me…	Let me help you! I will do that for you. I feel bad for you, let me fix this. You'll be fine, I'm here.
	DISCOUNTING ASPECT	
Discounts other's values and worthiness Feels nothing will be done properly without their intervention Views others as one down from them and "Not OK" In extremes they may bully, belittle and become emotionally abusive	Discounts themselves, he or she puts themselves in a one down position and feels they are "Not OK" Seeks out Persecutors to put them in their place or confirm their self-thoughts or, Seeks out Rescuers who will take over and offer help, confirming they cannot do it on their own. Often have an adapted Child EGO State mindset of "it's not fair" "it's not my fault" to place blame outside of themselves followed by inner self-talk on how useless they are.	Discounts other's ability to think for themselves or show initiative. Tends to see you as weaker or in need of constant support See's others as "Not OK" but by helping they help themselves move up to a better life position. Ties self-worth to ability to help others and beats up self when they can't fix someone. In extremes they can be intrusive or see themselves as martyrs and that they attract victims.

For those feeling they do not enter the drama triangle, I like to use an example from our workshops that resonates with many public safety professionals as a cultural norm. That is the use of sarcasm as humor. It is damaging to the victim. and if used excessively, shows as a sign of a bully with some deep anger issues. In a Psychology Today article author, Clifford N. Lazarus, Ph.D. wrote: *"The main difference between wit and sarcasm is that sarcasm is hostility disguised as humor. It is intended to hurt and is often bitter and caustic. Witty statements are usually in response to someone's unhelpful remarks or behaviors, and the intent is to unravel and clarify the issue by accentuating its absurdities. Sarcastic statements are expressed in a cutting manner; witty remarks are delivered with undisguised and harmless humor.*

Despite smiling outwardly, most people who receive sarcastic comments feel put down and usually think the sarcastic person is a jerk. Indeed, it's not surprising that the origin of the word sarcasm derives from the Greek word "sarkazein" which literally means "to tear or strip the flesh off." Hence, it's no wonder that sarcasm is often preceded by the word "cutting" and that it hurts.

What's more, since actions strongly determine thoughts and feelings, when a person consistently acts sarcastically it usually only heightens his or her underlying hostility and insecurity. After all, when you come right down to it, sarcasm is a subtle form of bullying and most bullies are angry and insecure."

We had one attendee in a recent workshop who was complaining about her peers, clearly coming from a Critical Parent State and using sarcasm to make her points. One of her gentler comments was:

"My team calls me dramatic because I get so angry with them, but I am surrounded by grown men who act like little babies. They always mess up their reports and I have to fix them, they are always demanding help, always whining and complaining and then they wonder why I lose my cool. I'm surprised they don't ask me to wipe their butts, it's like I'm everyone's mother and fixer!"[xliv]

By the end of training she understood Ego States and Drama Triangles and that her Critical Parent criticism and sarcasm triggered a Child State and victim response. If you make others feel they never do anything good enough, why would they bother trying? Then her Nurturing Parent actually did their work for them rather than asking them to review and correct on their own or coach them to fix their own errors. It was no wonder her communication style attracted Child State responses and victim mindsets. She had a tremendous ah-ha moment. By the end of the workshop, she was super excited to go back on shift and try out her new tactics on her peers, superiors, and her husband.

We can recognize when no drama triangle is triggered as the exchange is observable by an easy and low emotion exchange. An example is when a person seeks guidance and you offer some advice or share supports that help them find their own path to a solution. One of the best tactics for assessing where they are and what you need to offer advice on is to ask someone, "What have you tried?" when they seek help. When we come from a coaching perspective the goal is to bring the best out of them. Telling them what to do or doing it for them means you are in a Parent State and enticing a persecutor or victim emotional trigger from the exchange.

The Drama Triangle science goes much deeper as we have both outer and inner personality drama triangles. Dr. Karpman's latest book, A Game Free Life. is well worth the read for personal development and deeper interaction understanding. He shares this introduction; *"A Game Free Life takes you on a behavioral psychology journey through dozens of examples of stressful drama triangles in multiple familiar settings, including dysfunctional families, alcoholism, games in the courtroom, bedroom, and classroom, including the four rules of escalation, games of power and abuse in the workplace and at home, including child and elder abuse. Then from the outer personality drama triangles, we go deeper into the inner personality drama triangles illustrating rackets we use on ourselves. This includes generational and evolutionary trauma impacts in drama."*[xlv]

LIFE SCRIPTS AND EARLY DECISIONS

Some of us carry out subconscious life scripts which were formed very early in life and feed into our self-concept, our view of others, our biases and the path of life we expect to lead. These decisions about our lot in life are made at a time when the decision helped us adapt to the environment and the situations in which we were raised. Without in-depth analysis, they often do not make a whole lot of sense in our current world. Unless we take the time to discover what those decisive moments were and to decide whether they still serve us today, we will often repeat patterns in relationships and personal choices. This will prove to our subconscious that the early self-concept is still true. Think of it as your self-fulfilling prophecy.

Going back to the idea that our Parent Ego State is groomed by the adults responsible for our earliest care, whether parents, caregivers or other influencing adults, realize that the messages and strokes we received during that time feed into our self-perceived life scripts. These messages are verbal and non-verbal, and we interpret them and create decisions about ourselves based on these experiences. Much research on the cycle of poverty, abuse, and mental health can be aligned with this concept.

As we develop our sense of the world and our place within the culture and environment to which we are directly exposed has enormous impacts. We are born with the need to be connected to other humans. When a nurturing, loving bond is denied, it has significant implications on our wellness and survival. Babies denied touch and love as infants often die. This was discovered in a particularly gruesome experiment, as well as through historical information on lack of thriving in orphanages.

As parents and influential adults in a child's life, we want to aid their life script decisions on which they will base their self-concept. Those decisions that determine that they see themselves as good, lovable, and wanted as they grow and whether their actions and behaviors constitute a job well done, adequate intelligence and worthwhile competence. When these aspects are missing, children often grow up with a feeling that there is something wrong with them, that they do not fit within the world, and life decisions are based upon that subconscious life script.

Craig Groeschel, author of, Soul Detox, shares, *"There are four common categories of toxic thoughts. These are negative, fearful, discontented, and critical. Chances are you are struggling with toxic thoughts in one or more of these four ways". He emphasized the importance of "not allowing these thoughts to grab hold and consume you. The deeper you allow them to take root inside of you the harder they will be to shake off."*[xlvi]

Not everyone with adverse childhood trauma grows up negatively impacted by the influences of toxic parents. There are two key reasons a child will show significant resilience to adverse childhood inputs. The first is a child's natural personality. A happy, resilient, confident child is more apt to overcome harmful or toxic parenting than a child who is naturally withdrawn or prone to depressive personality traits. The second influence would come from the other adult influences in the child's life; this may be one good parent, or a close adult who counters the negative barrage of a toxic parent. For example, if one parent screams at a child that they are stupid, useless, a waste of flesh and then a close aunt counters that with consistent affirmations and negates the harsh words it can help significantly.

As a child who endured extreme emotional and physical abuse, Deirdre can confirm that there were five adults, including a couple of complete and unlikely strangers, whose words lifted her spirit and solidified a positive belief in moving beyond her abusive beginnings. She writes in her book, Unquiet Warrior; *"They had such an impact I dismissed the rants of my step-mother as crazy talk of an extremely cruel person and the critical and physical abuse of my father as a sad reflection of who he was as a man do to the unfathomable abuse he suffered as a child in an orphanage."*

This resilience was strong enough to withstand constant bullying and harassment in ghetto neighborhoods and helped keep self-esteem, strength and belief within to manage as a 14-year old run-a-way who survived eight months in survival mode, hiding from her father, not quite on the streets, but certainly not in a situation you would wish for any child. In Unquiet Warrior, she speaks to the power of resilience in creating a strong self-mastery and prosperous life.

For further communication strategies, we urge you to sign up for continuing information on our website. We will keep you apprised of further books, blogs and training events. Going Beyond the Call training programs can be found on GoingBeyondTheCall.com. Our non-profit organization will be holding Relationship Retreats and offering more personal development-based writings and programs. Follow up on GBTC911.com for these.

Versions of this content are developed for corporations challenged with toxic work environments, undergoing mergers or hampered with disengaged personnel. Check out DvKPartnerGroup.com for our corporate arm. Upcoming books are in planning for Disaster Relief, National Guard, and Recovery Teams; Medical Response and Emergency Room teams; and Military and Veterans. Programs are ready for these areas if you are interested in training please contact us.

For those public safety professionals seeking self-directed and fast acting therapy options for acute stress, we suggest you seek out Transactional Analysis Therapy in your local area. If you or someone you love is in crisis with PTSD or needs a solution to addictive behavior, then we strongly recommend in-house treatment centers that utilize trauma informed therapy techniques.

- **Twitter.com/GBTC911**
- **Facebook.com/gbtc911/**
- **Linkedin.com/company/gbtc**
- **Instagram.com/@gbtc911**
- **GBTC911.COM**
- **GoingBeyondTheCall.com**
- **info@goingbeyondthecall.com**

ABOUT THE AUTHORS

Deirdre von Krauskopf

Deirdre von Krauskopf developed her strong fortitude and resilience from necessity amid a traumatic childhood environment. A life in constant survival mode, abuse at home, severe bullying and forced participation in gang life to fight for her safety between school and home. Fighting became the one thing she excelled at, she took command at 14 and beaten savagely by her stepmother she resisted the violent urge to end another's life and ran away. Hiding in a friends cement basement, she worked to pay her board and used the family church to find and negotiate a custody release to her mother a few months later by leveraging her silence, as speaking up would put her handicapped half-brother in the system, which isn't kind to challenged kids. Similar to many child victims, threats had kept her and others quiet but there comes a time when you realize the only victor in silence is the abuser.

With the lessons of her past she drove herself to success. Desiring a better life, she realized a new family in Army Cadets at 14, Army Reserves at 17 and then marrying into the law enforcement family at 18 and working in that field. She attained her safe, secure, calm, loving home, locked her past in a vault and never looked back. With the addition of her son at 29 she was enjoying the best life could offer in career and family success until 26 year in, trauma came crashing in again.

She had nursed him through so many injuries and sleepless nights, together, they had always been okay. He had many near miss accidents, threats to him and our family by hardened criminals, even shot at but then one time, the last near-death incident hit harder. Slowly the man she loved stopped coming home and the stranger in his place set off long vaulted childhood triggers. It was devastating to be a top of her field human behavior "fixer" who failed her most important role. The unquiet in her head returned, unable to find a way to close the growing divide and no longer feeling safe, secure or calm, her crushed soul ran away once more. Needing to understand she educated herself in psychology and PTSD, found training to develop herself further then bought a license, and with combined education and life experience vowed to make a difference for other public safety professional families.

Her career spans Military, Law Enforcement, Senior Operational and Strategic Project Management. With a passionate drive to serve others Deirdre has developed her expertise in Human Behavior, Neuroscience, Emotional Intelligence, Body Language, Trauma-Informed Care and Strategic Communications through formal and informal education. She helps individuals and organizations achieve measurable, transformational change utilizing brain and behavioral sciences. She has written 5 books and over 30 training programs.

Sean Wyman

Sean grew up in poverty within the suburbs of Washington DC as a young child of an interracial relationship heated with underlying racial tension. Bullied as a minority, he is highly empathetic to generational and racial trauma of all kinds. Fighting for survival from a violent drug addicted and abusive stepfather Sean was quickly forced to learn how to manage daily mental and physical abuse. He adapted to survive using the streets as his guide. After three years of continual abuse, one night he came close to a fatal decision whose outcome changed his life forever.

Forced into a life of foster care and group homes he faced new problems along with old ones that were never resolved. Sean went from being bullied to becoming the bully. By the time he was a teenager, he had discovered damaging coping mechanisms to numb his pain. Ones that he became addicted to, and controlled by, for several years. A military Veteran with the Army Rangers, a Law Enforcement Officer with experience in many specialty units he kept swallowing down and pushing away the darkness. For over thirty years Sean's secret past was hidden in a vault while he privately suffered from denial, regret, anger, misery, and anxiety. It destroyed his first marriage and left him drowning in debt. The catalyst which pushed him to be a better man for his beautiful wife and family today. This goodness was the turning point in his life that at first he thought was just for him, but soon realized it was meant for millions of others like him.

Now, as the best-selling Author of THE MOVEMENT PROCESS, and a noted speaker he did not stop his passion for serving others. Sean achieved a certification in Trauma-Informed Care and further as a Trauma-Informed Professional. Sean is also a licensed provider of Verbal Aikido, a program of strategic communications, emotional intelligence and the philosophy of Aikido, staying calm, controlled and balanced in the moment. Sean has been street testing these tactics for years and making a significant impact in the community he serves with positive feedback from his partners and peers.

Today an 18+ year Law Enforcement Officer and Trainer, Army Ranger Veteran, father of 3, and husband of 14 years, Sean shares his story, the lessons learned, and most importantly teaches others as a trauma-informed care speaker, facilitator, and bestselling author with one purpose; help others realize that to them what is impossible with the right M.O.V.E.M.E.N.T. is possible. Sean is passionate about serving his brothers and sisters with the ground-breaking book, Going Beyond the Call because he has seen and battle-tested the contents and knows the benefits first-hand. His mission is to turn the increasingly devastating trend of suicides, PTSD and relationship failures within the ranks of the public safety professions. Everyone is calling for an answer … THIS is the solution! LET GO: THE MOVEMENT PROCESS

Appendix I

Self-Assessments ~ Crisis and Support links ~ Advocates

- QUALITY OF LIFE SCALE (PROQOL) - COMPASSION SATISFACTION AND COMPASSION FATIGUE (PROQOL) https://proqol.org/uploads/ProQOL_5_English_Self-Score.pdf

- BURNOUT: Test-stress.com has a series of free tests on stress and burnout.

- ANXIETY SCREENING TEST: https://psychcentral.com/quizzes/anxiety-quiz/

- DEPRESSION SCREENING TEST: https://psychcentral.com/quizzes/depression-quiz/

- PTSD: https://itherapy.com/interactive-ptsd-self-assessment/ (Also has a "find a therapist" link)

- The Diagnostic and Statistical Manual of Mental Disorders (DSM) determines the assessment criteria for PTSD.

- On the U.S. Department of Veteran Affairs site National Center for PTSD https://www.ptsd.va.gov/professional/assessment/documents/APCLS.pdf

- PTSD Treatment Decision Aid (https://www.ptsd.va.gov/apps/decisionaid/) helps to understand more about different therapies https://findtreatment.samhsa.

ADVOCATE LINKS: The following agencies have aided our research and advocate on our behalf. Please send us links to advocates for mental health and resiliency in your area, our website will have a growing list of links. We are happy to cross link with agencies working to help our public safety professionals.

Bluehelp.org - It is the mission of Blue H.E.L.P. to reduce mental health stigma through education, advocate for benefits for those suffering from post-traumatic stress, acknowledge the service and sacrifice of law enforcement officers we lost to suicide, assist officers in their search for healing, and to bring awareness to suicide and mental health issues.

Everyonegoeshome.com - Started at the 2004 Firefighter Life Safety Summit held to address the need for change within the fire service. At this summit, the 16 Firefighter Life Safety Initiatives were created, and a program was born to ensure that Everyone Goes Home. Our goal is to help the U.S. Fire Administration achieve its objective of reducing the number of preventable firefighter fatalities.

Thewoundedblue.org - The Wounded Blue, the national assistance and support organization for injured and disabled law enforcement officers, provides resources for officers that have experienced physical and emotional injuries on duty. Our mission is to improve the lives of injured and disabled officers through support programs that build unity, resiliency and wellness within the law enforcement community.

Naemt.org/initiatives/ems-mental-health - EMS practitioners face challenging and traumatic events that can impact their mental well-being each and every day. The mounting effect of patient needs, family, long workdays, nutrition, physical health, and sleep deprivation all contribute to an individual's sense of wellness. To assist EMS practitioners in recognizing, managing and seeking assistance for mental health issues, we have assembled the following resources.

911wellness.com/educationadvocacy/ - The Foundation's mission is to foster optimal health fueling resilience, peak performance, and a high Quality of Life (at work and at home) for our nation's 911 Public Safety Telecommunicators (PST). These 911 Professionals are the Very First Responders when citizens seek emergency help.

Correctional Peace Officers Foundation - cpof.org- The Correctional Peace Officers (CPO) Foundation is a national, non-profit charitable organization created in 1984. Its primary function is to preserve and support the surviving families of Correctional Officers who lose their lives in pursuit of their chosen profession of protecting the public from those remanded to correctional custody and supervision in the nation's prisons and jails.

National Volunteer Fire Council - FIRE & EMS
Nvfc.org/programs/share-the-load-program/ - Taking care of your mental health is as important as managing your physical health. The NVFC's Share the Load™ program provides access to critical resources and information to help first responders and their families manage and overcome personal and work-related problems. This includes the Fire/EMS Helpline, which offers free 24-hour assistance with issues such as stress, depression, addiction, PTSD, and more.

HELP AND CRISIS LINKS - PROGRAM IN YOUR PHONE:

- **The National Suicide Prevention Hotline** provides 24/7 confidential support for those in distress or in need of help for their loved ones.
  CONTACT: Call 800-273-8255 (TALK) or visit suicidepreventionlifeline.org
  In some States and growing 988 hotline will take you here.

- **Crisis Text Line** - A text will connect you with a trained crisis counselor, 24/7.
  CONTACT: https://www.crisistextline.org/ or text BADGE to 741741

- **Safe Call Now** is a resource for public safety employees to speak confidentially with officers, former law enforcement officers, public safety professionals and/or mental healthcare providers who are familiar with your line of work. CONFIDENTIAL, comprehensive, 24-hour crisis referral service for all public safety employees and families
  SAFE CALL NOW – 1-206-459-3020 OR 1-877-230-6060

- **1st Help** matches first responders with appropriate services based on a brief questionnaire, which determines what specific assistance you need (emotional, financial, religious, etc.).
  CONTACT: http://www.1sthelp.net/

- **National Volunteer Fire Council (NVFC)** teamed up with American Addiction Centers (AAC) to create a free, confidential helpline available 24 hours a day, 7 days a week.
  Fire/EMS Helpline: 1-888-731-FIRE (3473)

- **First Responder Support Network**
  FRSN provides educational treatment programs for first responders and their families.
  CONTACT: http://www.frsn.org/ or call 415-721-9789

- **CopLine:** 1-800-267-5463, available for the United States and Canada.

- **Serve & Protect**
  Serve & Protect helps connect public safety professionals with trauma services.
  CONTACT: https://serveprotect.org/ or call 615-373-8000 for the crisis line.

- **Treatment Placement Specialists**
  This program offers treatment guidance based on the individual needs of first responders.
  CONTACT: https://www.treatmentplacementspecialists.com/first-responders/ or call 877-540-3935

INTERNATIONAL ASSOCIATION FOR SUICIDE PREVENTION (IASP)
Has a global map that helps find crisis lines around the world:
https://www.iasp.info/resources/Crisis_Centres/

REFERENCES

i "Dealing with Trauma as a Paramedic." Emergency Services Health. Accessed November 21, 2019. https://eshealth.com.au/dealing-trauma-paramedic.

ii Heyman, Miriam, Jeff Dill, and Robert Douglas. "Study: Police Officers and Firefighters Are More Likely to Die by Suicide than in Line of Duty." Ruderman Family Foundation. Ruderman Family Foundation, April 2018. https://rudermanfoundation.org/white_papers/police-officers-and-firefighters-are-more-likely-to-die-by-suicide-than-in-line-of-duty/.

iii Barber, Erich, Chad Newland, Amy Young, and Monique Rose. "Survey Reveals Alarming Rates of EMS Provider Stress and Thoughts of Suicide." JEMS. Journal of Emergency Medical Services, September 2, 2019. https://www.jems.com/2015/09/28/survey-reveals-alarming-rates-of-ems-provider-stress-and-thoughts-of-suicide/.

iv "Suicide Facts at a Glance 2015 - Centers for Disease ..." www.cdc.gov/violenceprevention. Center for Disease Control and Prevention, 2015. https://www.cdc.gov/violenceprevention/pdf/suicide-datasheet-a.pdf.

v Pierce, Heather, and Michelle M Lilly. "Duty-Related Trauma Exposure in 911 Telecommunicators: Considering the Risk for Posttraumatic Stress." Journal of traumatic stress. International Society for Traumatic Stress Studies, April 25, 2012. https://www.ncbi.nlm.nih.gov/pubmed/22467384.

vi "911 Dispatchers at Risk for PTSD." ABC News Medical Unit. ABC News, March 29, 2012.

vii Denhof, Michael D., and Caterina G. Spinaris. "Depression, PTSD, and Comorbidity in United States Corrections Professionals: Prevalence and Impact on Health and Functioning." http://desertwaters.com/wp-content/uploads/2013/09/Comorbidity_Study_09-03-131.pdf. DESERT WATERS CORRECTIONAL OUTREACH, 2013.

viii Press, Associated. "Why Are Suicide Rates so High among Corrections Officers?" New York Post. January 9, 2018. https://nypost.com/2018/01/09/why-are-suicide-rates-so-high-among-corrections-officers/.

ix Nho, Seon Mi, and Eun A Kim. "Factors Influencing Post Traumatic Stress Disorder in Crime Scene Investigators." Journal of Korean Academy of Nursing. U.S. National Library of Medicine, February 2017. https://www.ncbi.nlm.nih.gov/pubmed/28262653.

x Carleton, R. Nicholas, Tracie O. Afifi, Sarah Turner, Tamara Taillieu, Sophie Duranceau, Daniel M. Lebouthillier, Jitender Sareen, et al. "Mental Disorder Symptoms among Public Safety Personnel in Canada." The Canadian Journal of Psychiatry63, no. 1 (2017): 54–64. https://doi.org/10.1177/0706743717723825.

xi Heyman, Miriam, Jeff Dill, and Robert Douglas. "Study: Police Officers and Firefighters Are More Likely to Die by Suicide than in Line of Duty." Ruderman Family Foundation. Ruderman Family Foundation, April 2018. https://rudermanfoundation.org/white_papers/police-officers-and-firefighters-are-more-likely-to-die-by-suicide-than-in-line-of-duty/.

[xii] Judd, Terri. "Now Ambulance Workers Fall Victim to Battlefield Stress." *INDEPENDENT*, November 7, 2008. https://www.independent.co.uk/news/uk/home-news/now-ambulance-workers-fall-victim-to-battlefield-stress-998218.html.

[xiii] "Majority of First Responders Face Mental Health Challenges in the Workplace." First Responders Face Mental Health Challenges - UOPX. University of Phoenix, April 18, 2017. https://www.phoenix.edu/about_us/media-center/news/uopx-releases-first-responder-mental-health-survey-results.html.

[xiv] Crawford, Alison. "Researchers Find Significantly Higher Rate of Mental Disorders among First Responders." *CBC News*. August 30, 2017. https://www.cbc.ca/news/politics/police-fire-fighters-ptsd-paramedis-1.4266720.

[xv] Sapolsky, Robert M. "Depression, Antidepressants, and the Shrinking Hippocampus." Proceedings of the National Academy of Sciences of the United States of America 98.22 (2001): 12320–12322. PMC. Web. 2 Sept. 2018.

[xvi] Walker, Anthony, Andrew Mckune, Sally Ferguson, David B. Pyne, and Ben Rattray. "Chronic Occupational Exposures Can Influence the Rate of PTSD and Depressive Disorders in First Responders and Military Personnel." *Extreme Physiology & Medicine*5, no. 1 (July 15, 2016). https://doi.org/10.1186/s13728-016-0049-x.
[xvii] . "Gun Violence Archive." Gun Violence Archive, November 24, 2019. https://www.gunviolencearchive.org/.

[xviii] Aboraya, Abe. "PTSD Currently Doesn't Qualify Parkland First Responders For Workers' Comp." *NPR Politics*. March 2, 2018. https://www.npr.org/2018/03/02/590207042/ptsd-currently-doesnt-qualify-parkland-first-responders-for-workers-comp.

[xix] Cunningham, Quinn. "Responding to a School Shooting." fortitudetrainingconcepts.com, April 23, 2018. https://www.fortitudetrainingconcepts.com/blog

[xx] De Marco, Heidi. "The Other Victims: First Responders To Violent Disasters Often Suffer Alone." *NPR Public Health*. July 4, 2018. https://www.npr.org/sections/health-shots/2018/07/04/625784687/the-other-victims-first-responders-to-violent-disasters-often-suffer-alone.

[xxi] / Chua, Jinnie. "Helping First Responders Recover After Las Vegas Shooting." *IN Public Safety*. October 3, 2017. https://inpublicsafety.com/2017/10/helping-first-responders-recover-after-las-vegas-shooting/.

[xxii]Morley, Jeff. "Badge of Life Canada | Police & Corrections Psychological ...," 2017. https://badgeoflifecanada.org/.

[xxiii] Brandt, Marisa, Robyn Bluhm, and MaryCatherine McDonald. "From Shell-Shock to PTSD, a Century of Invisible War Trauma." The Conversation, April 3, 2017. http://theconversation.com/from-shell-shock-to-ptsd-a-century-of-invisible-war-trauma-74911.

[xxiv] Linden, Stefanie Caroline, and Edgar Jones. "'Shell Shock' Revisited: An Examination of the Case Records of the National Hospital in London." *Medical History*58, no. 4 (October 9, 2014): 519–45. https://doi.org/10.1017/mdh.2014.51.

[xxv] "Shell Shock." *The British Medical Journal* 2, no. 3216 (1922): 322-23. www.jstor.org/stable/20420866.

[xxvi] Yealland, Lewis Ralph., and E. Farquhar Buzzard. *Hysterical Disorders of Warfare*. London: Macmillan and co., limited, 1918.

[xxvii] Kardiner, Abram, and . *The Traumatic Neuroses of War*. New York: Martino Fine Books, 2012.

[xxviii] Brandt, Marisa, Robyn Bluhm, and MaryCatherine McDonald. "From Shell-Shock to PTSD, a Century of Invisible War Trauma." The Conversation, April 3, 2017. http://theconversation.com/from-shell-shock-to-ptsd-a-century-of-invisible-war-trauma-74911.

[xxix] "The Florida Senate." Senate Bill 376 (2018). The Florida Senate, October 1, 2018. http://flsenate.gov/Session/Bill/2018/376.

[xxx] Aboraya, Abe. "Workers' Comp Benefits For Florida First Responders To Include PTSD." *NPR Politics*. March 9, 2018. https://www.npr.org/2018/03/09/592027551/workers-comp-benefits-for-florida-first-responders-to-include-ptsd-governor

[xxxi] Brown, Asa Don. "First Responders and Mental Health." *Psychology Today*, May 12, 2017.

[xxxii] Theofficernextdoor. "It's Not Normal." theofficernextdoor.com. The Officer Next Door , August 9, 2018. https://theofficernextdoor.com/2018/07/26/its-not-normal/.

xxxiii "National Survey on Drug Use and Health (NSDUH-2016)." National Survey on Drug Use and Health (NSDUH-2016) | SAMHDA. Substance Abuse and Mental Health Administrative Center for Behavioral Health Statistics and Quality, September 7, 2017. https://www.datafiles.samhsa.gov/study/national-survey-drug-use-and-health-nsduh-2016-nid17184.

xxxiv Haugen, Peter T., Aileen M. Mccrillis, Geert E. Smid, and Mirjam J. Nijdam. "Mental Health Stigma and Barriers to Mental Health Care for First Responders: A Systematic Review and Meta-Analysis." Journal of Psychiatric Research94 (August 5, 2017): 218–29. https://doi.org/10.1016/j.jpsychires.2017.08.001.

xxxv Felitti, Vincent. "Adverse Childhood Experiences (ACE)." APB Speakers. Accessed November 21, 2019. https://www.apbspeakers.com/speaker/vincent-felitti/.

xxxvi Perry, Bruce D. "ChildTrauma.org." ChildTrauma.org(blog). The Child Trauma Academy, 2003. http://www.fa-sett.no/filer/perry-handout-effects-of-trauma.pdf.

xxxvii Bellis, Michael D. De, and Abigail Zisk. "The Biological Effects of Childhood Trauma." Child and Adolescent Psychiatric Clinics of North America23, no. 2 (February 16, 2014): 185–222. https://doi.org/10.1016/j.chc.2014.01.002.

xxxviii Sanders, Robert. "New Evidence That Chronic Stress Predisposes Brain to Mental Illness." Berkley News. February 11, 14AD. https://news.berkeley.edu/2014/02/11/chronic-stress-predisposes-brain-to-mental-illness/.

[xxxix]*How Childhood Trauma Affects Health Across a Lifetime*. TEDMED 2014, 2014. https://www.ted.com/speakers/nadine_burke_harris_1.

[xl] MacNeil, James. "Verbal Aikido | Pure Communications Mastery." Verbal Aikido ~ Pure Communications Mastery. EQ Communications Inc., 2008. http://verbalaikido.com/ ©Fully Engaged and Fully Detached

[xli] "2014 Baker Act - Myflfamilies.com." Department of Mental Health Law & Policy, 2014. https://www.myflfamilies.com/service-programs/samh/crisis-services/laws/BakerActManual.pdf.

[xlii] Meuer, James. *Damaged: A First Responders Experiences Handling Post-Traumatic Stress Disorder*. Bloomington, IN: WestBow Press, a

division of Thomas Nelson, 2013.

[xliii] Craven, Allen B, Ray Hawkins, Tom Healy, JoAnne Fish Hildebrand, Murrey E Loflin, Lou Paulson, Ed Stauffer, and Marla Zipin. The United States Fire Administrations stress management model program for firefighter well-being, The United States Fire Administrations stress management model program for firefighter well-being § (1991). https://www.hsdl.org/?view&did=770552

[xliv] Backberg, Holly. "EMS World Leadership/Management." *EMS World Leadership/Management*(blog). EMS World, March 2019. https://www.emsworld.com/article/1222339/stress-silent-killer-ems-career.

[xlv]Coughlin, Steven S. "Post-Traumatic Stress Disorder and Cardiovascular Disease." *Post-Traumatic Stress Disorder and Chronic Health Conditions*, July 11, 2011. https://doi.org/10.2105/9780875530161ch07.

[xlvi] Luber, Marilyn. EMDR with First Responders Models, Scripted Protocols, and Summary Sheets for Mental Health Interventions. Springer Publishing Company, 2015. ISBN-13: 978-0826133380

[xlvii] Maté, Gabor. *In the Realm of Hungry Ghosts Close Encounters with Addiction.* London: Vermilion, 2018.
[xlviii] Substance Abuse and Mental Health Services Administration. *SAMHSA's Concept of Trauma and Guidance for a Trauma-Informed Approach.* HHS Publication No. (SMA) 14-4884. Rockville, MD: Substance Abuse and Mental Health Services Administration, 2014.

xlix Substance Abuse and Mental Health Services Administration. *SAMHSA's Concept of Trauma and Guidance for a Trauma-Informed Approach.* HHS Publication No. (SMA) 14-4884. Rockville, MD: Substance Abuse and Mental Health Services Administration, 2014.

[l] Maté, Gabor. *In the Realm of Hungry Ghosts Close Encounters with Addiction.* London: Vermilion, 2018.

[li]Center for Behavioral Health Statistics and Quality. (2015). *Behavioral health trends in the United States: Results from the 2014 National Survey on Drug Use and Health* (HHS Publication No. SMA 15-4927, NSDUH Series H-50). Retrieved from http://www.samhsa.gov/ data/

[lii] Williams, Timothy. "Long Taught to Use Force, Police Warily Learn to De-Escalate." *The New York Times*, June 27, 2015. https://www.nytimes.com/2015/06/28/us/long-taught-to-use-force-police-warily-learn-to-de-escalate.html.

[liii] Lerner, Jennifer S., Ye Li, Piercarlo Valdesolo, and Karim S. Kassam. "Emotion and Decision Making." *Annual Review of Psychology*66, no. 1 (September 22, 2014): 799–823. https://doi.org/10.1146/annurev-psych-010213-115043.

[liv] Hathaway, Bill. "Even-Healthy-Stress-Causes-Brain-Shrink-Yale-Study-Shows." *Yale News.* January 9, 2012. https://news.yale.edu/2012/01/09/even-healthy-stress-causes-brain-shrink-yale-study-shows.

[lv] PERRY, BRUCE. *BOY WHO WAS RAISED AS A DOG: and Other Stories from a Child Psychiatrists Notebook--What ... Traumatized Children Can Teach Us about Loss, Love.* Place of publication not identified: BASIC Books, 2017.

[lvi] Hanson, Jamie L., Alysha D. Gillmore, Tianyi Yu, Christopher J. Holmes, Emily S. Hallowell, Allen W. Barton, Steven R.h. Beach, et al. "A Family Focused Intervention Influences Hippocampal-Prefrontal Connectivity Through Gains in Self-Regulation." *Child Development*90, no. 4 (October 8, 2018): 1389–1401. https://doi.org/10.1111/cdev.13154.

[lvii] Kühn, Simone, Patrick Haggard, and Marcel Brass. "Differences between Endogenous and Exogenous Emotion Inhibition in the Human Brain." *Brain Structure and Function*219, no. 3 (May 5, 2014): 1129–38. https://doi.org/10.1007/s00429-013-0556-0.

[lviii] MacLean, Paul D. *The Triune Brain in Evolution: Role in Paleocerebral Functions.* New York: Plenum Press, 1990.
[lix] Roelofs, Karin. "Freeze for Action: Neurobiological Mechanisms in Animal and Human Freezing." *Philosophical Transactions of the Royal Society B: Biological Sciences*372, no. 1718 (February 27, 2017): 20160206. https://doi.org/10.1098/rstb.2016.0206.

[lx] Fenster, Robert J., Lauren A. M. Lebois, Kerry J. Ressler, and Junghyup Suh. "Brain Circuit Dysfunction in Post-Traumatic Stress Disorder: from Mouse to Man." *Nature Reviews Neuroscience*19, no. 9 (September 27, 2018): 535–51. https://doi.org/10.1038/s41583-018-0039-7.

[lxi] Shin, Lisa, et al. "Hippocampal Function in Posttraumatic Stress Disorder ..." *PubMed.gov*, US National Library of Medicine National Institutes of Health, 2004, https://www.researchgate.net/publication/8574168_Hippocampal_function_in_posttraumatic_stress_disorder.

[lxii] Moore, Michael Scott. "PTSD BRAIN STUDIES LOOK AT HIPPOCAMPUS." *Pacific Standard.* July 6, 2011. https://psmag.com/news/ptsd-brain-studies-look-at-hippocampus-33419.

[lxiii] Weiss, EM, et al. "Genetics of Posttraumatic Stress Disorders (PTSD)." *PubMed.gov*, NCBI, 19 July 2018, https://www.ncbi.nlm.nih.gov/pubmed/30025422.

[lxiv]NYU "Emotions Are Cognitive, Not Innate." http://neurosciencenews.com/cognitive-emotions-psychology-6117/ (accessed February 15, 2017).

[lxv] Hansen, Fawne. "Adrenal Fatigue: How to Recover Naturally." Adrenal Fatigue Solution. Perfect Health, 2014. https://adrenalfatiguesolution.com/.

[lxvi] InformedHealth.org [Internet]. Cologne, Germany: Institute for Quality and Efficiency in Health Care (IQWiG); 2006-. Depression: What is burnout? 2012 Dec 5 [Updated 2017 Jan 12].Available from: https://www.ncbi.nlm.nih.gov/books/NBK279286/

[lxvii]Javed, Afzal, and Konstanthos N. Fountoulakis. *Advances in Psychiatry*. Cham, Switzerland: Springer, 2019.

[lxviii] Siegel, Daniel J. *Mindsight: The New Science of Personal Transformation*. New York: Bantam Books, 2011.

[lxix] "Professional Quality of Life." www.proqol. ProQOL Office , 2019. https://www.proqol.org/.
[lxx] Gilmartin, Kevin M. *Emotional Survival for Law Enforcement: A Guide for Officers and Their Families*. Tucson, AZ: E-S Press, 2002.

[lxxi] Figley , Charles R. "Founder: Dr. Charles Figley." Tulane University Traumatology Institute, 1996. https://tulanetraumatologyinstitute.com/charles-figley.

[lxxii] Cell Press. "Pure Novelty Spurs The Brain." ScienceDaily. ScienceDaily, 27 August 2006. <www.sciencedaily.com/releases/20

[lxxiii] Lynn, Steven Jay, Anne Malakataris, Liam Condon, Reed Maxwell, and Colleen Cleere. "Post-Traumatic Stress Disorder: Cognitive Hypnotherapy, Mindfulness, and Acceptance-Based Treatment Approaches." *American Journal of Clinical Hypnosis*54, no. 4 (March 26, 2012): 311–30. https://doi.org/10.1080/00029157.2011.645913.

lxxiv BUBER, MARTIN. I AND THOU. New York, NY: New York : Charles Scribner's Sons, 1970. ISBN 0684717255

lxxv Chapman, Gary D. The 5 Love Languages: The Secret to Love That Lasts. Chicago: Northfield Pub., 2015.

lxxvi McKay, Matthew, Martha Davis, and Patrick Fanning. Messages: The Communications Skills Book. Oakland, CA: New Harbinger Publications, Inc., 2018.

lxxvii Sharma, N., Prakash, O., Sengar, K. S., Chaudhury, S., & Singh, A. R. (2015). The relation between emotional intelligence and criminal behavior: A study among convicted criminals. Industrial psychiatry journal, 24(1), 54–58. doi:10.4103/0972-6748.160934

lxxviii Wilcox, Laura. "Harvard Extension School, Professional Development." (blog). Harvard Division of Continuing Education, n.d. https://www.extension.harvard.edu/professional-development/blog/emotional-intelligence-no-soft-skill.

lxxix Plutchik, Robert. "The Nature of Emotions." American Scientist89, no. 4 (2001): 344–50. https://doi.org/10.1511/2001.28.739.

lxxx Rajeshwari, R. R., and S. John Mano Raj. "Opening of New Insights for the Researchers: A ..." Research Gate Publication. International Journal of Engineering and Management Research, August 2015. https://www.researchgate.net/publication/301894716_Opening_of_New_Insights_for_the_Researchers_A_Descriptive_Study_on_Emotional_Maturity.

[lxxxi] Colman, Andrew M. "Social Contagion - Oxford Reference." Social contagion - A Dictionary of Psychology (3 ed.). Oxford Reference, 2014. https://www.oxfordreference.com/view/10.1093/acref/9780199534067.001.0001/acref-9780199534067-e-7741.

[lxxxii]Marsden, Paul. "Memetics & Social Contagion: Two Sides of the Same Coin?" Social Contagion. Standford Edu, 2005. https://web.stanford.edu/~kcarmel/CC_BehavChange_Course/readings/Additional Resources/social contagion/Social Contagion.htm.

[lxxxiii] White, Rob. Swarming and the social dynamics of group violence, Swarming and the social dynamics of group violence § (2006).

[lxxxiv]Gelder, Beatrice De, and Julie Grezes. "Social Perception: Understanding Other People's Intentions and Emotions through Their Actions." *Research Gate*, January 1, 2009, - . https://www.researchgate.net/publication/237139986_Social_perception_Understanding_other_people's_intentions_and_emotions_through_their_actions.

[lxxxv]Fellous, Jean-Marc, Jorge L Armony, and Joseph E LeDoux. "Emotional Circuits and Computational Neuroscience." psychdept.arizona.edu. To appear in The Handbook of Brain Theory and Neural Networks, Second edition, (M.A. Arbib, Ed.), Cambridge, MA: The MIT Press, 2002. http://mitpress.mit.edu ©The MIT Press, 2002.

http://amygdala.psychdept.arizona.edu/pubs/Emotion-HBTNN2e-preprint.pdf.

[lxxxvi]Grezes, Julie, and Beatrice de Gelder. "Brain and Emotion Laboratory Maastricht University - Beatrice De Gelder." Brain and Emotion Laboratory Maastricht University - Beatrice de Gelder. Beatrice de Gelder, March 28, 2008. http://beatricedegelder.com/documents/SocialPerceptionUnderstandingotherpeoplesintentions.pdf.

[lxxxvii] Stein, Murray B, AN Simmons, JS Feinstein, and MP Paulus. "Increased Amygdala and Insula Activation During Emotion Processing in Anxiety-Prone Subjects." *American Journal of Psychiatry*164, no. 2 (February 1, 2007): 318–27. https://doi.org/10.1176/appi.ajp.164.2.318.

[lxxxviii] "The Unfortunate Connection Between Childhood Trauma and Addiction in Adulthood." *DualDiagnosis.org*, n.d. https://www.dualdiagnosis.org/unfortunate-connection-childhood-trauma-addiction-adulthood/

[lxxxix] Pontin, Jason. "The Importance of Feelings." *MIT Technology Review*. June 17, 2014. https://www.technologyreview.com/s/528151/the-importance-of-feelings/.

[xc] "Rule 403. Excluding Relevant Evidence for Prejudice, Confusion, Waste of Time, or Other Reasons." Legal Information Institute. Legal Information Institute, December 1, 2011. https://www.law.cornell.edu/rules/fre/rule_403.

[xci] Bandes, Susan A. and Salerno, Jessica M., Emotion, Proof and Prejudice: The Cognitive Science of Gruesome Photos and Victim Impact Statements (March 27, 2014). 46 Arizona State Law Journal 1003 (2014). Available at SSRN: https://ssrn.com/abstract=2416818

[xcii]Strets, Jan, and Jonathan H Turner. *Handbook of the Sociology of Emotions*. 1st ed. Boston, MA: Springer US, 2006.

[xciii] Pauen, Michael. "Somatic Marker Hypothesis." *Science Direct*, 2006.

[xciv] Covey, Stephen M. R., and Rebecca R. Merrill. *The Speed of Trust: the One Thing That Changes Everything*. New York, NY: Free Press, 2018.

[xcv] Gabriel, Roger, Roger Gabriel, and Chopra Center Educator. "Is the Ego Your Friend or Foe?" The Chopra Center, January 23, 2017. https://chopra.com/articles/is-the-ego-your-friend-or-foe.

[xcvi]Suhaimi, Farah Amirah Binti, and Norhayati Binti Hussin. "The Influence of Information Overload on Studentsâ□™ Academic Performance." *International Journal of Academic Research in Business and Social Sciences*7, no. 8 (September 1, 2017). https://doi.org/10.6007/ijarbss/v7-i8/3292.

[xcvii] Lynott, William J. "COULD THE EVENING NEWS BE BAD FOR YOUR HEALTH? The Dangers of Information Overload." *The Elks Magazine*, April 2003.

[xcviii] Toffler, Alvin. *Future Shock*. Bantam; Reissue edition, 1984.

[xcix] Geller, E. Scott. *The Psychology of Safety Handbook*. 2nd ed. CRC Press; 2 edition, 2000.

[c] Mathews, Kenneth E., and Lance K. Canon. "Environmental Noise Level as a Determinant of Helping Behavior." *Journal of Personality and Social Psychology*32, no. 4 (October 1, 1975): 571–77. https://doi.org/10.1037//0022-3514.32.4.571.

[ci] McNeil, James. "Verbal Aikido ." Verbal Aikido™. EQ Communications Inc., 2015. http://verbalaikido.com. *used with licensee contract permission

[cii] McNeil, James. "Verbal Aikido ." Verbal Aikido™. EQ Communications Inc., 2015. http://verbalaikido.com. *used with licensee contract permission

[ciii] McNeil, James. "Verbal Aikido ." Verbal Aikido™. EQ Communications Inc., 2015. http://verbalaikido.com. *used with licensee contract permission

[civ] Ueshiba, Kisshomaru. *Spirit of Aikido*. Kodansha International, 2013.

[cv] McNeil, James. "Verbal Aikido ." Verbal Aikido™. EQ Communications Inc., 2015. http://verbalaikido.com. *used with licensee contract permission

[cvi] McNeil, James. "Verbal Aikido ." Verbal Aikido™. EQ Communications Inc., 2015. http://verbalaikido.com. *used with licensee contract permission

[cvii] Davis, Eric. "Habits of Heroes." Habits of Heros. Accessed n.d.. https://www.ericdavis215.com/habits-of-heroes.

[cviii] Kolk, Bessel van der. *The Body Keeps the Score: Brain, Mind and Body in the Healing of Trauma*. New York: Penguin Books, 2015.

[cix] Csikszentmihalyi, Mihaly. *Flow: The Psychology of Optimal Experience.* New York: Harper Row, 2009.

[cx] Bassham, Lanny. "With Winning in Mind." Mental Management Systems. Lanny Bassham , 2002. https://mentalmanagement.com/.

[cxi]Csikszentmihalyi, Mihaly. "Finding Flow: the Psychology of Engagement with Everyday Life." Amazon. Basic Books; 1st edition, March 20, 2007. https://www.amazon.com/Finding-Flow-Psychology-Engagement-Masterminds/dp/0465024114.

[cxii] Csikszentmihalyi, Mihaly. "The Pursuit of Happiness, Bringing the Science of Happiness to Life." Pursuit of Happiness. Accessed n.d..https://www.pursuit-of-happiness.org/history-of-happiness/mihaly-csikszentmihalyi/.

[cxiii] Mehrabian, Albert. "Nonverbal Betrayal of Feeling." *Nonverbal Communication*, 2017, 84–103. https://doi.org/10.4324/9781351308724-5.

[cxiv] Mehrabian, Albert. "'Silent Messages' -- A Wealth of Information About Nonverbal Communication (Body Language)." Personality, Psychological Articles & Books of Popular Interest. Albert Mehrabian, 1995. http://www.kaaj.com/psych/smorder.html.

[cxv] McNeil, James. "Verbal Aikido ." Verbal Aikido™. EQ Communications Inc., 2015. http://verbalaikido.com. *used with licensee contract permission

[cxvi] McNeil, James. "Verbal Aikido ." Verbal Aikido™. EQ Communications Inc., 2015. http://verbalaikido.com. *used with licensee contract permission

[cxvii] frontiersin.org/articles/10.3389/fpsyg.2017.02278/Matching Your Face or Appraising the Situation: Two Paths to Emotional Contagion

[cxviii] Martin Bruder, Dina Dosmukhambetova, Josef Nerb & Antony S. R. Manstead (2012) Emotional signals in nonverbal interaction: Dyadic facilitation and convergence in expressions, appraisals, and feelings, Cognition and Emotion, 26:3,480-502, DOI: 10.1080/02699931.2011.645280

[cxix] Mumenthaler, Christian, and David Sander. "Automatic Integration of Social Information in Emotion Recognition." *Journal of Experimental Psychology: General*144 , no. 2 (April 2015): 392–99. https://doi.org/https://doi.org/10.1037/xge0000059.

[cxx] Remmers C and Michalak J (2016) Losing Your Gut Feelings. Intuition in Depression. *Front. Psychol.* 7:1291. doi: 10.3389/fpsyg.2016.01291

[cxxi] White, Rob. Swarming and the social dynamics of group violence, Swarming and the social dynamics of group violence § (2006).

[cxxii] "Bengt's Notes." *Bengt's Notes*(blog), July 22, 2009. http://bengtwendel.com/your-teacup-is-full-empty-your-cup/.

[cxxiii] McNeil, James. "Verbal Aikido ." Verbal Aikido™. EQ Communications Inc., 2015. http://verbalaikido.com. *used with licensee contract permission
[cxxiv] Frankl, Victor E. *Man's Search for Meaning.* 1st ed. Beacon Press, 2006.

[cxxv] Gottman, John Mordechai. *What Predicts Divorce?: the Relationship between Marital Processes and Marital Outcomes.* 1st ed. New York: Psychology Press, 1993.

[cxxvi] Bloom, Linda, and Charlie Bloom. "12 Steps to Getting Someone to Open Up." *Psychology Today*, September 8, 2014. https://www.psychologytoday.com/us/blog/stronger-the-broken-places/201409/12-steps-getting-someone-open.

[cxxvii] Mayer, John D., Peter Salovey, and David R. Caruso. "Emotional Intelligence: Theory, Findings, and Implications." *Psychological Inquiry* 15, no. 3 (2004): 197-215. www.jstor.org/stable/20447229.

[cxxviii] Goleman, Daniel. *Emotional Intelligence: Why It Can Matter More Than IQ* . New York: Bantam Books, 2005.

[cxxix] Martsvishvilli, Khatuna. "Boell.org." *Boell.org*(blog). Heinrich-Böll-Stiftung, 2010. http://ge.boell.org/sites/default/files/uploads/2015/11/khatuna.pdf.

[cxxx] Mandel, Mike. "The Ultimate Live and Online Hypnosis Training." Mike Mandel Hypnosis Academy. Accessed n.d..https://mikemandelhypnosis.com/.

[cxxxi]Porges, Stephen. "Home of Dr. Stephen Porges." Home of Dr. Stephen Porges. Accessed

n.d..https://www.stephenporges.com/.

[cxxxii] Goleman, Daniel. *Emotional Intelligence: Why It Can Matter More Than IQ* . New York: Bantam Books, 2005.

[cxxxiii] Tumlin, Geoffrey. *Stop Talking Start Communicating: Counterintuitive Secrets to Success in Business and in Life.* New York: McGraw-Hill Education, 2013.

[cxxxiv] Maslow, Abraham H. *TOWARD A PSYCHOLOGY OF BEING.* Place of publication not identified: Wilder Publications, 2013.

[cxxxv] Nieves, Brain. Captain Your Ship Speech "GURU Builder Tour with Deirdre von Krauskopf." *The Benson Hotel, Portland,* OR

[cxxxvi] McRaven, William H. *Make Your Bed: Little Things That Can Change Your Life... and Maybe the World.* 2nd ed. Grand Central Publishing, 2017.

[cxxxvii]Berne, Eric. "Eric Berne Books: Transactional Analysis in Psychotherapy (1961), Games People Play (1964), The Principles of Group Treatment (1966) and What Do You Say After You Say Hello." Eric Berne M.D., 1999. http://www.ericberne.com/.

[cxxxviii] Karpman, Stephen. "Karpman Drama Triangle." Karpman Drama Triangle, 2005. https://www.karpmandramatriangle.com/.

[cxxxix] Harris, Thomas. "History and Impact of the Book I'm OK - You're OK Dr. Thomas A. Harris." Thomas A. Harris M.D., 2019. http://www.drthomasharris.com/im-ok-youre-ok-book-thomas-harris/.

[cxl] Karpman, Stephen B. "Intimacy Analysis Today: The Intimacy Scale and the Personality Pinwheel." *Transactional Analysis Journal*40, no. 3-4 (2010): 224–42. https://doi.org/10.1177/036215371004000308.

cxli Harris, Thomas. "History and Impact of the Book I'm OK - You're OK Dr. Thomas A. Harris." Thomas A. Harris M.D., 2019. http://www.drthomasharris.com/im-ok-youre-ok-book-thomas-harris/.

[cxlii]Levin, Pamela. "Ego States and Emotional Development in Adolescence." *Transactional Analysis Journal*45, no. 3 (2015): 228–37. https://doi.org/10.1177/0362153715599990.

[cxliii]Levin, Pamela. *The Cycle of Life: Creating Smooth Passages in Every Life Season.* Ukiah, CA: Nourishing Co., 2007.

[cxliv] Berne, Eric. "Description of Transactional Analysis and Games by Dr. Eric Berne MD." Eric Berne M.D. Eric Berne MD, 1999. http://www.ericberne.com/transactional-analysis/.

[cxlv] McNeil, James. "Verbal Aikido ." Verbal Aikido™. EQ Communications Inc., 2015. http://verbalaikido.com. *used with licensee contract permission

[cxlvi] Harris, Thomas. "History and Impact of the Book I'm OK - You're OK Dr. Thomas A. Harris." Thomas A. Harris M.D., 2019. http://www.drthomasharris.com/im-ok-youre-ok-book-thomas-harris/.

[cxlvii] LAWRENCE S. KUBIE, A THEORETICAL APPLICATION TO SOME NEUROLOGICAL PROBLEMS OF THE PROPERTIES OF EXCITATION WAVES WHICH MOVE IN CLOSED CIRCUITS, Brain, Volume 53, Issue 2, July 1930, Pages 166–177, https://doi.org/10.1093/brain/53.2.166

[cxlviii] Bates, Laura. *Shakespeare Saved My Life: Ten Years in Solitary with the Bard: A Memoir.* Naperville, IL: Sourcebooks, Inc., 2013.

[cxlix]Chapman, Gary D. *The 5 Love Languages: the Secret to Love That Lasts.* Chicago: Northfield Publishing, 2017.

[cl] Twomey, John. *Matters of Love: Unraveling the Mysterious Energy Patterns of Attractions and Relationships.* Dr. John Twomey , 2017.

[cli] McNeil, James. "Verbal Aikido ." Verbal Aikido™. EQ Communications Inc., 2015. http://verbalaikido.com. *used with licensee contract permission

[clii] "Common Games." changingminds.org, 2002. https://changingminds.org/explanations/behaviors/games/games.htm.

[cliii] Karpman, Stephen. "Karpman Drama Triangle." Karpman Drama Triangle, 2005. https://www.karpmandramatriangle.com/.

[cliv] Lazarus, Clifford N. "Think Sarcasm Is Funny? Think Again." *Psychology Today*, June 26, 2012.

[clv] Karpman, Stephen. "Karpman Drama Triangle." Karpman Drama Triangle, 2005. https://www.karpmandramatriangle.com/.

[clvi] Groeschel, Craig. *SOUL DETOX: Clean Living in a Contaminated World.* Place of publication not identified: ZONDERVAN,

2013.